365 Science of Mind

365 Science of Mind

A YEAR OF
DAILY WISDOM

FROM

Ernest Holmes

EDITED BY KATHY JULINE

JEREMY P. TARCHER • PUTNAM
A MEMBER OF PENGUIN PUTNAM INC.
NEW YORK

Most Tarcher/Putnam books are available at special quantity discounts for bulk purchase for sales promotions, premiums, fund-raising, and educational needs. Special books or book excerpts also can be created to fit specific needs. For details, write Putnam Special Markets, 375 Hudson Street, New York, NY 10014.

Jeremy P. Tarcher/Putnam
a member of
Penguin Putnam Inc.
375 Hudson Street
New York, NY 10014
www.penguinputnam.com

Library of Congress Cataloging-in-Publication Data

Holmes, Ernest, 1887–1960.
[Science of mind. Selections]
365 Science of mind : a year of daily wisdom from Ernest Holmes /
Ernest Holmes ; edited by Kathy Juline.
p. cm.
ISBN 1-58542-121-9
1. United Church of Religious Science—Doctrines. 2. Spiritual life—United Church of
Religious Science. 3. Devotional calendars—United Church of Religious Science.
I. Title: Three hundred sixty five Science of mind. II. Title: Three sixty five Science of
mind. III. Juline, Kathy. IV. Title.

BP605.U53 H652   2001   2001033214
299'.93—dc21

All materials by Ernest Holmes used by permission of
The United Church of Religious Science, 3252 West Sixth Street,
Los Angeles, CA 90020-5096

Printed in the United States of America

1   3   5   7   9   10   8   6   4   2

BOOK DESIGN BY DEBORAH KERNER

CONTENTS

365 Science of Mind

INTRODUCTION

In 1927 a little magazine called *Religious Science,* later renamed *Science of Mind,* began what has now been more than seven decades of continuous publication. The early issues, collector's items today, contain language that to our contemporary ears occasionally sounds flowery or old-fashioned. Yet ideas as current as tomorrow's headlines radiated from those now-brittle pages—and still do.

The words that appear in today's issues are more contemporary, but the truths conveyed remain perennial. The ideas taught by *Science of Mind*— particularly in a section called "Daily Guides to Richer Living"—have captured the attention and imagination of a growing movement of people who are striving to live fully and freely.

Ernest Holmes, founder of the Science of Mind philosophy, taught that through the power of our mind we are continually creating the conditions of our life. We are always making use of this innate creative power, whether consciously or unconsciously; the thoughts, attitudes, and beliefs we hold are shaping our tomorrows. The desire for a richer life has always been at the heart of human striving. Something within each of us, in our innermost being, knows that greater possibilities exist for us. Though we may sense these possibilities only faintly, they evoke a deep longing for fulfillment. This longing is the essence of what makes us both human and divine. To be divine means to possess the power of creativity, to be capable of expansion that is progressive and eternal.

Holmes saw beyond the veil of outer appearances, and he challenged us to do the same. He exhorted us to use the power at the center of our being for improving our own life and the world around us, asking, "We are chemists in the laboratory of the Infinite. What, then, shall we create?" Holmes believed that we possess the opportunity in each moment to use our power of choice in bold and imaginative ways.

In the philosophy he developed, which he originally called the Science of Mind *and Spirit*, Holmes focused attention on an idea that, though not new, seems somehow revolutionary: "There is a power for good in the universe greater than you are and you can use it." These words offer the assurance that you can change your life for the better. Through your ability to tap a power for good within yourself, you can find solutions to problems relating to health, finances, relationships, and other aspects of life. You can be free of loneliness, guilt, and resentment. You can find peace and purpose.

Holmes prophesied that the ideas he formulated into the Science of Mind teaching would become the spiritual impulse of the twenty-first century. The 365 daily meditation readings in this book—from "Daily Guides" written by Holmes for early issues of *Science of Mind*—state over and over again in a variety of ways, the central idea of this spiritual impulsion: that each of us is part of a unified whole. We are one with all others and one also with a dimension of wholeness sometimes called the Divine or God. We can never be separated from one another nor can we be separated from the whole. So, lack or limitation of any kind is merely the result of a restricting belief we have accepted and does not reflect our true nature. The greater good that *is* our true reality arises when we focus on the transcendent and true, recognizing our unity with it.

Holmes stressed that even more important than knowledge of spiritual truth is its daily application in the normal course of life. In his classic work *The Science of Mind,* he asserts that "what the world needs is spiritual conviction, followed by spiritual experience. I would rather see a student of this Science prove its Principle than to have him repeat all the words of wisdom that have ever been uttered." Knowing that beliefs in lack and limitation would not release their hold unless habitually supplanted by right thinking, Holmes taught his students to spend several minutes each day training their thought, refocusing their attention, and aligning with wholeness. Old attitudes are altered only through the consistent and conscious affirmation of new ones; persistence is required for these new ideas to become second nature.

A few minutes each day of retraining our thought in this way is all it takes, according to Holmes. In this way, daily meditations play a unique role in living the Science of Mind. Over the course of a year of daily recognizing and practicing the reality of wholeness instead of limitation, Holmes taught, our beliefs and expectations are profoundly altered. When we become attuned to oneness and its harmonizing power, wondrous events occur. How could they not, since our experience springs forth from the mold, or form, we create in our imagination—from the image we keep uppermost in our mind? The good that we would achieve, says the Science of Mind, we must first conceive. Then, once conceived, no matter how high the aim may be, so long as we hold fast to it in our thought, it will be realized.

Now to begin. The best time for working with these daily meditative readings is morning, when you are setting a tone for the rest of your day. Start with a few minutes of quiet stillness and read the daily message first for content. Then read it a second time to absorb it more deeply. Look for ideas that apply to you in some specific way and reflect for a few minutes on them. Allow them to take root in your mind until they feel real and right to you. As you go through your day, maintain an awareness of the main idea introduced in the day's reading, knowing you are being changed and enlarged by it. Ask yourself how these ideas call upon you to release an old attitude or belief, and then make a conscious choice to expand your thinking. Be alert for opportunities to practice and apply the new attitude or insight you have chosen. If this practice seems difficult, remember that you are breaking entrenched patterns of behavior and that resistance to anything new is normal. Yet be assured that your impulse toward wholeness and healing is stronger than any resistance you may feel. Remember that your mind deals with the realm of *causes* and that you have the power to introduce new causes, which will in turn result in new effects. "Thought is the instrument of Mind," Holmes said. "New thoughts create new conditions. We must learn to think in the Absolute. This means to think independently of any given or experienced effect."

So, as you move through the daily readings in this book—represented here as they originally appeared in *Science of Mind* magazine—endeavor to clear your mind of set or preconceived beliefs. Holmes—who did not view the past as precedent—taught the promise of eternal renewal. He spoke with great conviction when he told his students in the classes he taught, his rapt audiences in the great lecture halls where he spoke, and the numerous readers of his books and articles, that life *can* be changed for the better. Nothing is more certain or more necessary. If you practice and apply the ideas and teachings contained in *365 Science of Mind,* your life *will* change. You will become prosperous, happy, successful, and—the best part of all— a blessing to yourself, to others, and to the world.

I first encountered the Science of Mind philosophy in 1979. In 1984 I was offered employment with the magazine founded by Ernest Holmes, *Science of Mind,* and have worked for that magazine in various capacities ever since. Over the years I have read countless reports from people for whom the promise of the Science of Mind way of life has been fulfilled beyond imagining. Every one of their letters and stories attests to the truth that we are creative centers and can realize a more harmonious experience of life, through the power of our thought. We can be lights unto the world.

— KATHY JULINE
Senior Editor, *Science of Mind* Magazine
Los Angeles, 2001

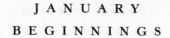

JANUARY
BEGINNINGS

New arts, new sciences, new philosophies, better government, and a higher civilization wait on our thoughts. The infinite energy of Life, and the possibility of our future evolution, work through our imagination and will. The time is ready, the place is where we are now, and it is done unto all as they really believe and act. —ERNEST HOLMES

When I dipped into the future far as human eye could see,
Saw the vision of the world and all the wonder that would be.
——ALFRED, LORD TENNYSON

Divinity is in its omniscience and omnipotence like a wheel, a circle, a whole, that can neither be understood, nor divided, nor begun nor ended.
——HILDEGARD OF BINGEN

Are you in earnest? Then seize
    this very minute.
What you can do, or dream you can,
    begin it;
Boldness has genius, power and magic in it;
    only engage then the mind grows heated;
Begin, and then the work will be completed. —GOETHE

NEW YEAR'S DAY

I Enter into a Newness of Life

> . . . I create new heavens and a new earth. —ISAIAH 65:17

We have been given the ability to initiate a new chain of causation. There is but One Mind and we use It. The laws of nature are universal, but our use of them is individual and personal. Our thought is operated on by a universal Creativity that is infinite in Its capacity to accomplish. Thus, in taking thought we do not force anything; we merely decide what thought to follow, knowing that the result is automatic. Spirit is forever unfolding Its own nature. In the physical universe It does so independently of our thought; in our personal lives It must do Its renewing activity through our thinking. To the degree that our thinking accords with the original Nature, the same harmony will operate in our affairs that already operates in that larger world that we experience but neither create nor control.

Everything is continually being re-created. Spirit is forever making all things new. Today is the time to prove to ourselves that It knows how to bring the right things to pass for us. Let us confidently affirm the Divine Presence and actually believe that It is guiding us as we consciously bring a problem we are facing into our thought, not as a problem, but as though we were receiving the answer, saying:

I believe that Divine Intelligence, which is the Mind of God, is guiding, guarding, and directing my thoughts and actions. I believe that God already knows the answer to this particular problem; therefore, I am letting go of the problem and I am listening to the answer as though it were sure. The answer to this problem exists in the Mind of God and is revealed to my mind now. Something in me does know what to do. I joyfully accept Its guidance. I am open to new ideas, new hopes, and new aspirations. This which so recently seemed a problem no longer exists, for the Mind of God, which knows the answer, is quietly flowing through my thought and feeling. Great peace and joy come over me as I accept this answer from the Giver of all Life.

I Am Conscious of the Currents of Life

And the prayer of faith shall save the sick,
and the Lord shall raise him up. —JAMES 5:15

When we say that our body is spiritual we are not denying our physical body. The physical is included within the spiritual. If the Spirit, or Divine Intelligence, has seen fit to give us a physical body it would be absurd to think of our body as an illusion unworthy of our attention. Rather, we should think of our body as a spiritual instrument, and every statement we make about our body, or belief we hold about it, that accepts spiritual Perfection as the substance of the body, tends to heal.

My body is the temple of the living Spirit. It is spiritual substance now. Every part of my body is in harmony with the living Spirit within me. The Life of this Spirit flows through every atom of my being, vitalizing, invigorating, and renewing every part of my physical body. There is a pattern of perfection at the center of my being that is now operating through every organ, function, action, and reaction. My body is forever renewed by the Spirit.

I am now made vigorous and whole. I possess the vitality of the Infinite. I am strong and well. The Life of the Spirit is my life. All of Its Strength is my strength. Its Power is my power. I feel that my whole being is renewed, invigorated, and made alive. There is complete stillness and perfect peace at the center of my being as I wait on that Presence that makes all things perfect. Every breath I draw is a breath of perfection, vitalizing, upbuilding, and renewing every cell of my body. I am born of the Spirit. I am in the Spirit. I am the Spirit made manifest.

I Enter into the Gladness of Living

Give, and it shall be given unto you; good measure, pressed down . . .
and running over, shall men give into your bosom. —LUKE 6:38

Who would not be a child again? Who would not again have the simple
faith and childlike trust that somehow or other we seem to lose on the pathway of human experience? Things crowd in on us until we lose some of the
greatest of all gifts—the simple, spontaneous joy of living and a trust in the
Power of good, which alone is able, ready, and willing to meet all our needs.
Let us, then, again return to the place of assurance that comes with the simplicity of faith.

I now release the multitude of doubts and fears that crowd into my
mind, and I become quiet so that the Divine miracle may take place in my
life. I let every good I possess become multiplied as Divine Love acts upon
my faith to bring into my experience everything necessary to my well-
being. I know that the Divine Good includes all things that are necessary:
food and shelter, love and friendship, and the accomplishment of every
right purpose.

And so my faith, the faith of the little child in me, rises with expectancy
to meet this new day in joy and to accept the bounty of heaven. With the
faith of a little child I place my human hand in the invisible hand of the all-
sustaining Good, and I let the miracle of Life and Love take place. I break
my bread with thanks and distribute such good as I have to everyone I meet.
I say of my own household and the households of all others: God bless the
four corners of this house, and be the lintel blest, and bless the bed and bless
the board, and bless each place of rest. And bless the door that opens wide
to stranger as to kin, and bless each crystal windowpane that lets the sunlight in.

From Prayer to Performance

Yea, the darkness hideth not from thee . . . the darkness
and the light are both alike to thee. —PSALM 139:12

To be effective, prayer must be affirmative, but it is not enough merely to affirm the Presence of God. We must add to this realization the thought that Divine Intelligence is acting in and through us now. Prayer is not a wishful or wistful longing, nor is it an escape from objective reality. To become lost in our prayers might give us an unconscious desire to escape the activities of life. Therefore, we affirm that Divine Intelligence not only knows what to do, but also impels us to act on Its knowing.

I hand my life and affairs over to Divine Intelligence, to the Power that knows how to do everything. I do this in the complete conviction that I receive only good into my experience. I know there is nothing in me that can doubt either the Divine Goodness or the operation of Its Law in my affairs. I believe that everything necessary to the fulfillment of every good desire is now in full operation, that all the circumstances in my life are tending to bring it about.

If there is anything I ought to do about this, I accept the action and know that I receive guidance and am impelled to act intelligently. Therefore, I have a complete sense of ease and assurance. I look forward joyfully as I anticipate the good that is to come into my life. I believe that all who are now praying with me will receive the answer to their desires from the same Source. My faith goes out to them even as their faith reaches back to me. For I believe that out of the great Good in which we live there will surely come to all of us an answer to our particular need.

I Am at Home in the Universe

And all mine are thine, and thine are mine;
and I am glorified in them. —JOHN 17:10

This meditation may be considered an all-inclusive prayer because it includes ourselves and others. It is truly doing unto others that which we would like them to do unto us, and it establishes a unity between ourselves and those around us, a feeling that we all are some part of the kingdom of Good. This all-inclusive prayer, then, is one that expands our consciousness of the true self and at the same time blesses all others.

Believing that there is a Divine Presence closer to me than my very breath, that I live in perfect Spirit, that the God around and the God within me is One God, I say: My Father, which art in heaven within me, hallowed be Thy name. Thy kingdom come, now, and I accept it. And, looking about me, I say to all people: Your Father, which is in your heaven within you, hallowed be His name, for you are One with Him forevermore. There is One Life, that Life is God, that Life is Perfect, that Life is your life now.

Looking upon the circumstances that surround me, I bless them even as Jesus blessed the bread and broke it. Even as the loaves and fishes multiplied in the outstretched and upturned hand of his love, so I know that everything in my experience that is good is multiplied and increased. Even as I feel the increase pressing into my own experience, I give it out that it may feed and bless and multiply the good of others, who are some part of me because God is in them and in me, and we are in each other.

I Accept My Inheritance of Wholeness

Ye shall have a song, as in the night . . . and gladness of heart, as when
one goeth . . . into the mountain of the Lord. —ISAIAH 30:29

Let us see if we cannot take the flute of faith and go into the mountain of the
Lord, which is the secret place of the Most High within us, and let the whole
harmony of our lives flow from that perfect Spirit that is at the center of
everything.

I am One with the infinite and perfect Spirit, the Giver of all good and
perfect gifts. I open my mind and my heart, and, indeed, my body, to the inflow of this Divine Presence. I know that this living Presence is in every cell
of my body and every function of my being. I accept It as my health of body,
here and now. I accept It as that which looses from me all that is unlike the
perfect expression of Life. There is no doubt or fear in my mind that rejects
in any way all that God is, right here and right now.

My conscious acceptance of the fullness of the Presence of God flows
out in joy and love to bless those whom I would help, those with whom I
would share this inner joy. And I decree that the loved one I now bring into
the scope of my thought is blessed and healed through the Presence of Good
that is within. The radiance of Joy in my own heart brings happiness into
the lives of all those around me. The Abundance that benefits me supplies
everyone around me with the good things of life. The Light that warms the
center of my own being so shines forth that all may find guidance and
warmth and comfort in Its rays. This is the Light that lighteth every man
that cometh into the world. This is the Fount from which spring the living
waters. I drink, and will not thirst again. And even as I drink I hand the
chalice of my faith to all.

I Experience the Creativity of Faith

*Thou shalt also decree a thing, and it shall be established unto thee:
and the light shall shine on thy ways.* —JOB 22:28

Faith acts like a law, because it is a law. It is the law of mind in action. When we realize this we no longer feel that we must have faith in ourselves as isolated beings, but, rather, that as human beings we are included in the great Law of Life. Then we can rest in complete confidence that our words, spoken in this faith, are the presence and the power and the activity of the Spirit in us. All effort to make things happen or to concentrate the mind is put aside, and with quiet childlike acceptance we make known our requests with thanksgiving. We are One with God. Nothing can separate us from the Source.

Letting our faith be of God's Presence and Power we can each say: All that I am, and all that I do, is the Divine Presence expressing Itself through me. The thoughts I think and the words I speak are Life and Truth because God speaks them through me. Of myself I give no authority to my prayer, but the child of God in me knows that the authority of the Almighty brings to pass the words that I speak.

I speak the word of health for my body, my feelings, and my thoughts, knowing that the Father within is the Power that brings this wholeness into complete being. I speak the word of Divine Guidance, and the Wisdom of the universe wells up as a beacon to lead me into paths of right-use-ness, to make straight and clear my everyday paths. I speak the word of joy, and the Father within frees me from loneliness and sadness. I speak the word of peace to the world and know that the Peace of God reaches into the hearts and minds of the people of all nations.

My Thought Is Inspired by the Most High

And the Lord, he it is that doth go before thee; he will be with thee,
he will not fail thee, neither forsake thee: fear not,
neither be dismayed. —DEUTERONOMY 31:8

We should believe that God is the invisible Partner in our lives and affirm that Divine Love goes before us and prepares the way. We should permit ourselves to be guided for there is Something within us, deep at the center of our being, which knows what we ought to do and how we ought to do it.

I am listening to the Divine Presence and permitting It to direct my path. Thoughts and ideas will come to me and I shall be led to follow through on them in my everyday life. I shall be impelled into right action. I know how to meet every situation in calm trust and with the complete conviction that Divine Intelligence is guiding me. I wish to do only that which is constructive and life-giving; therefore, I know that everything I do will prosper. Everything I touch will be quickened into a newness of life and action. Every constructive purpose in my life will be fulfilled.

I have a deep sense of inner calm, a complete assurance that all is well. The same Intelligence that governs the planets in their course is now acting as a Law of Good in my personal experience and in the experiences of everyone around me. I do thank God for this increase that is mine. I do accept Divine guidance. I do believe that I am in silent partnership with all the Power, all the Presence, and all the Love there is. I place my life entirely and completely under the protection and guidance of this Power, and I rest in complete assurance that everything I do will prosper.

I Am Filled with Confidence and a Sense of Security

For he shall give his angels charge over thee,
to keep thee in all thy ways. —PSALM 91:11

Deep within the consciousness of each of us there is a center of peace and security where trouble and accidents do not occur, where truth and love reign
supreme, where good is the only power. It is to this center that we go in the
silence of our own minds to commune daily with the Spirit that is both
around us and within us. Truly this is the Most High within, always immediately responsive to us. In our meditation we seek to make this Presence
more real to us and more personal. And as we do, an inward sense of calm
comes over the mind, a feeling of security and safety that every human being needs.

I know that all the Power there is and all the Presence there is, is Love,
the Spirit Almighty. I know that Love protects me and that I am guided and
guarded into the pathways of peace, of joy, and of security. I know that this
is true of all people. This is what I believe about everyone. This is what exists for the whole world. This is my prayer of acceptance today and every
day. I feel myself safe in the keeping of the Divine Love. I feel the soft enveloping Presence of the living Spirit.

I know there is no confusion or doubt in the Mind of God, and God's
Mind is the only mind there is. This Mind is my mind now, directing everything I do, guarding every movement I make. For all Thy ways are ways of
blessedness, and all Thy paths are peace. I trust. I live and move and have
my being in that which is completely perfect and wholly joyous.

I Accept the Divine Gift

The Spirit itself beareth witness with our spirit,
that we are the children of God. —ROMANS 8:16

Affirmative prayer means that we clear the mind of all doubt and fear and turn in faith to the great Giver of life. It means that we become aware of the Presence of God within and around us, here and now. It means that we affirm this Presence and accept It—quietly, calmly, and peacefully—in all of Its fullness.

I now let go of every anxious thought. I now surrender any doubt or fear into the great heart of Love. I look out upon the world and say that it is my world because it is God's world. I think of all people as my friends because they live and move and have their being in the Father of us all. I now receive confidence and inspiration from the Source of all life. I believe that Love is guiding me. I believe there is a Divine Power that goes before me and makes perfect my way in joy and happiness. I believe this Power is flowing through me, to the joy and happiness of those around me.

I have a faith, a conviction, an assurance that cannot be moved, for I am established in a Love that envelops everything I contact and every person I meet. I have a Friend who knows all my needs. I accept the life that He has implanted in me, and this life reaches out to everything around me, in joy and gladness, and with the blessed assurance that all is well. And believing that God is Love, I affirm that there is nothing in me that could hurt or harm or hinder those around me from entering into the fullness of their own joy, into the completeness of their own self-expression, into the perfection of their own being.

The Impersonal Law of Personal Good

All power is given unto me in heaven and in earth. —MATTHEW 28:18

It is interesting to note that while Jesus said that all power was given to him in heaven and earth, at another time he said that he of himself could do nothing. This sounds like a contradiction until we understand the subtlety of its meaning. Jesus realized that there is but One Power and One Presence and he knew that we all live in this Presence and by this Power. He also knew that when he surrendered himself to the Presence, that is, when he thought the thoughts of God after Him, then the Power would automatically respond to him. Therefore, in surrendering himself to the Presence of Good he commanded the Law of Good. This is fundamental to our whole concept of what we believe and the way we use it. For we use the Law of Good, which of Itself is entirely impersonal and independent of us, like all other laws of nature. Responding to the Presence of Love, we use the Law of Good. This is what meditation, affirmation, and prayer mean.

I am now depending on the Power that is greater than I am and upon the Law of Good that is available right here and now. I identify my life with the Presence and the Power and the Love of God. I recognize the Divine Presence within and around me, and in all people.

If there is anything in me that denies this Presence or this Power, I loose it and let it go. I surrender myself to the complete conviction that everything necessary for my well-being, for my physical, mental, and spiritual self-expression, is now operating in, through, and around me. I know that everything I do will prosper. I know that the One Life, which is God, is my life now. Therefore, I accept this gift of Life and Love, for myself and for all people.

I Accept the Outpouring of Spirit

Hereby know we that we dwell in him, and he in us,
because he hath given us of his Spirit. —I JOHN 4:13

How could we better explain this than to use the words of Robert Browning, "'Tis Thou, God, who giveth, 'tis I who receive"? Or Emerson, who said that we are "beneficiaries of the Divine fact"? The thoughts of both Emerson and Browning were thoughts of acceptance and recognition. Like all men of great spiritual insight, they knew that the gift of Life is an eternal reality, that it is our office to accept it.

Today I accept this gift of Divine Life and Love that God has eternally given to me and to everyone. With deep gratitude and a childlike simplicity I enter into the joy and the peace that come from the realization of Divine Guidance, for I know that Love guides my thoughts even as It guards my life and action. I know that the eternal Presence is really embracing everything. In this Presence I serenely and confidently rest, placing all my hope and aspiration in Its loving care. In this Love I embrace the world and affirm that peace shall come on earth and goodwill exist among people everywhere.

I also realize that I belong to the universe in which I live, and it belongs to me. It is the gift of God. I am unified with everyone I will ever meet, and they with me. For we all are manifestations of the One Presence. Gratefully acknowledging and gladly receiving this benediction from heaven, I live and love and accept Life in Its fullness.

I Know the Active Power of God

One God and Father of all, who is above all, and through
all, and in you all. —EPHESIANS 4:6

The key thought for our meditation today is the idea that there is an active
Presence of the creative Spirit in all our affairs—not something passive, but
something that is moving in and through everything we do. We should affirm that this Divine Presence is everywhere, that It is always active in,
around, and through us.

Believing that the Spirit is at the center of everything and at the very
center of my own physical being, I recognize this Presence harmoniously
acting in every cell, every organ, and every function of my physical body. I
praise my body-temple, bless it, and know that every activity within it is in
harmony with Divine Life. One Mind governs everything, and I now affirm
and accept that this same Intelligence governs my affairs. It is within me
and around me at all times, directing, guiding, governing, controlling, and
leading me happily to the fulfillment of all good purposes.

I salute the God-Presence in everyone I meet, and I know that as surely
as I do this, the Love dwelling in them responds to the same Presence that is
within me. We act in a unison of peace and understanding. Recognizing all
of nature as the handiwork of God, I see the beauty of His activity in everything—in the wind and the wave, in the sunshine and cloud, and in everything that God has created.

∾

The Spirit in Me Is Perfect

The Spirit of God hath made me, and the breath of
the Almighty hath given me life. —JOB 33:4

Each of us is a spirit, but we don't always recognize this greatest of all truths about ourselves. We do not always consciously invite communion with the Spirit or open all the doorways of our thought in complete acceptance. The Bible tells us to let that mind be in us that was in Jesus, which, of course, is the Mind of God and the invisible Guest in every person.

I know that this invisible Guest within me, the Angel of God's Presence, is counseling me wisely, leading me unerringly, directing my thoughts and actions in harmony, in peace, in poise, in love, and in cooperation. And because God cannot fail, and because the Divine Presence within me is God as my real self, I know that there is Power flowing through my word of faith, which makes straight the way before me. I know that the great Giver of life is giving, through me, that gift which is gladly made, which returns multiplied and goes out again to increase its blessing and to multiply its own good as it blesses others.

I know there is a Presence that came with me when I entered this life, and I know that this same Presence will go with me when I leave this physical form, for It is the Presence of eternal Life, the Life that cannot die. And so I have no fear of the past, the present, or the future, but I am living today as though God really were over all and through all. I feel this Presence as life, love, and goodness, and experience Its action as power and certainty. It is with me today, making my life whole and complete.

I Lift Up My Cup of Acceptance

And God is able to make all grace abound toward you; that ye, always
having all sufficiency in all things, may abound to every
good work. —II CORINTHIANS 9:8

We lift up our cup of acceptance to the Divine Bounty when we think affirmatively and give thanks to the Giver of all life. Daily we should practice affirming that our cup is filled and running over, always remembering that
what we affirm for ourselves we must affirm for others. Living and letting
live, giving and receiving, loving and being loved, our cup of acceptance
will be filled from the horn of God's Abundance.

I am living in the continual expectancy that every good thing in my experience shall be multiplied. There is neither doubt nor uncertainty in my
mind. Every denial is transformed into an affirmation, every negation into
an acceptance, every no into a yes. I know that the Spirit of God has made
me, and the breath of the Almighty has given me life. I have complete confidence in this Spirit. I know that I am beloved and needed. I feel at home
with God.

Today is filled with blessing for myself and others. The past is gone and
I gladly loose it and let it go. The present is filled with peace and joy and the
future with hope. Gratefully I accept of the Divine Love and Givingness
and gladly extend them to everyone I meet. I am made whole with the
Wholeness of the Spirit. Gently, but with complete certainty, I am guided
into right action and successful accomplishment of all good desires. This I
accept. This I experience.

Good Is Forever My Experience

And he said unto him, Son, thou art ever with me;
and all that I have is thine. —LUKE 15:31

Realizing that we are in the midst of an ever-present Good, and believing that there is a Law that brings everything of Its nature into our lives, we should learn to think and act as though every wrong condition of yesterday were converted into something new and better today.

I believe that all the mistakes I have ever made are swallowed up in a Love, in a Peace, and in a Life greater than I am. Therefore, I surrender all past mistakes into the keeping of this ever-present and perfect Life. I affirm that Love is guiding me into a real and deep cooperation with Life and into a sincere affection for everyone.

Today is a fresh beginning, a new start, a joyous adventure on the pathway of eternal progress. Today is bright with hope and happy with fulfillment. Therefore, I affirm that this is the day that God has made, that it is good, and that I find fulfillment in it. The Law of Mind responding to this word of good makes everything in my life simple, effective, and whole. The action of Wisdom through me arranges every circumstance so that success and happiness will come from it. I express the Spirit within so that only love and confidence go out to everyone I meet, blessing everything I touch, and bringing peace and comfort and joy to my world. In every thought, in every deed, in every act, I am sustained by an infinite Power and guided gently into an increasing good, for myself and for others.

I Loose All Condemnation

And forgive us our debts, as we forgive our debtors. —MATTHEW 6:12

When Jesus said that we should not judge lest we be judged, he was stating the action of the law of cause and effect. If we wish a complete clearance from any sense of condemnation about ourselves, we must first be certain that we have released all condemnation of others from our own minds. When we do this we meet others in a new light and, reaching past all judgment and criticism, establish a relationship between the Spirit that is within them and the same Spirit that is within us, for God is One in all people.

Knowing that God must be at the center of everything, and realizing that God's Love is the great motivating power of life, today I know I am meeting this God in everyone and seeing the manifestation of Love in everything. If there is any condemnation or animosity in me, I gladly loose it. I loose it and let it go as I turn to that silent Presence within me that gives all and withholds nothing.

Giving and receiving, loving and being loved, I rejoice with all creation and find in field and flower and running brook, in the sunshine and in the stillness of the night, that One Presence that fills everything. I enter into the harmony of eternal peace, into the joy of knowing that I am now in the kingdom of God, from which no person is excluded. My yesterdays are gone forever; my tomorrows stretch forth into an endless future of pure delight. And from out of the Invisible there come to me these words: Today thou art with Me in Paradise.

The Argument That Wins

He that saith he is in the light, and hateth his brother, is in darkness. . . .
He that loveth his brother abideth in the light. —I JOHN 2:9–10

When St. John said that it is impossible for us to remain in the light while we hate someone else, he was pointing out the same truth that Jesus had in mind when he said for us to forgive that we might be forgiven. We should not expect the Law of Good to operate for us alone, shutting all others out. It is only that which we share with others that really is ours. We are so constituted that when we think evil of others or condemn them it is impossible to escape this condemnation for ourselves. This is why Jesus said: "Judge not, that ye be not judged. For with what judgment ye judge, ye shall be judged." Everything that goes out comes back again. Our thoughts and acts move in circles.

I bless myself for the good I would do and I bless everyone for the good they would do. I recognize the Presence of God at the center of my own being, and I know that the Divine Spirit within me responds to the same Spirit in others, comforting, unifying, and making whole. There is no criticism, no false judgment, no unkindness in me. My whole thought and feeling is one of praise, of thanksgiving, and of blessing.

Today I live as though this moment were eternity. I recognize that the kingdom of Good is at hand. Seeing the Divine in everything, I know that the Divine in all things responds to me. Receiving the silent blessing of the Spirit, I permit this blessing to enrich the life of everyone I meet, to bring comfort, faith, and good cheer to everyone I contact. I walk in that Light in which there is no darkness, in that Love in which there is no fear, in that Life in which there is no death.

"He Restoreth My Soul"

The Lord is my shepherd. . . . He restoreth my soul. —PSALM 23:1, 3

As we take this thought for our meditation today, "The Lord is my shepherd. . . . He restoreth my soul," let us feel that we are One with the Divine Presence and enter into conscious communion with It. This is spiritual meditation and affirmative prayer. It is through spiritual meditation that we reach out, or in, to that Divine Presence, which has Its dwelling place in the sanctuary of our own hearts and is also everywhere.

"The Lord is my shepherd. . . . He restoreth my soul." Believing that God is everywhere, and knowing that the Divine Life can and does restore my soul, I now affirm and deeply accept Divine Guidance. I believe that I am sustained by an infinite Power, guided by an infinite Intelligence, and guarded by an infinite Love. I feel this Presence in, around, and through me, and through all people. There is a Power greater than I upon which I may rely. I am relying on this Power and I am letting this Intelligence govern and guide me. I am fully aware of the protection of Divine Love.

I lay aside every doubt or fear and gladly enter into the newness of life. I do believe that the Lord is my shepherd. I do believe that He restoreth my soul. I am lovingly aware that the Divine Presence is not only close to me, It is now only right where I am. It is also within me and what I am. It is this inner "I Am," this Spirit of God within me, that is my shepherd. I not only shall not want, but my cup will run over. A table is prepared before me. This is the table that God has spread and I gratefully acknowledge this Divine Bounty, this Feast of Life. For God's Abundance is my abundance. His Good is my good, and His Life is my life, now.

I Accept the Heritage of Happiness

Thou wilt shew me the path of life: in thy presence is fulness of joy;
at thy right hand there are pleasures for evermore. —PSALM 16:11

We should daily feel a deeper union with Life, a greater sense of that in-dwelling God, the God of the everywhere, within us. When we speak into this Mind we have sown the seed of thought in the Absolute and may rest in peace. Nothing in our thought about God should produce sadness or de-pression; rather, it should be quite the reverse, because our faith in and love of God should give us such confidence and such a sense of security that we should indeed be able to say: Joy to the world, the Lord has come.

Realizing that the Lord is not far-off, that God is an inward intimate Presence closer to me than my very breath, I affirm that there is nothing in me that can doubt this Presence or limit the Power of Good. There is noth-ing in me that can separate me from the Love of God and I accept the joy of living in the very midst of It.

The Divine Presence leads me on the pathway of peace. It directs my thoughts, my words, and my actions into constructive channels of self-expression. It unites me with others in love, in kindness, and in considera-tion. Today I accept this action gratefully and realize that it brings into my experience everything necessary to my happiness. Knowing there can be no good to myself alone, for God is in all people, I affirm for others that which I accept for myself.

I Walk in the Joy of Increasing Good

He shall call upon me, and I will answer him: I will be with him in
trouble; I will deliver him and honour him. —PSALM 91:15

This passage contains a great promise. It is not of something that is to transpire in the future, but of a good that is transpiring in the present moment
in which we live—right here and right now. We are the center of the divine
activity. All things are made of Spirit, and we must know that the Spirit not
only can manifest through us, but that It wishes to do so. Struggle belongs
to the old order; in the new order peace takes the place of confusion, faith
answers the cry of doubt and fear, and the Spirit is supreme.

I now accept the promise of spiritual fulfillment. I do believe that every
good thing necessary to my success already belongs to the kingdom of God,
which I know is at hand. I am expecting good to happen; I anticipate success. I believe that Divine Intelligence guides me in all my right activities,
and, because I know that God always succeeds, He now succeeds in and
through my endeavors. I know that right now everything necessary to my
success is being brought about. I look through the eyes of Spirit, which sees
and knows the complete fulfillment of every worthwhile idea.

I accept that God is active in my affairs. And, knowing that God is in all
people, there is joyous cooperation with others. Therefore, I help and I am
helped. Knowing that God is the great Giver, I accept His gift and myself
become a giver to life. In all I do I seek to be of service and assistance to others. The kingdom of God is at hand today and I enter into it with joy. It contains all that belongs to the life of Good. It encompasses all people and all
things. Its abundance flows through me and manifests in increasing good.

Constructive Thought Fills My Day

And I, if I be lifted up from the earth,
will draw all men unto me. —JOHN 12:32

When Jesus spoke of being "lifted up from the earth" he meant that that which is human about us must consciously become united with the Divine. In ancient writings the earth stood for the lowest form of life, while heaven represented the highest. Therefore, being lifted up from the earth means uniting earth with heaven. This daily lifting up of our thought is necessary if we wish to so unite ourselves and everything we are doing with the Divine spiritual Power that flows through us and into all our acts.

I now turn to the Spirit within me. I know that It is close to me, It is what I am, and It governs my life in harmony and in peace. And I know that through me It brings joy and happiness to everyone I meet. Through the Power of this indwelling Spirit I am a blessing to myself and to others.

I lift up my whole mind to the realization that the Spirit of God is within me and that this perfect Spirit is my real self. I invite the Spirit to direct my thoughts and acts, and I believe that It is doing so. I expect new ideas to stimulate my imagination and direct me into new ways of doing things. I invite and expect new circumstances and situations, and I know that as they present themselves, the Intelligence within me will accept them and act upon them. I know that the Divine Presence within me makes Itself known to every person I meet, to every situation I encounter. I know that It brings life and joy and happiness to everything and everyone.

My Affairs Are in the Hands of Divine Action

Thy kingdom come. Thy will be done on earth,
as it is in heaven. —MATTHEW 6:10

When Jesus said, "Thy kingdom come. Thy will be done on earth, as it is in heaven," he was again affirming that there is a Perfection at the center of everything. He was telling us that when we reach toward this inward Perfection, It will be revealed to us and that It must finally establish the kingdom of God on earth, as It most certainly will.

Realizing that the kingdom of God is a kingdom of joy and that the heart of the Eternal is most wonderfully kind, I place all my affairs in the keeping of Divine Love and I permit all of my thoughts to be directed by Divine Wisdom. The Spirit within me guides me and directs my path—guides me into peace and prosperity and happiness.

God's perfect kingdom is established in me today. And the Fatherhood of God is revealed through me as the brotherhood of man. This brotherhood I help establish on earth today, for I know that it is within all people. The indwelling Love and Peace draw me close to everyone I meet, in joy and in friendship. Therefore, my prayer for the kingdom of God on earth is a communion of my own soul with that universal Soul that overshadows and dwells within everyone. This is the kingdom I am recognizing as I affirm: "Thy kingdom come. Thy will be done on earth, as it is in heaven."

I Accept My Individuality

Now there are diversities of gifts, but the same Spirit. And there are differences of administrations, but the same Lord. —I CORINTHIANS 12:4–5

It is right and necessary that we should be individuals. If two persons were exactly alike, one would be unnecessary in the scheme of things. Emerson said that imitation is suicide. The Divine Spirit never made any two things alike—no two rosebushes, two snowflakes, two grains of sand, nor two persons. We are all just a little unique, for each wears a different face but behind each is the One Presence—God. Unity does not mean uniformity. Unity means that everything draws its strength, its power, and its ability to live from One Source. One Life does flow through everything, but this Life is never monotonous; It is forever doing new things in you and in me.

I affirm that I, too, am of this original Spirit and that It is doing something new through me today. Therefore, everything I do is original; it is a new creation. There is a new enthusiasm, a new zest for life. Even the old songs I sing are different because of a renewed influx coming from "the Maker of all music."

The Divine Spirit is flowing through me in an individual way and I accept the genius of my own being. Since the original Artist is doing something new through me today, I do not imitate others. Each is a king in his own right; each is a Divine Being on the pathway of an eternal unfoldment. Gladly I recognize and unite with the genius in others, but always keep the uniqueness of my own personality. All the Presence there is flowing through me in an original manner. I invite the inspiration, the illumination, and the guidance of God and gladly cooperate with them.

I Acquaint Myself with Peace

Thou wilt keep him in perfect peace whose mind is stayed on thee:
because he trusteth in thee. —ISAIAH 26:3

When we give a spiritual mind treatment, or affirmative prayer, we are recognizing the Presence of God in, around, and through us. It is this closeness of the Divine Presence that gives us the feeling of peace that is accompanied by a consciousness of power. And it is because we do believe that we can have this feeling, this inner conviction, this sense of certainty that all spiritual teachers have told us is necessary to effective living.

I know that there is a Power greater than I am. I know that there is a Love that casts out all fear. I know that there is a faith that overcomes all obstructions. I now enter into this Love. I now use this faith and know a great peace of mind, a deep sense of belonging, a complete realization that God is right where I am.

I believe that the Spirit within me, which is God, makes perfect and peaceful the way before me. I enter into conscious union with everything that lives. I commune with the Spirit in all people and in all things. I feel an intimate relationship to the Presence and the Power that control everything. I put my whole trust in God. I know that the Spirit gently leads me, wisely counsels me. I know that the Love that envelops everything flows through me to everyone and with it there goes a confidence, a sense of joy and of peace, as well as a buoyant enthusiasm and zest for life. There comes back to me today everything that makes life worthwhile, everything that flows from the inner realm of fathomless Peace—the indwelling Presence of God.

Right Action Prevails in My Affairs

Therefore I say unto you, What things soever ye desire, when ye pray, believe that ye receive them, and ye shall have them. —MARK 11:24

There could be no more explicit technique for effective prayer than this, laid down by the Master himself. We actually are to believe that we already possess the object of our desire when we ask for it. We are to accept it even as we believe in the harvest that follows the spring planting. Therefore, every spring should be one of hope and every harvest one of fulfillment. We must learn to accept the good we desire and affirm its presence in our experience.

Realizing that there is a Law of Good that governs my affairs, I loose every thought of doubt, fear, or uncertainty and accept the good that I desire, here and now. Realizing that this Law of Good not only knows how to create, but must contain within Itself all the details of its own creation, I let go of the need to say how my good shall come and accept the perfect answer today. Feeling a deep sense of gratitude and joy because of this, I live enthusiastically and with calm and happy anticipation of more good yet to come.

And because there is no sense of strain in this, I relax in quiet contentment, while at the same time realizing that what the Law of Good does for me It must do through me. I declare that I not only know what to do but I am impelled to act, to move objectively. I move into a greater sphere of action and life with complete certainty, calm confidence, and limitless trust. Today everything of good in my experience is reanimated, reborn, and increased. Gladly I accept this and place no limit on the Divine Givingness.

The Spirit Lives Within Me

Then shall thy light break forth as the morning, and thine health
shall spring forth speedily: and thy righteousness
shall go before thee. —ISAIAH 58:8

Spiritual mind healing has long since passed the experimental stage. We now know that we cannot tell where the body begins and the mind leaves off, and many of us believe that the actions, organs, and functions of the physical body really are activities of the infinite Intelligence within us. To come to realize, then, that there is One Body, which is the Body of God and which at the same time is our own body, is to accept a greater influx of the One Life.

We should daily affirm: There is One Life, that Life is God, that Life is my life now. Every organ, action, and function of my physical body is in harmony with the Divine life. There is perfect circulation, perfect assimilation, and perfect elimination. If there is anything in me that does not belong, it is removed. If there is anything that my physical being needs that it does not appear to have, it is supplied. My body is daily renewed after that image of perfection of it that is held in the Mind of God. "Be ye therefore perfect, even as your Father which art in heaven is perfect."

I affirm, then, that my body is the Body of God; it is a body of right ideas all working in harmony with each other. The Life of the Spirit does circulate through it; the Law of the Spirit does govern it; the Love of the Spirit does sustain it. Therefore, I sleep in peace and wake in joy and live in the continual acceptance that life is good. My whole experience is of God. My whole life is God in action, for I am One with All-Life and All-Power.

Goodness Flows from Me

If we love one another, God dwelleth in us,
and his love is perfected in us. —I JOHN 4:12

Every heart responds to the warmth of love. Every mind yearns for its embrace and no life is complete without it. Love really is the fulfillment of the Law of Good. Love alone can heal the world and enable people to live together in unity and in peace. Believing that love is the great lodestone of life and that love alone fulfills the Law of Good, quietly I say to myself: I believe that God is Love. I believe that Love is at the center of everything; therefore, I accept Love as the healing power of life. I permit Love to reach out from me to every person I meet. I believe that Love is returned to me from every person I meet. I trust the guidance of Love because I believe it is the power of Good in the universe. I feel that Love is flowing through me to heal every situation I meet, to help every person I contact. Love opens the way before me and makes it perfect, straight, and glad.

Love forgives everything unlike itself; it purifies everything. Love converts everything that seems commonplace into that which is wonderful. Love converts weakness into strength, fear into faith. Love is the all-conquering power of Spirit. As a child walks in confidence with its parents, so I walk in confidence with Life. As a child, through love, trusts its parents, so I put my whole trust in Love, which I feel to be everywhere present, within, around, and through me—within, around, and through all people. In that Love I am safe, secure, and cared for.

All Things Are Made Whole

And thou shalt love the Lord thy God with all thy heart, and with all thy soul, and with all thy mind, and thy neighbour as thyself. —MARK 12:30–31

When we let the love that is within us go out to the God who is in all people and the Divine Presence that is in all things, then we are loving God with all our heart and with all our soul and mind, because we are recognizing that the Spirit within us is the same Spirit that we meet in others. This is loving our neighbors as ourselves.

The love that is within me goes out to the God who is within all people. I recognize the Divine Presence everywhere. I know that It responds to me and I know that there is a Law of Good, a Law of Love, forever giving of Itself to me. This Divine and Perfect Law is circulating through me now. Its rhythm is in my heartbeat; Its perfection is manifest in every organ, action, and function of my physical body. Love and Perfect Life circulate through everything. This Love and this Life I accept as the truth about myself, now and forever.

This same Love, this same Presence, this same Law of Good, I recognize in others. It is a Divine Presence, a Holy Presence, and a Perfect Presence. It is a Law that heals and makes whole, that prospers and makes happy. This is the Law of my life. This is the Good that I meet everywhere. I know that the only Power there is and the only Presence there is is Love, the Spirit Almighty. There is no condemnation, no judgment, and no fear in me. I feel that I belong to the world in which I live, that I love people and am loved of them. I have a deep sense of confidence and trust. I feel that I am secure in life and am no longer anxious about anything.

I Surrender All Fear and Doubt

Fear not, little flock; for it is your Father's good pleasure
to give you the kingdom. —LUKE 12:32

We should always keep in mind that we are beneficiaries of Life. We do not put the chicken in the egg, nor the oak tree in the acorn. Rather, we take them out. We did not create the Divine Presence nor the Law of Good; we commune with this Presence and use this Law. Therefore, Jesus said that "it is your Father's good pleasure to give you the kingdom." It is our business to receive it. And in doing this we follow the same method that any scientist would, for the scientist knows that he did not create the laws that he uses or the principles that he employs.

It is my Father's good pleasure to give me the kingdom. Today I accept this kingdom, and I accept it in its fullness. Because of it, the day contains joy and happiness and is filled with peace. Running through it all is the silent power of spiritual Wisdom and Love, harmoniously and happily governing my thoughts, decisions, and acceptances so that everything I do is done with ease.

I lay all weariness aside and accept the life-giving, invigorating, dynamic activity of the Spirit, knowing that it vitalizes every organ of my body; it flows with power and strength and purpose through everything I do, as it leads me gently down the pathway of life. Today is the day that God has made, and I am glad in it. And when evening comes, the cool shadows of peace will fall across my pathway and the quiet of the night will enter into my soul, while the beatitude of the Spirit flows through me as a river of life.

My Thought Establishes New Beginnings

For behold, I create new heavens and a new earth: and the former
shall not be remembered, nor come into mind. —ISAIAH 65:17

Nothing is ever twice alike. It is said that the physical body is never more
than a year old, that we discard many bodies through this life. Everything is
continuously being re-created, and it literally is true that the creative Spirit
is forever making a new heaven and a new earth. We must permit It to make
them new for us.

I empty my mind of every thought of fear and doubt. I condemn no one
and no thing, not even myself. Forgetting that which is past and having no
fear for the future, I live today as though the new heaven and the new earth
were already accomplished facts in my experience. I live in harmony with
people and with all the situations that surround me. I see and feel the Presence of Good running through everything. I have complete faith that this
Divine Presence reveals Itself to me in every thought, in every word, and in
every act.

There is nothing in my past experience and nothing in my thought
about the future that can in any way deny me the pleasure and the privilege
of living today as though everything were complete and perfect. "For behold, I create new heavens and a new earth: and the former shall not be remembered, nor come into mind." My whole expectancy is of much and
more, of good and of better. The future is bright with hope and fulfillment.
The present is perfect, and no past failure mars today's understanding.

FEBRUARY
LOVE

Love is the self-givingness of the Spirit through the desire of Life to express Itself in terms of creation. —ERNEST HOLMES

Love is the central flame of the universe, nay, the very fire itself.
—ERNEST HOLMES

We may think of the Divine as a fire whose outgoing warmth pervades the Universe. —PLOTINUS

Love is a fire and I am wood. —RUMI

All's love, yet all's law. —ROBERT BROWNING

Some day, after we have mastered the winds, the waves, the tides and gravity, we shall harness . . . the energies of love. Then, for the second time in the history of the world, we will have discovered fire.
—PIERRE TIELHARD DE CHARDIN

God's Presence in Me Is Love

He hath made everything beautiful in his time. —ECCLESIASTES 3:11

The Divine Presence within me is everlasting Love. The action of love is expressed in my world. God's Wisdom holds me steady, and the Peace of God fills me. I am His creation, understood, wanted, and cared for. From this Infinite Source I give and receive love in my world. If petty emotions seem to trouble me, I immediately turn to the Source within me of strength and peace. God in me does the loving, and I have no fear.

Kindness and understanding are shown to me. I bless anyone who seems to disturb me. I know how to love those who are dear to me and love them more each day. As our loves grows so we grow as individuals.

God in me is never troubled. Nothing can take love from me or keep it out of my heart. Love enters freely, and there is no restriction to it. I came into this world to love, and I am loving. I express my love for God, a boundless gratitude, because I live. God rejoices for me, because of and by means of me.

I Have Limitless Imagination

Open thou mine eyes, that I may behold wondrous things
out of thy law. —PSALM 119:18

The greatest satisfaction in using the Law of Life is in the consciousness
that such a Power is available, rather than in any use we make of it. For any
particular use we make of It is a passing thing, whether it be healing oneself
or others or producing any other temporary good. All of these are transitory,
and there is something in everyone that longs for permanency.

The artist knows that even though he has created something beautiful,
it can be destroyed. His real and innermost satisfaction is not in the object,
but in the subject; that thing within him that penetrates the mystic splendor
of Beauty itself. So it is with all our temporary creations. Empires may rise
and fall. Chance and change, the comings and goings of human events, inevitably must give way to something bigger. You are greater than the sum-
total of all the experiences you have had.

I know that a Law of Life exists and that I am one with It and inseparable from It. I am part of an infinite Energy from which I draw limitless creative imagination. This Energy is the invisible essence and substance of
every visible form. Its nature is goodness, truth, beauty, and love, and that
is my nature, too.

ॐ

The Activity of God Heals My Life

Now faith is the substance of things hoped for, the
evidence of things not seen. —HEBREWS 11:1

If we carry a light into a darkened room, the darkness is dissipated without
effort on our part. So it is the experience of one who has a deep consciousness of Life. Something invisible but all-penetrating will flow through his
every look and gesture. People will feel better by sitting in his presence.
Healings will take place automatically.

The Divine Spirit is not a mythical, abstract being, living somewhere
above this Earth. God is a Divine Presence revealing Himself to everyone
who believes. Where God is recognized, there is life. Where the power of
God is realized, there is action. Where the goodness of God is acknowl-
edged, there is peace.

I understand that God works through me, for I know that God is the
God of all life, of everyone's life, of everything that lives. God is the intelligence, the beauty, the love, the order, and the animating principle in and
through everything. God is my life.

I Use the Power of God

The God of love and peace shall be with you. —II CORINTHIANS 13:11

Have we really tried God? Since all the other methods have failed, a divine compulsion is laid upon everyone to find the power of God and make use of it. It is not merely a new theory about God that we are looking for; rather, it is the actual power of God that we must harness. Our trouble is that we have not really believed that this Presence exists and operates in human affairs. We have not realized the Divine Presence as a living and dynamic reality. What we need is the direct experience of a conscious contact with the Divine.

God is pure Spirit, filling all space. This pure Spirit animates your every act. There is a real you, which lives in a real God, and the two are one. To know this is to understand the secret of life. To realize this is to understand your relationship with the Divine Presence. To realize that the Law of God is written in your own mind is to make available to you a power that can meet every need.

Right now I feel a flow of Energy, Light, and Love filling my entire being. I know I am one with an infinite Presence that fills my life with peace, harmony, and joy. I let go of all negative beliefs and affirm that Love is transforming my life today.

I Know That Life Responds to Me

The desert shall rejoice, and blossom as the rose. —ISAIAH 35:1

The Law of Life operates through your affirmation. Nothing can hinder Its working but yourself. There is no more of It on the desert than there is on the busiest street corner, and It will not respond any more quickly because we go up into the temple. It is everywhere; therefore, It is where you are, and, most of all, It responds where you recognize It.

Your recognition makes possible Its response through you. This is the secret of faith. Faith is the supreme affirmation. It is the unconditioned affirmation. It is the affirmation that makes all things possible to the one who believes in the Power of God. Know that nothing can hinder you but yourself. If you believe you can, you can. You cannot fail if you start with the proposition that Life is all there is. It is the substance of every form. As the invisible, It is the cause. As the visible, It is the effect.

Right now I move from fear to faith. I let go of all doubt, distrust, worry, and fear. I change the direction of my life by focusing my thoughts on God, the Life within me, everyone, and everything. I have supreme faith in the Power of God to still the troubled waters and make the crooked places straight.

I Am One with My Source

Neither shall they say, Lo here! Or, lo there! for, behold,
the kingdom of God is within you. —LUKE 17:21

The good things we seek from life are but echoes of the true self knocking at
the door of consciousness. Everyone seeks an inward sense of certainty. We
all seek an inner awareness of something greater than we are; something so
complete that we can find completion in it; something so vast that we may
anticipate exploring its nature through endless eternities.

Someone has said that the soul is homesick and that it cannot recover
until it finds complete union with its Source. Intuitively we know that such
a union with a Source of power must exist. If the pipe that conducts water
from a high reservoir to our homes becomes disconnected, it does not mean
that the water has dried up at its source. So it is with our life. Its Source is an
infinite sea of energy, power, love, and wisdom. That which connects us
with the Source is our inner life, those thoughts and feelings that make up
our consciousness. Through the spiritual practice of meditation, we are able
to unite consciously with our infinite Source and so allow the cosmic stream
of Good to flow to us in an unobstructed channel.

I am filled with the spirit of love and gladness. I am filled with an expectancy of good things. The energy of life flows through me. I have no anxiety for the future, no regrets for the past. Today is God's day in which I live
and in which I greatly rejoice.

I Contemplate the Presence

Pray without ceasing. —I THESSALONIANS 2:17

It doesn't matter what we call it, so long as we remember that there is a "secret place of the most High" within us and that we may consciously enter it by merely knowing that we are already there. This is the place where the universe meets us in its wholeness without any restriction whatsoever. This is the place where the All delivers everything that It is to us.

Anything that helps you to enter here is good. If you say prayers, make affirmations, repeat beautiful passages, or just sit in the quiet contemplation of your thought, realizing the presence of life, you will do well, for all of these methods lead to the conclusion that the Power exists and is available.

All life, all health, all love, all peace exist in this Power. Our loneliness, our sense of isolation, our poverty, our doubt, and our sickness are results of being disconnected in consciousness from this Divine Self.

I let go of every inharmonious, limiting thought. I quietly turn within and acknowledge that Inner Presence of my own being. Beautiful, uplifting feelings of harmony, peace, and love flow through me like a river, elevating my consciousness to a new and higher level of acceptance and unity.

I See the Divine Presence in All Others

Behold, how good and how pleasant it is for brethren
to dwell together in unity! —PSALM 133:1

The best way to make friends is to realize that we meet Life in everyone. The God in us meets the God in others. Proclaiming the Divine Presence, believing in It, we shall meet It. Love will find a perfect way. Our faith in the Divine Presence in others will overcome the fear of being misunderstood or hurt. If the mind is calm and serene, there will be less liability toward pain. Therefore, at all times we should be serene and poised.

Confidence and love alone cast out fear. The person without fear is the only truly whole person. It is ours to decide whether we shall live in fear or in faith. Let us decide to live in faith. Let us learn to practice faith until all fear disappears, until life ceases to be a funeral dirge and becomes a song of joy. To find peace in the midst of confusion, we must realize our center in pure Spirit. To reach this place of confidence and faith in the midst of doubt and uncertainty, we should consciously unite our thought with the Divine Mind.

I know that God is within me. I know that the Spirit within me is perfect. I enter into Its peace and am secure in Its protection. The unerring judgment of Divine Intelligence directs my way. The presence of Love uplifts me and lights my life today.

I Give Form to the Invisible

Let your light so shine before men that they shall see your good works and glorify your Father which is in heaven. —MATTHEW 5:16

Life at the center of your being is a silent Power. Physical facts, form, and conditions are no obstruction to this Power. It flows through them and takes a new form in them. It remolds them. That which makes can re-make; that which molds can re-mold; that which creates can re-create. Remember, what you see comes from what you do not see. The visible is the Invisible made manifest. It is the Invisible caught in temporary form. Every time you think, you are giving form to this Invisible Power.

The question arises whether any limit can be placed upon the possibility of the conscious use of spiritual Power. Theoretically it would seem impossible to place such a limit. The only limitation would be that which proceeds from lack of belief or understanding. The Spirit Itself must be ever-present with us. If we could strip our mind of fear, superstition, and all sense of separation from this Divine Presence, approaching It quite simply and directly, we would probably be surprised at the results that would follow. In using spiritual Law, the one having the greatest faith obtains the best results.

I am surrounded by a spiritual Presence that responds to my word. Today I take charge of my thinking. Knowing that the Divine appears to each only as a measure of his own imagination, I enlarge the concept I present to It for fulfillment. I wait calmly and expectantly for new and greater experiences to come to me.

I Dwell in the Household of God

Know ye not that ye are the temple of God, that the Spirit
of God dwelleth in you? —I CORINTHIANS 3:16

The Household of God is the Household of Perfection. It is the Secret Place of the Most High. The inhabitants of this Household are all Divine Beings. Nothing can enter the consciousness of any of these inhabitants that contradicts the unity of Good. Each and every member of this Household is at peace with all other members. There is a community of peace, of understanding, of fellowship, and of love and unity.

In this Household of God—which is any person's household who declares it to be such—there is no bickering, no jealousy, and no avenue through which any littleness or meanness may operate. It is not only a household of peace, but also a household of joy; it is a place of happiness and general contentment. Here is warmth, color, and beauty. This earthy household symbolizes the Divine Harmony of the Kingdom of God. No one is a stranger within this household. Nothing is alien to it. It is protected from all fear, from every sense of loss. Nothing can enter it but joy, integrity, and friendship. This same good I realize belongs to everyone else.

I do not desire a good for myself that is greater than the good I desire for all people. Neither do I deny myself the good I affirm for all others. In this Household, the Host is God, the Living Spirit Almighty. All are invited and all who dwell in this Household are guests of the Eternal Host. I dwell here in peace, joy, and love.

I Am a Creative Center

Commit thy way unto the Lord; trust also in him;
and he shall bring it to pass. —PSALM 37:5

Let your consciousness rise above the sense of separation from the power of God, and in a few moments you will feel as though you were sitting in the midst of an infinite sea of unobstructed Life. This place in Mind where you are now is the Source of all action, the center of all creativity. It is also the innermost part of your own being.

Just as a plant turns to the sun, your thoughts turn to the Power and draw It down through your being, causing It to manifest through your word. In this act you are not losing your identity, you are more intensely self-conscious than every before, but you are conscious in a larger, less obstructed manner. Whatever you decree, state, or affirm from this altitude of thought will produce definite results. The Law of Life exists in all of us at all times, and we are using It whether or not we are conscious of the fact. If we wish to make a specific use of this Law of Life, then we must use It specifically.

I now climb a ladder of thought that takes me above all confusion. Climbing joyously, I pass through the clouds of fear and doubt. I behold light everywhere. I sense the enveloping presence of Love everywhere. The good that I desire, I now affirm and accept, knowing that my definite intentions produce definite results.

The Fullness of Life Flows Through Me

The water that I shall give him shall be in him a well of water
springing up into everlasting life. —JOHN 4:14

Your place in Life is to become an outlet for Its wisdom, intelligence, love, beauty, and creativity. Your relationship to Life is that you are of like nature to It. You are in it and It is in you. Some part of you exists as pure, unmanifest Spirit. This side of your nature has never been troubled. Since you are fashioned from the stuff of the Invisible, Its nature is incarnated in you. Because of this, your word has the power in your world of localizing itself, of manifesting itself in concrete form. You are in Life. Life is flowing through you. It is you. It decrees, affirms, knows, and imagines. That which it decrees transpires. You are like it. You rule your own world.

Every idea you have automatically sets the Law of Life in motion in such a way as to produce the definite form of that idea. There is something involved in a sunflower seed that acts upon the creative energy of nature in such a way as to produce a sunflower and not a cabbage or a potato. Definite ideas produce definite results. This means that if you are using this Law to bring loving friendship into your life, then you are specializing it for this definite purpose and not for something else.

I choose to live the kind of life I deeply desire. Accepting and affirming the truth of my being, that God and I are one, I free myself of beliefs in limitation and lack, and move forward into a new life of loving friendship and joy.

I Know Only Right Action

A new heart will I give you, and a new spirit
will I put within you. —EZEKIEL 36:26

Remaining constantly open to the Love of God within ourselves can produce great results. Though the essence of Love may be elusive, It pervades everything, renewing our soul and uplifting our emotions. We can all live happily, harmoniously, and successfully with one another when each of us practices a conscious recognition of the presence of Love within ourselves and within everyone. We can overcome the troubles and difficulties that we have allowed to enter our lives when we remember that Love is that creating and sustaining Presence within all.

God loves, moves, gives, and exists in me. As I eliminate anger and resentment, the Divine Nature flows freely through me. The Life-giving qualities are forever in motion. There is nothing in me that can stop, even for a second, the flow of Divine Energy, and there is only loving right action. The warmth of Love circulates through my mind, my body, and my world. The energy that I would have used in being angry, I now release in love. I dismiss all tendency to be angry, fearful, or resentful. In exchange I am filled with faith, love, and trust.

I Accept My Good

Go thy way, eat thy bread with joy, and drink thy wine with a merry heart; for God now accepteth thy works. —ECCLESIASTES 9:7

God speaks when we listen. God is there when we open the door. And when we listen there is a response from something greater than ourselves that is the infinite Person, the limitless Possibility. God speaks wherever and whenever we listen to our Inner Voice.

There is a Presence in the universe that is personal to us. It is the Spirit of which we are the direct individualizations. Whenever we create an idea, it is because a demand has been made upon the Mind of God that is incarnated in us. We mentally measure out what we shall receive in terms of the limitations of our previous experiences. But little by little we see that we can grow, and experience adds to experience until we accumulate an ever greater possibility. Each one of us is a direct inlet and direct outlet to God. This infinite Personalness residing within us is never limited by or separated from us except by the degree of our own ignorance. Our Inner Voice is always instantly available to guide and direct us through the vicissitudes of living.

I listen with complete faith and trust to the voice of Love guiding me today. I accept the abundant good that flows easily and freely to me. In return I am loving and generous to all others, knowing that we are joined in Spirit. My whole mind is open to the Divine influx of joy, love, wisdom, and guidance. My life prospers.

I Allow More Good into My Life

Blessed are they that have not seen and yet have believed. —JOHN 20:29

There is one ultimate Thinker, yet this Thinker thinks through all of us. This is why our thoughts are creative. The Universal Mind is incarnated in everyone. Every person has access to It; every person uses It, either in ignorance or in conscious knowledge. The mind of each one of us is the Mind of God functioning at the level of our perception of life. Consciously using It, we bring into our experience today something we did not appear to have yesterday—a better environment, a happier circumstance, more love, more joy.

In such degree as I know that the God in you is the God that is in me, I cannot seek to do you ill. It would be unthinkable, because all that I could do would be to hurt myself. When all of the nations of the world see God incarnated in one another, then we will no longer have use for weapons. We must stop believing that God is somewhere apart from us, or somewhere apart from the person or situation that is still in bondage of some kind. We must not be disturbed by the contradiction of objective experience. Rather, we need to know that the Truth of God's ever-present activity in our life is superior to the condition that we want to have changed.

I sense the Eternal Presence within me. Discarding any thoughts and attitudes that limit my inner awareness of this Presence, I accept the One Life as my life and see all around me the expression of love, peace, and harmony. I rejoice in the wondrous gifts of an unlimited Universe.

A Creative Spirit Expresses Through Me

*Eye hath not seen, nor ear heard, neither have entered into
the heart of man, the things which God hath prepared
for them that love him.* —I CORINTHIANS 2:9

Let us take a very simple lesson from nature. Perhaps from where you are sitting you can see a tree in full bloom. If so, remember that the tree's roots, from which it draws its life, are entirely invisible. Unless the tree drew on this invisible source, it would never flourish. We have roots in the Mind of God. Our personality, our individuality, everything we are and do that the world sees is really a result, in effect, of our continually drawing on the Infinite.

We must come to believe that the Creative Spirit in back of all things also flows through us. If we think of ourselves as rooted in God and expect Divine Power to flow through us, our every thought and action will be animated by the same life and power and beauty that clothe the lily of the field. God has imparted our life to us, placing no limitation or condition that would restrict us, other than this: Our life must be lived constructively, in unity and love and sympathy with everything around us, if we expect to live it to the fullest. I believe that every person is born to be creative and to live to the fullest and to be happy and glad and prosperous and whole.

It is the Father's pleasure to give me the Kingdom of Good. I accept it with joy and thanksgiving, knowing that I am called to be a creative center of Life. All that I wish for myself, I wish for others as well. Sensing the presence of Love guiding and protecting me, I go forth to spread this Love to all those I meet.

Love Is the Essence of My Being

Let us love not in word, neither in tongue;
but in deed and in truth. —I JOHN 3:18

Since God is Love, and God is All-in-All, Love must be the underlying principle of life, and therefore in all. This Life is my life. This Love is me. It is the very essence of my being. Love heals everything, every imperfection of mind or body or environment. Love alone may overcome hatred, anger, envy, and criticism. Where Love is, there is no room for any negative emotion. Love is the Great Adjuster.

I know that Love is harmony and peace and joy. In it is all good, all that is true, all that is beautiful. It is perfect balance, perfect poise. I empty my mind and heart of all but Love. I let Love express in me and through me. I let Love flow out into my world of thought and action. I am Love. The Love in me shines forth as harmony, peace, joy, freedom, and wisdom. Love binds me to the whole of creation. I find fulfillment through loving.

Each New Day Is a Fresh Beginning

*Now are we the sons of God, and it doth not yet appear
what we shall be.* —I JOHN 3:2

While there is a place that dwells in eternal stillness and inaction in the innermost recesses of our soul, there is also a place at the circumference of our being that, animated by the inner Spirit, goes forth to accomplish. If we will take time daily to sense this Presence, believe in It, and accept It, before long the life we have known until now will gradually disappear. Something new and wonderful will be born—a bigger, better, and more perfect life. We will pass from sadness into happiness, from lack and want into greater freedom, and from fear into assurance. Through the continual emergence of the Creative Principle, any last finality proves to be but the beginning of a new creative series. This eternal spiral, finding its base in the everlasting Reality, will never cease to emerge. Our increased awareness of spiritual truths will make each day a fresh beginning, a new approach to Reality, a spiritual adventure arising fresh and new from the original Creative Principle active within us.

I enjoy my present experiences and joyously anticipate each day's increasing good. Opening my heart and mind, I allow the creative action of God to express through me, aware that as my capacity to accept good expands, I become a blessing both to myself and to the world in which I live. I rejoice at the greater possibilities of my future unfoldment.

The Divine Presence Within Me Is My Authority

Thou wilt keep him in perfect peace,
whose mind is stayed on thee. —ISAIAH 26:3

The Divine Presence within each of us is both the center and circumference of our real being. It is the Infinite Presence that inhabits eternity and finds a dwelling place in our own consciousness. We recognize It as the only authority there is. We know we are one with It and in It, for there is no separation from It. Our own consciousness is the very depth and height of Its Being and is one with all that It is.

There is an infinite self-knowingness, which we call the Spirit. It is ruled by law and impelled by love. Each of us is an individual center in it, without being an individual separate from It. We are rooted in the One, which produces limitless variety. Therefore, God is uniquely individual and uniquely personal to each one of us.

We are not one in God or one with God, but we are one *of* God. Although the identity is the same in essence, it is not the same in degree. If there were a sameness in degree, we would have already exhausted the possibility of the Infinite; and having done so, our continual existence would be a cosmic tragedy, because there would be no place to go and nothing to see. Everything would have been used up. Let us keep our thoughts turned to the Divine Presence within us and within one another. Deeply desiring that we become more aware of the love we have for one another and the world, may our consciousness be opened to a deeper understanding of Life.

In the beauty and quiet of this moment, I commune with the Divine Presence. The certainty of love and friendship flows into my consciousness, and I feel a deep peace. I give thanks for my increasingly beautiful life.

I Recognize the Indwelling Spirit

Be still, and know that I am God. —PSALM 46:10

A belief in the Invisible is the very essence of faith. Prayer, or spiritual communion, demands a complete surrender to the Invisible. It knows that because the Creative Power of God is at hand, all things are possible.

Whatever our idea of God may be, the perception of Reality is always an inner perception. As Moses tells us, the word is not afar off but in our own mouths, and Jesus taught that the Kingdom of Heaven is within us. The prayer of power is not so much a petition as it is an inner recognition.

We cannot doubt that the Spirit has already made the gift of Life—since we live. Ours is the privilege of acceptance. Thus we are to assume the attitude of a grateful beneficiary of the Divine gifts. This should be done simply and directly. The Spirit is not something that was, or that is going to be or become. The Truth is that which is; it exists at the very center of our being. To pray in spirit and in truth means to recognize this indwelling Spirit and to declare the truth about its activity through us.

Today I directly experience the reality of Spirit, allowing It to renew my mind, guide my decisions, and direct my affairs. I know that in the eternal act of creation, everything passes from the Invisible to the visible to be temporarily experienced. I rest in peace, assured that my needs are met by this play of Life upon Itself.

I Let My Light Shine

A new heart also will I give you, and a new spirit
will I put within you. —EZEKIEL 36:26

People who spend a great deal of time in prayer, meditation, or communion with the Spirit gradually take on a new atmosphere, a new sweetness, a love and light that all others sense. The Old Testament often refers to a light always shining over the altar in the temple. This light, of course, is a symbol of the Life that is never extinguished. The light of Jesus has been sensed by artists so completely that they have depicted it as an aura, at atmosphere of light.

Now this light is real. There is such a light at the center of everything. This is the Divine Stuff of which we are all made. There is nothing outside this light. Everything exists in it. There is light at the center of everyone. It is never obliterated, but it does seem that it is often obscured for various reasons. Jesus said never to put your light under a bushel, but to let it shine.

I feel a deep sense of unity with everyone and with everything. I know that all is Love and I am filled with the goodness of Life. Love and Light flow in and through me. I give thanks for the radiance of Spirit within me.

Deep Within Me Dwells Infinite Love

A good man out of the good treasure of the heart
bringeth forth good things. —MATTHEW 12:55

God is the giver of all things—by means of love. The Spirit is always at
peace. There is no argument in Divine Mind. The Spirit has never doubted
Itself, opposed Itself, or disagreed with Itself. This is the Oneness that is
God. Deep within me is that which never gets angry, troubled, or afraid.
When I seem to be in conflict, I become still so that I may listen.

All the Love there is is right here, right now with me. I now cease all
self-opposition. I hear only the voice of Love, speaking to me. I hear nothing but the words of Wisdom, guiding and inspiring me. And when I listen
there is a response from something greater than myself. It is the mysterious
energy of Love, the active principle of unity. Everything loves, and everything responds to love. It is a universal quality, shared alike by all, the central flame of the Universe.

Desiring to be loved, I allow myself to love greatly, to feel warmly in-
clined toward all people, and to be helpful on their behalf. I give as I wish to
receive. As I love and cooperate with other people, so do they love me and
give me their cooperation. My loving thoughts attract caring friends to me.

A Certain Future Awaits Me

Let us hold fast the profession of our faith without wavering;
for he is faithful that promised. —HEBREWS 10:23

We are not enough at home in the universe. We are afraid of it—afraid to live. If the time ever comes to you and to me when we see God in everything and in everybody, we will never be alone or lonely. Every experience will but more vividly reveal the warmth and color and beauty and responsiveness of the Universe in which we live; its entire nature is given to us.

We are on the verge of a vast possibility. The individual or nation without a vision must perish until the vision is reborn. What is our vision going to be in the midst of confusion, doubt, and uncertainty? It is either going to fall before the confusion and be destroyed, or something transcendent within us is going to rise and look to a certain future, to an eternal Reality, to a God-Principle—to an Infinite Presence, responding to us according to our acceptance.

There is no individual good. Good belongs to everyone. Good fulfills itself only as it multiplies itself; therefore, there is no good that belongs to you and to me alone, no final peace to us only as individuals. The watchword is not exclusion but inclusion, and the more good we release, the more good we experience.

I am part of one tremendous Whole whose nature is of God. It is in this Divine Nature, this inevitable union, that I consciously walk and talk with the Infinite, until it becomes dynamic and real to me. I am thankful for every opportunity to let God's Life be expressed through me.

I Open Myself to Greater Love

Though I speak with the tongues of men
and of angels, and have not charity, I am become
as sounding brass, or a tinkling cymbal. —I CORINTHIANS 13:1

Love is more than a sentiment. It is a need, a hunger, a thirst that is perfectly natural. Anyone who thinks he can live and be happy without it does not know what he is talking about—psychologically, emotionally, or spiritually. Love is the beginning and end, the impulse in nature that will not be denied.

Let us think back beyond the individual to the Source of all life. I believe that the whole universe is the givingness of the Creative Spirit—to the delight of Its own Being—into the creation that is Itself in that creation. Love is the principle of Life, for it is the nature of everything to give. Only the one who loves so much that there is no longer any room for hate will ever arrive at the place where, if there may be hate, he will never know it. We are afraid of greatness because we are so tied down to littleness. We clutch the littleness anxiously and jealously, but so precariously, to our hearts. It is essential to see beyond the littleness to something bigger. None of us is as perfect in expression as we ought to be. So the challenge to each of us is to be great enough to rise in love, in charity, through understanding and compassion. Love is the lodestone of life.

I respond lovingly to all persons. Recognizing that the spiritual life is the real life, I surround myself with love, the key to joyous living.

I Clear My Mind of Discord

Peace I leave with you, my peace I give unto you. —JOHN 14:27

How are we going to heal ourselves and others? By first becoming convinced that love is a principle of nature. We have ample evidence scientifically, logically, and intuitively that there is no need for anyone in the world today to speak of love as mere sentimentality. We have to practice the Presence of God as love, as friendship, as peace, as joy, if we would know the fullness of the adventure of living.

It is a terrible burden to dislike people and to be critical. All it does is cover up a perpetual pain in our own heart. It is a whistling in the dark to keep up our own courage. How much easier it is to love people, to learn to forgive rather than to hold grudges. We should not go to bed at night until we have cleared our mind of every animosity. Love is the greatest healing agent on Earth for our body as well as for our affairs.

To be a friend is the greatest privilege I can experience. Therefore, I extend loving friendship to all I meet. I identify myself with the givingness of God's own nature, knowing that I am in league with the highest force in life.

I Make Intelligent Use of Universal Laws

I have given thee a wise and an understanding heart. —I KINGS 3:12

The Universe is impersonal. It gives alike to all. It is no respecter of persons. It values each alike. The philosopher, the priest, and the professor, the humanitarian and the empire builder, all have caught some gleam of the Eternal God. The world of knowledge needs to be knit together and not pulled apart.

The road to freedom lies, not through mysteries, but through the intelligent use of natural forces and laws. We do not create laws and principles, but discover and make use of them. Our mind and spirit is our echo of the Eternal Thing Itself, and the sooner we realize this fact, the sooner we will be made free and happy.

Don't we all agree that the world is tired of mysteries, does not understand symbols, and longs for Reality? We should take truth wherever we find it, making it our very own. Intellectual freedom and religious liberty are necessary to the unfolding spirit in man.

I Keep My Thought Clear

Be ye transformed by the renewing of your mind. —ROMANS 12:2

We are surrounded by a receptive and creative medium that receives our thought and acts upon it. There is nothing harder than keeping the thought straight, and nothing else so desirable. It is not easy in our contacts with the daily world to keep our thoughts so clear that we never become unpoised, that we never accept anything we do not wish to accept, and that we always control the intellect so the emotions do not respond unless the intellect says to respond. But whenever we can do this, our destiny will be in our own hands, backed by an immutable Power. But before we do this, we must relate and harmonize ourselves with the Infinite. We oppose It when we admit that anything opposes us. We deny it when we admit that a good is denied to us.

When we find ourselves in discordant conditions, we should never say, "Oh, what's the use?" Rather, we should say, "There is Something in me that is greater than this condition and It can dissolve it." We have the privilege and power to do this, and if we use this ability properly, it will produce wondrous results. Remember that the cause of everything is an idea and that the thought is the mold in which our tangible experience is cast.

I have the power to live the life of good. My thought reflects the good that I desire. I am conscious of the focus of my thinking, and my own is manifesting itself to me now. There is nothing in me that can hinder it from entering and taking possession of my Soul. My own is now expressed.

I Form a New Concept of God

We shall be changed, in a moment, in the twinkling
of an eye. —I CORINTHIANS 15:51–52

The Power of Life within you is a spiritual power, able to bring to you permanent peace, increasing happiness and joy, and greater material abundance. These things that have made man miserable can be eliminated through the conscious use of this Power. God could not visit fear or hate or impoverishment upon us, because God transcends these things. The world needs a new concept of God; a new idea must be born in the minds of people everywhere about the nature of God and their relationship to this Divine Creative Spirit.

The only thing that can bring love, joy, peace, and prosperity to the world is a direct experience of the Invisible. We must sense the immediate presence of Life. With simplicity and directness, we must sense that the Spirit is at the center of our own lives. We must learn to recognize that It is at the center of all people and working in human affairs. While it is true that the Power of God is always within us, it is not true that we have always realized Its presence. To realize this is to be able to make conscious use of it, to direct It, for ourselves and for others.

I rely on my Inner Power to work with me in creating the kind of life I deeply desire. I know that within myself I can find the guidance I seek and the strength I need. With Love in my heart, knowing I am unbound and unlimited, I accept myself as a happy, healthy, strong, and successful person right here and now.

MARCH
FAITH

Faith is a mental attitude that is so convinced of its own idea—which so completely accepts it—that any contradiction is unthinkable and impossible. —ERNEST HOLMES

> There is no chance, no destiny, no fate,
> Can circumvent or hinder or control
> The firm resolve of a determined soul.
> —ELLA WHEELER WILCOX

> All shall be well
> And all shall be well,
> And all manner of things shall be well.
> —JULIAN OF NORWICH

Any anxious thought as to the means to be employed in the accomplishment of our purposes is quite unnecessary. If the end is already secured, then it follows that all the steps leading to it are secured also.
—THOMAS TROWARD

Faith

A spiritual mind treatment or affirmation of Truth, or a prayer of faith, once made and completely accepted, is then acted upon by the Law of Mind, and the effect or result is independent of the person who has made the prayer. In order to understand this idea more clearly let us take a simple fact in nature. We bury an acorn in the ground and walk away from it knowing that some-day an oak tree will grow. In the same way our word is acted upon creatively by some kind of intelligent Force, or Law, which knows how to create the form the word implies. Every scientist follows the same method in dealing with the principles of nature.

We have every reason to believe there is a creative Law that acts upon our acceptance. This Law already is equipped with the know-how to do what we accept It is doing. It is the same Law that has governed all prayers of faith throughout the ages and brought about the results that have always been looked upon as miracles. They are miracles in the sense that it is a mir-acle for an egg to hatch. Faith, affirmation, and acceptance are acted upon by some creative Intelligence.

Today I have faith in my own affirmations. I know that there is a Power flowing through me, taking the form of my belief, acting upon my accept-ance, answering my prayer, and fulfilling my affirmation. Therefore, I am calling upon myself for a deeper faith, a broader conviction, a higher ac-ceptance, a more complete realization. I affirm that every good thing I do will prosper, every person I meet will be blessed, every situation I touch will be helped. Everywhere I go some subtle influence of love and joy and peace will diffuse itself as a glow from the eternal Light of Heaven itself.

> Seest thou how faith wrought with his works, and
> by works was faith made perfect? —JAMES 2:22

Unifying with the Spirit

"Hear, O Israel: The Lord our God is one Lord." This is a statement of the unity of all life. Einstein believed in one physical law that comprehends, co-ordinates, and synthesizes all physical laws. This, from the greatest mathematician of modern times, philosophically and spiritually viewed, is no different from saying that there must be one final Mind, Power, Spirit, or Reality in the universe flowing in and through all things and governing all things. This is what we mean when we say that God is all there is.

Science, logic, mathematics, reason, and revelation are on the side of the one who boldly proclaims the Allness of God. We shall do well to follow this path because it means that in the last analysis right has no opposite, good cannot be denied. Feeling and thinking and sensing this Allness, we enter into conscious communion with It, and in some subtle way we do not understand, Its essence flows out into our acts, spilling Itself in and through everything we do and bringing to bear upon the problems of life an Intelligence greater than the human and a Power that is transcendent.

Today I am affirming the supremacy of Good and everything within me responds to this thought, understands Its meaning, and announces Its presence. There is a Power flowing through me into everything I do and think, automatically making everything whole. There is a Transcendence coordinating, unifying, causing all the experience of my life to blend into Its unity, into Its oneness, and proclaiming the power of Its might. As a child accepts life without question and love without argument and action without anxiety, so do I spontaneously accept the operation of this Power as the Divine Governor of everything I do, the Divine Provider of all my needs, and the Divine Presence diffused through all my thinking.

They seek me daily, and delight to know my ways . . .
they take delight in approaching to God. —ISAIAH 58:2

Affirmative Prayer

Today thousands of people are coming to believe in, and use, the power of affirmative prayer. We are entering into a new era of spiritual acceptance. Something definite is happening in the field of spiritual thought and endeavor. From all sources we are coming to realize that affirmative prayer is dynamic. It should be easier today than ever before for people to accept the simple teaching that there is a Power greater than ourselves that desires our good, and a Law of Mind that we may consciously use for definite purposes. We shall be both inspirational and scientific when we come to believe this— inspirational in the belief and scientific in the use of the Law. For while the belief is personal, the Law is impersonal and acts upon our thought regardless of who we are.

We should come to believe in the exactness of this Law. We should use It definitely and consciously. This requirement applies in every science and it applies equally to the Science of Mind, for we are not dealing with chaotic laws that may or may not respond to us. We are dealing with the certainty of a reaction that is equal to the action or a response that is equal to our own conviction. We are dealing with a definite principle, but the conviction is personal, a thing of warmth, of color, and of feeling.

Today I affirm the All-Good. I know that my word, being acted upon by a Power greater than I am, is sure to accomplish its purpose. Therefore, I find peace, joy, and an inward tranquility in my own acceptance. Knowing that the Law of God is perfect, I know that my word is certain. My faith is complete; my affirmation cannot be denied. Living in this continual acceptance, finding security in this complete trust, in gratitude I accept every good thing Life has to offer and in love I share it with all.

> I will pray with the spirit, and I will pray with the
> understanding also. —I CORINTHIANS 14:15

Acceptance

Spiritual mind treatment, or affirmative prayer, really is something we do to ourselves. The only direction we give to this treatment, this prayer, this affirmation of acceptance, is that we identify it with the person we are working for or the condition we wish to help. This is neither willing, concentrating, coercing, nor compelling anything or anyone. It is, rather, a quiet inward acceptance, an affirmation of our conviction, based on the theory that there is a spiritual Perfection at the center of all things in the universe and that there is a fundamental Good governing all things.

There is One Life, that Life is God, that Life is our life now. Consciously we identify ourselves with It, definitely we affirm the One Presence and the One Power operating in, around, and through us. Anything that denies the supremacy of Good is itself but a mistake in judgment. As we come to open up our thought to a greater acknowledgment and acceptance of the Divinity that resides within us, we find ourselves on the pathway to achieving the purpose for which we were created: to express the nature of the Divine, the Source of our being.

Today I accept my own affirmations. There is nothing in me that can contradict them. I have a deep inward sense, feeling, conviction, and complete faith that there is a Power of Good governing everything; that It is governing completely, with absolute certainty, without deviation, without exception and that there is nothing to oppose It, to change It, to limit or circumscribe Its action. I abandon myself to this faith, live in its atmosphere, and accept its conclusion. I know that I am a Divine being on the pathway of an endless self-expression and that the eternal God is my host, now and forevermore.

> I am the Almighty God; walk before me,
> and be thou perfect. —GENESIS 17:1

Human Relations

There is One Spirit incarnated in everyone, an immortal Presence forever expanding everything, causing everything to grow. What a difference it would make in our human relations if we tried to sense the meaning of this Divine incarnation in all people and adjust our viewpoint to the truth that all are bound together in the unity of God. While it is true, as the Scripture says, that now we see through a glass darkly, there still is hidden within each one the Cause of all life, all aspiration, and all faith.

We are so used to thinking of ourselves as separate from one another that we suspect the very feeling and emotion that causes us to embrace everything in love. The one who loves the most will live the most. We meet each other only in fragments, only partially, only in a miserly way when we refuse to open the whole avenue of our consciousness to the realization that there is but one living Spirit. If our human relations are to mean the most to us, we must sense that there is hidden within, around, and through each of us a Divine Presence manifesting Itself in infinite variations—the same impulse, the same Love and Life, but never quite alike in any two persons.

Today I am going to meet each experience as I feel it really is. I will endeavor to see the Divine Presence in everything. I am demanding of myself that I see and sense and feel the One Life that flows through all things. I affirm this Presence and accept Its beneficent action because It already is. As I go forth today and embark on the wonderful experience of living, I am on a journey of self-discovery and also of the discovery of the self hidden in everyone and the Power in back of everything.

That they all may be one; as thou, Father, art in me, and I in thee, that they also may be one in us. —JOHN 17:21

Living Today

It is not the particular negative experiences we have gone through in the past that destroy our happiness, but rather our emotional reaction to those experiences carried in the reservoir of memory. Many people suffer complete defeat without having really been defeated; others succumb the first time anything goes wrong. It is one of the aims of psychosomatic medicine, analytical psychology, and psychiatry to drain out the negative and emotional reactions to previous experiences. There is just as real an infection of the mind as there is of any part of our physical body.

Almost invariably our negative reactions to life, our unhappiness, and perhaps most of our physical disorders are based on unhappy experiences that are buried, but buried alive, in our memory. But yesterday can have no reality to us other than as our reaction to it. It can have no real existence of its own in today other than as the lengthened shadows of yesterday. And so it is that as the impulsions of yesterday are carried over into today, making today happy or disconsolate, so the reactions of today are prophetic of what we will experience tomorrow.

Yesterday is gone, tomorrow has not arrived, and I live in an eternal present filled with an everlasting good. There is nothing unhappy or morbid in my consciousness. I have no fear of yesterday nor do I anticipate tomorrow with anything other than enthusiastic expectation. Everything good in my experience will create my future. I have no fear in looking backward or forward, but realize the eternal day in which I now live. Today is big with hope fulfilled, with love and life well lived. Tomorrow will provide its own blessings.

Be renewed in the spirit of your mind. —EPHESIANS 4:23

Individualization

Everything in the universe is a unique individualization or expression of the One Thing that is the Cause of all things. No two blades of grass are alike, no two grains of sand, no two thumbprints; no two of anything are alike and nothing ever exactly reproduces any other thing. This means that the one ultimate Cause is pressing against every individualization, flowing through it or him or her and that every event in the finite has an infinite possibility behind it.

We have to link all of this with our everyday actions because we cannot live by theories alone. They must be brought down to earth and applied to our daily life, but it is wonderful to realize that we do not have to imitate; we do not have to compete. All we have to do is to be ourselves and realize that the One Self, the Universal Being, expressing Itself in us in a unique way, is absolute and available. This is the secret that every person has with Life and with God: that God shall be to each one of us what we are to God.

Today I practice being myself. I think simply and directly from the center of my own being, which is one with the living Spirit. I realize that all the Good there is, all the Presence there is, all the Power there is, is immediately available and responsive to my acceptance. I enter into the faith of believing, the joy of knowing, and the act of living that proclaim the One Presence and Power in all things. This Presence—warm, personal, and colorful—responds to me. It is within, around, and through me, and It embraces all things. Today I accept my partnership with the Infinite.

> If ye have faith as a grain of mustard seed . . . nothing
> shall be impossible unto you. —MATTHEW 17:20

Our Right to Self-Expression

It is right to enjoy life. It is normal and natural to desire a more abundant life. Jesus said, "I am come that they might have life, and that they might have it more abundantly." In the unity of humankind with Spirit, there can be no lack or limitation; each of us is entitled to all that our Father has. The realization that God is an infinite Source is dawning upon our awakened thought, expanding our acceptance of greater abundance and dispelling all lack.

This impartation of livingness to everything is the very nature of the God who gives. Selfishness enters only when our good would exclude or hurt others. Nothing is selfish if it is done from the viewpoint of expressing the hidden splendor in all things, revealing it through all things and in all occasions. It is this more abundant life that we all seek, and we have a right to experience it. We have a right to be filled with joy, to desire the good things of life, to expect "manna from heaven" and good from every source. But at the same time we must know that good is not for us alone.

Today I express myself with joy and enthusiasm. I want to live more abundantly and I accept such possibility. I want to look more deeply into the heart of all people, finding there the pulsation of the Heart of the Universe. I want to penetrate all externals and reveal the Divine Presence hidden there. I know in my self-expression of the abundance of the Whole, there is nothing mean or little, nothing separate from the All-Good. As I lift high the chalice of my hope and faith I know that it will overflow, that everything I do will be blessed, that every good I seek will be expressed through me. Everyone I meet will proclaim that God is expressing through all humanity and rejoicing in that which He does.

> Ye shall eat your bread to the full, and dwell in
> your land safely. —LEVITICUS 26:5

Relaxation in Treatment

If we feel that our thought—by our own will and through the power of concentration—must go out somewhere in the invisible and compel things to happen, then we will put strain into our prayer or treatment. This is one of the things we must avoid. Our prayers are spoken in faith, then released to the Power of the Law.

Through the use of faith and belief in affirmative prayer, which we call spiritual mind treatment, something greater than ourselves acts upon us. If we had the same faith in spiritual laws that we have in physical ones, our faith would be complete and miracles would happen every day. As we turn to the Divine Center within us, then, realizing the fullness of the activity of the living Spirit is working through us, let us announce our good. Without effort or strain, and in a relaxed receptivity, let us know that the Law of Mind acts upon our word. Not asking how or why, but with simple acceptance and complete belief, let us permit this good to be established in our experience.

Knowing that the Divine Presence has given me of Its nature, I accept that everything of good is right where I am and is active in all of my affairs. Today, everything in my life comes under the control of God's Intelligence. Everything is harmonized by It and unified with It. Consequently, my faith is complete. I know that I will be guided in everything I think, say, and do. I know that peace and joy and happiness will flow from me to everyone I meet. Today everything in my experience is made glad, and joy goes before me making every experience happy and radiant with life.

Be still, and know that I am God. —PSALM 46:10

Divine Patterns

There is a Divine pattern for humanity, and within this pattern there is a variation that individualizes each one of us. This is why the Bible says that we should act in accordance with the pattern shown us on the mount, a symbol of high consciousness. When we lift our thought above the confusion of the material world, we become aware of the spiritual Cause behind all things.

It is no idle statement to affirm the Perfection of God as the center of all things, manifesting in and through each and every thing in a unique way. We should spend more time meditating upon the harmony, the beauty, the peace, and the joy that exist at the center of our own being. We cannot believe that our inner wholeness was created by us or came into being through a process of evolution. Quite the reverse. All evolution is a result of the action of an imprisoned splendor that exists at the center of all things.

Today I seek the Divine pattern at the center of my own being. Affirming its reality, I permit its essence to flow through me. Claiming it as my very own, I embrace it. Believing in its beauty, I sense its harmony. Accepting its peace, I am calm. Living in its love, I am unified with life. Believing in its power, with childlike faith, I accept the authority of its action in my everyday affairs. And looking at the God in humankind, I see in everyone the pattern of God's Perfection. I see God's image and likeness.

And there are diversities of operations, but it is the same
God which worketh all in all. —I CORINTHIANS 12:6

Givingness

There can be no real gift unless the giver goes with it. Giving includes more than the giving of money or things, it includes the giving of service or whatever we have to others, but always the gift and the giver must go hand in hand. The surrender of everything we have and everything we are into the joy of its own self-expression—this is the way that God gives. This is the way we should give.

Real giving is the art of transmitting ourselves to others and to the conditions and situations that surround us. This kind of giving is not something for special occasions only; for it should become a habit growing out of our desire to live life to the fullest extent. Only that which becomes an inward habit of thought can spontaneously flow from the heart and transmit itself to everything we touch. Just as life belongs to the one who lives it, to the one who takes it, so the fuller life belongs only to the one who scatters every good he has. It is by giving of oneself to every person, every project, and every association with zest, love, and friendliness that one sees the larger possibility in all things: beauty instead of ugliness, love instead of hate, the Divine hidden within the human.

Today and every day it is my desire that what Life has given to me so abundantly shall be shared with others. I desire to share this realization of the indwelling Presence with everyone. In this consciousness I say, Bless you, my friend. I desire for you health, happiness, and success. I desire for you love, peace, and joy. I desire for you the benediction of the kingdom of God here upon earth.

There is that scattereth, and yet increaseth. —PROVERBS 11:24

Identification

Spiritual mind treatment is an affirmation of the Divine Presence in and through all things, all people, and all events. There is one intelligent Law governing all things. We live in this Divine Presence and may consciously use this Universal Law. But someone might ask, How does our prayer, our treatment, or our affirmation reach the person, place, or the thing we wish to help? This question is answered when we come to realize that we are individualized expressions of the One Life.

Whenever we identify our thinking with some person or thing, we identify him or her or it as the object of that thinking, and automatically, because there is One Law operating, the result of that thinking will be for that person or thing. Since the focus of our treatment or prayer is in the One Mind, the mere act of identifying our affirmation with that person or thing brings about an effect upon him, her, or it.

Today I am identifying myself, everyone else, and everything I do with the Divine Presence. I am not trying to influence people. I am not holding thoughts to make things happen. I am not concentrating Divine energies for any purpose whatsoever. Rather, I am still, knowing that God is over all, in all, and through all. Through my affirmation I am watching, expecting, and knowing that there will be a reaction through whatever I identify with my word. Therefore, I am at ease; I am at peace. I affirm the Divine Presence and Its manifestations as happiness, prosperity, and well-being for everyone.

> We dwell in him, and he in us, because he hath
> given us of his Spirit. —I JOHN 4:13

Forgivingness

It is only when we have completely forgiven others that we can get a clearance in our own minds, for we are judged by the judgment with which we judge. If we criticize, condemn, and censure, these are the attitudes that occupy our thinking. They will not only reflect themselves outwardly, they will also reflect themselves inwardly. They must, for the without is but an extension of the within, and the within is the determinor of that extension. If we want a complete clearance of our attitudes, we must forgive everything and everyone. Whether we like it or not, or whether we accept it or not, this is one of the great truths of life.

Not only should we forgive others but we should equally forgive ourselves. Until we release all of our own previous mistakes and failures, pain and suffering, we shall merely be monotonously repeating them today. A great deal of our trouble, both mental and physical, is built on an unconscious sense of rejection and guilt. It is necessary that each of us seek complete forgivingness toward both ourself and others.

Today I affirm that I forgive everyone and am forgiven by everyone. I affirm that the eternal Spirit harbors no malice toward me or anyone else. Forgiving and being forgiven, I have an inward sense of peace and tranquility. There is no anxiety, no sense of guilt, no fear of judgment. All mistakes of the past are now wiped out in my consciousness and I no longer carry any burden from them. I look forward to the future with joy, in peace and gladness, and live in the present with an inner assurance of being one with all life.

And when ye stand praying, forgive, if ye have ought against any:
that your Father also which is in heaven may
forgive you your trespasses. —MARK 11:25

Immutability of the Law

There is a Power to which all things are possible. This Power or Law of Mind is right where we are and we use It with every thought we think. To come into the greater possibility of Good that is open to each of us we must use It constructively. This is what we do in giving a spiritual mind treatment, which we call practicing the Science of Mind. Taking our inspiration from God's Spirit dwelling within us, we cause the Law to operate for us at this level of consciousness.

When Jesus said that we should seek the kingdom of heaven first and everything else would be added, he was telling us that when our consciousness lifts itself above confusion and enters the peace of the Spirit, then our word spoken from this center is acted upon immutably, producing the desired effect. We are not making the prayer work or using spiritual mind treatment to force things to happen any more than we would be compelling a reflection of our likeness to be cast from a mirror when we stand in front of it. Such reflection is automatic; it is certain to look exactly like the image. In just such a manner our thought reflects into a creative medium that returns its image.

Believing in the immutable Law of Mind and knowing that I am not coercing, I do now completely abandon myself to the realization that I am one with the living Spirit, one with the eternal Good, one with the everlasting God. I am steadfast in my affirmation, letting nothing limit or obstruct its reflection in my experience. There is nothing in me that need compel my word to operate, nor is there anything in me that can hinder its operation. Standing still, operating from the Divine center of my own consciousness, I announce the Truth and the Truth makes me free.

Open thou mine eyes, that I may behold wondrous
things out of thy law. —PSALM 119:18

Love

Love is the lodestone of life, the great and supreme Reality. Love is the highest gift of heaven, the greatest good on earth, and the treasure of all our search. It is the end and aim of everything. We cannot doubt that God is Love, because love renews and reinvigorates while hate kills. People who love animals and understand them are not afraid of them, for love transmits some subtle essence of life to everything it touches, awakening within all things an equal awareness and response. This is true also of human relationships. Love is the greatest healing power there is and no one feels whole without it.

But love is something that need not be confined to only a few persons; that love that we have for the few can be extended to more without losing the love of the few. And what a wonderful experience and realization it would be if we learned to love everyone as we love the few! Right now our vision is hardly great enough to include this larger good. But when love becomes more complete it will take in a larger territory and we will experience a greater degree of livingness.

Today my love goes out to all people and to all things. There is no fear in this love for perfect love casts out all fear. There is no doubt in this love for faith penetrates all doubt and reveals a unity at the center of everything that embraces all things. This love flowing through me harmonizes everything in my experience, brings joy and gladness to everything, brings a sense of security and well-being to everyone. I realize that the love flowing through, in, and around me and all things is one vast all-enveloping essence and force forever emanating from the living God.

As the Father has loved me, so have I loved you.
Now remain in my love. —JOHN 15:9

Affirmation and Denial

By far the larger part of our thinking processes are automatic, casting the images of their acceptances into the Universal Mind that reacts upon them. Thus it is that fear can bring about a condition of failure, while faith can reverse it. In spiritual mind treatment, affirmation and denial are for the purpose of erasing the wrong thought patterns and establishing correct ones. This practice is both scientific and effective in that a denial tends to erase the negative conviction, while an opposite affirmation tends to establish a new thought pattern that works as automatically as the negative one did.

The whole theory of affirmation and denial in spiritual mind treatment is built upon an understanding that the Mind-Principle accepts the inward meaning and feeling of the words that our conscious mind utters. The Mind-Principle is like a mirror; therefore, the argument must bring out an evidence that causes our whole inward being to accept the affirmation we make, whether it be a declaration of supply, health, happiness, or success. If we practice this method and watch the result of this simple process, we will discover that an argument logically presented to this Mind-Principle will produce a definite result.

Today I affirm the All-Good, and in this affirmation I accept the presence of love and repudiate every belief that hate has any power. I affirm peace and deny confusion. I affirm joy and declare that sadness has no place in my consciousness. I affirm that God is over all, in all, and through all. There is nothing in my past that can limit me or limit my future. There is One Life, that Life is God, that Life is the only life there is, and that Life is my life now.

> So shall my word be that goeth forth out of my mouth:
> it shall not return unto me void. —ISAIAH 55:11

Power of the Word

The universe seems beyond our comprehension. The slightest fact in nature is a miracle we cannot perform. All we can do is recognize that there is a way to work with the spiritual law of the universe. We may rely upon It, for It will not fail us. We must come not only to believe and accept, but also to know that we are one with the living Spirit, that God is all there is.

Our word, being the presence and the power and the activity of God's Spirit, activates the Law of Mind, which cannot fail to operate. Let us feel that there is something permanent about the word we have spoken. Just as we plant a seed and walk away from it, nature takes it up, and the law of its own being evolves it, so let us believe the same thing about our word—something takes it up, something evolves it, and it will manifest.

"So shall my word be that goeth forth out of my mouth: it shall not return unto me void." I affirm that it is the word of Truth establishing harmony as my experience. With utmost simplicity I accept and believe in the answer to my own prayer because it is a prayer of acceptance. There is an Intelligence, a Divine Presence operating in and through my life, guiding, directing, governing, bringing me good. This affirmation of acceptance endlessly repeats itself in my experience and in the experience of others, for whatever I identify my word with is lifted up in consciousness and made manifest.

> He that doeth truth comes to the light, that his deeds may be made manifest, that they are wrought in God. —JOHN 3:21

Expectancy

In spiritual mind treatment we are dealing with a Law as definite as that which takes a cabbage seed and makes a cabbage out of it instead of a cauliflower. We are dealing with a creative Power that acts upon our thinking. This Power we did not make, but we may use. It operates upon us like all other forces in nature. With this in mind, we have every right to expect all that is desirable. We should daily affirm that new ideas are coming to us, new ways of doing things; that we are meeting new and wonderful friends, new situations; that joyous things are going to happen to us.

The creative Power is always reacting to us as we act in It. It is always creating in our bodies and in our affairs. Consequently, we should all learn to live in a state of joyous and enthusiastic expectancy. This is the principle upon which faith or the answer to prayer is based. Let us, then, bless everything we do and everyone we meet, knowing that the limitations of the past need not be carried into the future. Nothing is too good to be true. Nothing is too much to ask of the Power that can do anything.

Today I go forth in joy, knowing that everyone is my friend, knowing that I am a friend to all. I believe that Divine Love is protecting me and Divine Intelligence is guiding me. It is my sincere desire to share everything I have with others and to expect the greatest good for everyone. Knowing that the same Spirit, the One Spirit of the living God, is in all, over all, and through all, I expect more good than I have ever experienced. I am keeping my mind open to Divine intuition, the instinctive knowledge that is the omnipresent Wisdom that ordains, governs, and controls everything.

> My soul, wait thou only upon God:
> for my expectation is from him. —PSALM 62:5

Personality

Personality is the use or misuse we make of a unique something back of us that is expressing through us. Within each of us there must be a Divine pattern of individualization that we but dimly perceive and even more inaccurately interpret. Personality has a possibility far beyond anything that is merely physiological or psychological, for it has the possibility, not of becoming a mask to hide Reality, but rather an open countenance through which Reality becomes expressed.

We have many personalities if we understand that each is but some reflected form of that behind it which is greater and which may express warmth and color and love, unity and peace, joy and happiness. We should learn to sense this greater Self, for it is what the Bible means when it speaks of Christ in us. There is a pattern of God behind our personality, seeking unique expression through it, and to this we should surrender everything we are, for this surrender will not lead us away from Reality. It is not an escape but a revelation and an instrumentation of something greater than we appear to be.

Today I live in the knowledge that there is a Presence hidden within me that is both the Reality of my true being and the Presence of God. I consciously unite my personal self and all of its actions with this overdwelling and indwelling Reality. I know that the vitality of the living Spirit flows through my personality, invigorating it. I know that all the warmth and color and beauty this is is pouring through it. All its impulses and actions flow from the Presence of God in me as what I am and reveal to me the same exalted Divinity manifesting Itself through all the faces of humanity.

Your life is hid with Christ in God. —COLOSSIANS 3:3

Divine Guidance

We believe that the Mind of God governs all things. We believe that God's Intelligence in the midst of us is governing and guiding, counseling and advising, causing us to know what to do under every circumstance and at all times, if we will but trust It. Therefore, every seeming problem has a right solution, and we may turn to the infinite Knower for the answer. In our human ignorance, we often make unwise decisions, but there is nothing that God cannot set right, if we permit Him to do so.

If we will but take our personal problem to a high place in our consciousness, it will disappear as the answer to it takes its place. This is the way a problem is solved. We should know that there is nothing in us that can keep this from happening. There is no thought of doubt or limitation. We should feel that the answer is established in our consciousness and will make itself known to our mind, right now, in our present experience. This can be done only as we let go of the problem, as a problem, and definitely expect and accept its answer.

Since the whole secret of Divine Guidance lies in the ability to accept it, today I affirm that I do accept it. I do believe that the Spirit goes before and prepares the way. I do know that every thought and act is governed and guided by a superior Intelligence. There is something in me that knows what to do. It not only knows what to do, It impels me to act upon what It knows. This very acceptance flows forth into action through me. Always there is an inner, quiet, persistent confidence, a nonresistant but complete acceptance, an inward flowing with the stream of Life, knowing that It carries me safely and surely to my destination and to the accomplishment of every good purpose. This is Divine Guidance and I surrender to it.

And the Lord shall guide thee continually. —ISAIAH 58:11

Authority

If we were to ask a modern scientist what authority he has for believing in a certain principle in nature, his only answer would be: "Because I can do something with it, it must exist. Since it reacts to the use I make of it, there must be something real about it." This is equally true of our faith in God. Because something does react to our faith, there must be something real that can react. Even after Jesus had demonstrated the authority of his faith in God through so many wonderful acts, one of his disciples asked him to show them the Father. He told them to believe him "for the very works' sake."

If Jesus was the first or only person to multiply loaves and fishes and make the wind and wave obey his will, it was not because God or the Supreme Creative Cause had withheld this same power from others. It was merely because Jesus was the first, and perhaps the only one, who completely accepted his oneness with the Spirit and then acted on that basis. When we make our affirmation in the silence of our own consciousness, we are facing the Divine Reality, dealing with It directly, using Its power consciously.

Today I affirm my faith in God's Presence dwelling within me. And I ask no one for any justification of my conviction. Boldly I proclaim this Presence and humbly I accept Its authority in my life. The Divine, governing everything out of Itself, knows how to guide my life toward happiness, toward peace, toward perfect fulfillment. There is no barrier or bar to the possibilities of Its expression, no restriction to Its dynamic creativeness because It is Self-existent in all things. This is the secret I hold with the Invisible. Alone with God I make my claim, and, in the integrity of my own soul, I fear no opposition to it.

> Believe me that I am in the Father, and the Father in me:
> or else believe me for the very works' sake. —JOHN 14:11

Omnipresence

The Universe is a spiritual system of complete consciousness, entire wholeness, the sum total of which is present everywhere. We are both scientifically and inspirationally, spiritually and philosophically in accord with the great intuitions, the spiritual revelations of all the ages, that have always announced that God is over all, in all, through all, and is all. There is not God and something else. There is only God, and God is in everything, constituting the only Reality to anything that is, proclaiming Itself as all things; therefore, God knows things only as Itself.

There is an Intelligence in everything, from the smallest atom to whatever we think of as big, and that Intelligence must of necessity respond to us intelligently. Then, automatically, we will have to assume that It can only respond to us at the level of our belief in, knowledge of, feeling about, acceptance and embodiment of, and identification with It. In other words, God is all there is, but to each of us individually, the God that is all there is must be the God believed in.

Since there is but One Life present everywhere, I must be in that Life and of it, and It must flow through me. It must be what I am; therefore, I accept this Omnipresence as something real, definite, immediate. At the very center of my own being I realize the Divine Presence. At the center of my own consciousness I recognize a transcendent Principle forever animating, sustaining, vitalizing, re-creating, guiding, directing, inspiring. There is within me that which knows what to do and impels me to act in accord with its perfect Law and Order and its complete Peace. This I accept, and even as I affirm it I know that this Omnipresence is alive and awake and aware within me.

And behold, I am with thee, and will keep thee in all places
whither thou goest. —GENESIS 28:15

Nonresistance

Gandhi built his whole philosophy of life around the theory of nonviolence. An ancient Chinese sage said that all things are possible to the person who can perfectly practice inaction. And the Bible exclaims: "Be still, and know that I am God." Surely some great truth must be contained in these simple thoughts. There is a spiritual consciousness that, through the power of nonresistance, can change a condition that appears solid. By way of illustration let us think of an iceberg. When the sun's rays daily fall on it, it will dissolve; that which was an obstruction becomes liquid. Such is the power of nonviolence.

There is something flowing in, around, and through all things that nothing can resist. This is the something that the great and the wise have known about and have used, but too often our way is the way of resistance. We try to change the outer without changing the inner first.

Today I practice nonresistance. Disregarding everything that seems to contradict the Reality in which I believe, I affirm that It is operating in my life. Turning resolutely from everything that denies the good I wish to experience, I affirm that good. There is no situation or condition that resists this transcendent thought; for I proclaim the omnipotence of God, the guidance of the Mind that knows all things, and the Peace that is beyond every confusion.

I say unto you, that ye resist not evil. —MATTHEW 5:39

Abundant Living

Why go through life as though it were something to be endured, as though there were not enough good or joy to go around? Are we not always limiting the possibility of love and affection, of appreciation, and of the common everyday good things of life? If we really are in union with a Divine Source then there should come a feeling of abundance in everything we do—an abundance of friendship, of self-expression, of everything. The abundant life contains all things whether we call them big or little.

We should sense the flow into our consciousness of the Divine Intelligence, a feeling that the creative imagination of the whole Universe is centered in us and flowing through us. We should consciously practice this more abundant life, not necessarily for any specific thing or good we desire, but for the realization of the All-Good flowing through everything and everyone. Attuning our consciousness to this Divine abundance, automatically we find a betterment in everything we do, a broader and deeper experience, a higher realization, and a greater good.

Today I expect a more abundant life. I am keeping my whole mind and thought and expectation open to new experiences, to happier events, to a more complete self-expression. Giving out more love, I expect greater love in return. Sharing with others whatever good things I have, I expect all life to share with me the good that it possesses. Seeing beauty everywhere, I expect a revelation of still more beauty. Seeing joy in everything, I expect more laughter. More deeply sensing the Divine tranquility in which all things exist, I expect a deeper consciousness of peace and security. Through it all I feel that I am in the embrace of a warm, loving Presence forever seeking an outlet through me.

> Thou openest thine hand, and satisfieth the
> desire of every living thing. —PSALM 145:16

Treating for Others

People frequently ask how they can help others and how their prayer or treatment reaches the other person. The method, the technique, and the approach are no different from that of helping oneself. For when you treat for yourself you affirm the spiritual Truth about yourself, recognizing the activity of Spirit in your life and affairs; when you treat for another, you affirm that same Truth about that person. The same procedure is followed concerning a group of people or a specific situation.

After having made this identification of the person or condition with the activity of God's Love and Wisdom, your affirmation should contain an idea of the required good or right action. And your denials, if any, should repudiate that which denies this activity. You need never wonder how your thought gets to the other person, because it does not have to go anywhere. Every person is already established in the Universal Mind, whose creative Law must manifest the ideas presented to It. So the whole action takes place in your own consciousness. Your treatment, working through the Law of Mind, produces results according to your faith and conviction.

Today I affirm that every person I meet will be helped, every situation I contact will be harmonized, every activity I am engaged in will be made prosperous and complete. In addition to my specific treatment, the silent affirmation of my whole thought automatically reflects itself wherever I am, whatever I may be doing. Consequently, I know that a blessing rests upon everyone I meet in my experience and goes out to the whole world to benefit all humanity.

> Whither can I go from your spirit? Whither can I flee
> from your presence? —PSALM 139:7

Dominion

Each one of us has access, immediately, in our own consciousness, to that absolute, unconditioned Presence that molds and makes things out of Itself by Itself directly becoming the thing It makes. The secret of effective prayer lies in the realization that there is a Power for Good in the universe and that we can use It. That subtle Presence we call Mind or Spirit is the Giver and we are the receiver. But how can it make the gift unless we accept it? One of the first things to do is to learn to expect and to accept the Divine nature flowing through everything we do. God is eternally present, and we are the instruments of Its expression. But only as much of the Divine Essence is ours to use as we permit to flow through our complete and unrestricted faith.

To understand our unity with God is the beginning of wisdom. To realize that we can express our Divinity today should be the start of a conscious practice that will gradually conduct us to a greater and greater experience of life. Thus, we will demonstrate not only that an infinite Good exists, but that it is now operating in our experience. This is the purpose of the practice of the Science of Mind. Our consciousness of the indwelling Spirit and the embodiment of Its gifts bring us into the dominion of Good.

Believing in the universal Presence as Power for Good, I now accept Its action in my life. I know that there is a strength and a vitality, a livingness flowing through me and out into everything I do or say or think. I am the very embodiment of this Divine Essence. There is no sense of weakness or lack of strength; rather the fullness and the completion of It is always present, always activated. I combine the belief I have in It with the conscious use I make of It, completely accepting and no longer rejecting the flow of this Power through me.

> When wisdom entereth into thine heart, and knowledge
> is pleasant unto thy soul; Discretion shall preserve thee,
> understanding shall keep thee. —PROVERBS 2:10–11

Subjectivity

The Mind of God is the only Mind there is and we all use this Mind. But in the use of It we create a mental atmosphere that surrounds us and that is often thought of as the unconscious or the subconscious. This is not a separate mind, it is merely a reaction of the One Mind–Principle to the use we have made of It. You and I could no more have an individual mind than we could have an individual ownership of the principle of mathematics or of harmony or of beauty. Each of us is creating in an individual way; we are individualizations in this One Mind and no two of us are exactly alike. But we all are immersed in the collective thought of the whole human race. Jung has called this the collective unconscious.

Just as we have an individual subconscious reaction to life, we also have a collective subconscious reaction to life. And just as we are more or less automatically influenced and perhaps too much controlled by our individual subconscious reactions, we also are influenced by the subconscious reactions of the ages. Tradition too largely governs us. But we should never forget that back of all this is the Divine Mind or Intelligence Itself in which there is no bondage, no fear, and no evil. It is toward this greater center within us that we must travel if we wish to become emancipated from the unconscious reactions of our own being.

Today I affirm freedom from the limitation of my own thought. I am no longer hypnotized by the mind of history. The Divine Intelligence within me is transcendent of all previous experience; free in Its own right, existing in Its own being, and creating and manifesting from the center of Its own perfection. This radiant center in me is making everything new in my life and in the lives of those around me.

> His compassions fail not. They are new
> every morning. —LAMENTATIONS 3:22–23

Simplicity

In the complete simplicity of Jesus we find thoughts more profound than those of the world's greatest philosophers, yet so simply stated: "As thou hast believed, so be it done unto thee." What is this but saying there is a Power greater than we are and we can use It? All the art, all the science, and all the wit of humankind can neither add to nor take from Life Itself. We are obliged to assume that there is a Presence or Principle, a creative Power and Intelligence that responds to our word.

But let us not try to be profound about this or put on a long and sober face as though we were carrying around some mystery too great to bear. Rather, let us accept the simple fact with utmost simplicity, and let us believe, and believe in our hearts, that which the intellect cannot and need not explain—the mystery of Life. For all the rational analysis and all the apparent synthesis of every analysis known to the mind of man has not, and cannot, and never will explain Life. The Divine Gift is made, and as we awake to the realization of It, It is ours. This is the only secret of any power we may possess, though in reality we do not possess the power at all. We merely use it.

Today I accept that Life desires me to have everything that is good merely because It could not desire anything else. I accept everything that is good and I rejoice in the simple realization that I am one with Life, one with God, one with people, one with human events and the passing show of life. I have nothing to explain, nothing to be profound about, nothing to become lost in. Life is and I live it. Peace and joy exist and they are mine. I love and am loved. In joy, then, greet each day and rest at night with a calm confidence in Spirit.

When I sit in darkness, the Lord shall be a light unto me. —MICAH 7:8

Physical Perfection

When we speak of physical perfection we are not saying that no one is sick or no one has pain. We are merely implying that of necessity there is an essence of Perfection at the center of everything, including the physical body. If that which is whole within itself were not already here, neither medicine, psychology, nor affirmative prayer could in any way benefit us physically. For whatever the medication or manipulation or emotional adjustment or prayer or affirmation may do, it does not and cannot create life, it may only reveal it.

This is what we mean when we say that every organ, action, and function of our physical body is rooted in a Divine Life and that in this Divine Life there is no congestion, no wrong action; there is always perfect circulation, assimilation, and elimination. Through such statements we are trying to sense the greater Reality. Believing as we do in all of the healing arts that help humanity, we definitely affirm that toward which they and we all reach—the spiritual center of things.

Therefore, I affirm that my body is the body of right ideas. It now is the Body of God. Every organ, action, and function of it is in harmony. Whatever does not belong to this body is eliminated. Whatever does not belong is removed. All the energy and all the action and power and vitality there is in the universe is flowing through this Divine Creation now. My word does actually eliminate that which does not belong. It does establish the action of that harmony that already exists. There is One Life—perfect, harmonious, whole, complete. That Life is my life now—not yesterday, not tomorrow, but today.

According to your faith be it unto you. —MATTHEW 9:29

Living Without Fear

Fear robs memory of happiness because it dwells upon the limitations and morbidities of the past. It robs the future of pleasurable and enthusiastic anticipation because it casts a shadow of its past into the future. It robs today of the possibility of fulfillment because it denies the good we might experience in the moment in which we live.

How much better it would be if we could think as a child thinks, abandoning ourselves to the integrity of the miracle-working universe in which we live. If the warmth of the sun can melt an iceberg, why should it not follow that there must be something in us or operating through us that can dissolve any difficulty, remove any obstruction, or renew any human relationship that has been impaired. We should consciously practice having faith just as we would practice to become a musician. We should do mental exercises to build up our acceptance of Good. The process is simple enough since it finally resolves itself into very simple affirmations of conviction, but there must be a persistency until finally old thought patterns melt and give way to new ones.

Today I cultivate the art of having faith. I affirm the reality of the Divine Presence in my life and deny everything that refutes it. As a child turns to its parents, so do I turn to that infinite Presence whose creative Law can do all things, and I accept the influx of all that makes for richer living. Because nothing is impossible to God, I believe that nothing is impossible to me through God's Power in me. I am daring to believe in the greater good. I am forsaking all that has held me in bondage, and, uniting myself with faith, with expectation, and with the joy, I now live without fear.

Be not overcome by evil, but overcome evil with good. —ROMANS 12:21

Substance and Supply

Spiritual mind science cannot promise something for nothing. It does not teach that you can have anything you want, no matter what it is, or that your thought can precipitate a million dollars. It does, however, teach, and it can demonstrate, that a betterment of circumstances and conditions and relationships can be brought about through spiritual mind treatment. We believe that the great Intelligence of the Universe cannot lack for anything or that It can plan for Its creation to lack what expresses Its own Being.

We may be certain that the Divine intends only good, only abundance for Its creation because It is the very essence of life and givingness. In spiritual mind treatment for success, for right action, and for right compensation, we work to know that Divine abundance is forever flowing into everything we do. We are guided by a Divine Intelligence and impelled to act on this guidance. While we do not expect someone suddenly to thrust a fortune upon us, we do expect that we shall be gradually led to something better and more abundant. We should expect a greater good than we have ever experienced or than we have ever known of anyone experiencing.

Divine abundance is forever manifesting in my affairs. I desire to do only that which is good and constructive, life-giving and life-expressing. Therefore, I know that I shall prosper in everything I do. I exist in limitless possibilities, and infinite Good is right where I am. I believe that everything for complete self-expression is the law of my individual being. New thoughts, new ideas, new situations are forever unfolding before me. There are new opportunities for self-expression and for abundant life and love and happiness. This I expect, and this I accept.

For every one that asketh receiveth; and he that seeketh findeth;
and to him that knocketh it shall be opened. —LUKE 11:10

APRIL
RENEWAL

Whatever the mind holds to and firmly believes in, forms a new pattern of thought within its creative mold, as whatever thought is held in the mind tends to take outward form in new creations. —ERNEST HOLMES

The natural healing force in each one of us is the greatest force in getting well. —HIPPOCRATES

We must be the change we wish to see. —GANDHI

You could not step twice into the same river; for other waters are ever flowing on to you. —HERACLITUS

The house of the Divine is not closed to any who knock sincerely at its gates, whatever their past stumbles and errors. —SRI AUROBINDO

I come that they might have life. —JOHN 10:10

Let us turn toward the sun of eternal Life, the spiritual sun that cannot set and forever rises on the horizon of our own experience. Definitely and deliberately, we let go of every lost hope, every fear of want, every sense of lack, every hurt, because today we leave the tomb of doubt and enter the sanctuary of certainty. We roll away the stone of uncertainty from our consciousness; we find the resurrected, the Divine, and God-intended perfection and wholeness. We let go of every belief that we are lost or forlorn, because we know that the doorway from that tomb leads us away from all morbid thought. We are standing forevermore in the glory of an everlasting protection of the One Presence.

We let go of all disease and disharmony. They slip back into the tomb of oblivion, for the spiritual body now rises trimphant in every cell; we are instantly renewed by the creative principle of eternal Life that is within us. We are alive and aware, and we know that the kingdom of God is here and is within us this moment.

Thou art the center and circumference of my life, the beginningless and endless part of me, the eternal Reality of me, the everlasting Power within me. Thou art my whole being.

Create in me a pure heart, O God, and renew
a steadfast spirit within me. —PSALM 51:10

Life is an adventure in which we never know what is going to happen just beyond the turn of the road. But too often our today is filled with regrets over the past. If we could convince ourselves that the limitations of the past need not be carried into the future, what a happy outlook we would have.

One of the outstanding things that Jesus taught was that the mistakes of yesterday can be canceled, that God's creation is always taking place, and, no matter what the experiences of yesterday may have been, they can be changed.

Jesus did not seem to think that this change required months and years of strenuous effort. Unlike those around him, he knew that God, or the Divine Spirit, wishes only Good for everyone. He knew that we are all rooted in Pure Spirit, in Perfect Life, and that at any moment we can so unify ourselves with the Power of Good that evil will disappear from our experience.

For my yoke is easy and my burden is light. —MATTHEW 11:30

If we make every day a day of praise and thanksgiving, a day in which we recognize the Divine Bounty and the Eternal Goodness, and if we live today as though God were the only Presence and the only Power there is, we would not have to worry about tomorrow.

We are all human, and we have all made mistakes. The starting point for creating a better future for ourselves is to deliberately free our minds from the mistakes of yesterday and feel that they need no longer be held against us; they need no longer be a liability.

Too often our minds are so burdened because of the mistakes we have made that we do not take time to forgive ourselves and others and to start over again. And so it is wise to occasionally review the past and try to find out just what we have been thinking and doing to create this burden in our minds.

We cannot go back over the past and relive it. We cannot make adjustments in the past. We have to make them in the present. It is not going to do us any good to sit around and cry over the past and bemoan our fate, because in the very day in which we are living, we are creating our tomorrows, which will become monotonous repetitions of our yesterdays.

> We are the clay, and thou our potter; and we are
> all the work of thy hand. —ISAIAH 64:8

How can we expect to realize God in the emptiness of space if we have refused to see God in those we meet? And how can we find God in those we meet and in the events that transpire around us unless we have first discovered God at the center of our own being? We cannot.

The starting point is at the center of our own being. When we awaken to the Divine within us, It will reach out and embrace everything around us, and It will discover the same Presence in people and in events and in all nature. For God is not separate from what He is doing. The Divine Life is in everyone and in everything.

This is the secret that Jesus discovered. This is why he was able to speak as no other person ever spoke. This is why he was able to perform the miracles of love and healing, and in so doing prove a fact so simple, so fundamental, but so powerful that people stand in awe before it—the simple fact that God is right where you are.

Before they call I will answer;
and while they are still speaking,
I will hear. —ISAIAH 65:24

There is an inner meaning to everything, an inside to every fact, a hidden Cause within every visible effect. This Cause is Spirit.

If we spiritually discern this hidden Cause, if we inwardly know that It is operating for us, then we are thinking from the recognition of the Allness of Good. We all have direct access to the Parent Mind, but we do not all use this direct access because we are so used to judging from external facts. It is difficult for us to get away from the apparent long enough to judge the real.

When we know that there is but One Spirit in the entire Universe, we shall know that there is but one Source for all forms. We shall know that every form is some manifestation of this Source.

When we have found that this Source is also centered in us, we will know that we can come directly to It, and discerning that Its Spiritual Nature is Love and Truth and Beauty, we will make known our requests with thanksgiving, with complete mental abandonment.

A merry heart doeth good like a medicine,
but a broken spirit drieth the bones. —PROVERBS 17:22

All of us are rooted in the Mind of God. We did not plan it this way; this is
the way it is. God is still the Supreme Power, and the Divine Spirit is still
present with us no matter where we are. We must learn to tune in to the
Mind of God, for when we do, we are turning in to the most dynamic Reality in the Universe.

Do not be afraid to talk to God, always remembering that God speaks a
certain kind of language and there is nothing negative in it. We believe in
prayerful, affirmative meditation above everything else. We believe in actually talking to God and then letting God answer. But perhaps in our confusion we talked *at* God rather than *to* Him. We have told God how terrible
everything is, how unhappy we are.

Try this: Sit in complete repose, and then tell God how wonderful He is
and how glad you are and how grateful. It is at times like these that we are
really tuning in to the Divine, and the Divine will always respond to us. We
will always receive the comfort and consolation we need, the inward sense
of security and well-being that everyone must have to be happy and whole.

If the tree fall toward the south, or toward the north, in the place
where the tree falleth, there it shall be. —ECCLESIASTES 11:3

We are all spiritual and mental broadcasting stations. There is a Silent Force
flowing from us in every direction at all times. How necessary it is that we
assume the role of the announcer and the broadcaster. How necessary it is
that we write our own program and deliver it ourselves.

When a person speaks into a microphone in a broadcasting station, his
words are carried to the far corners of the Earth, where they are reproduced.
But the force that carries them is mechanical. It is a law, a vibration. And it
is a law that actually reproduces the words he speaks, the intonations, the
inflections.

And now along with this word that is broadcast goes a picture, an image
of his personality. This is what we see in television, as though he were suddenly present everywhere, and the picture looks like him because it was his
image, his likeness, that created it.

And so it is with the reaction of the Law of Good from a Power greater
than ourselves. It always tends to bring back to us exactly what goes out.
But we are always the broadcasters, and we can always change the pictures
if we will.

And I saw a new heaven and a new earth:
for the first heaven and the first earth were passed away;
and there was no more sea. —REVELATION 21:1

Fear is the great enemy of man. It is impossible for a person to do his best if he is filled with anxiety. Unless we live without fear today, we will dread tomorrow. Those who live in the dread of tomorrow generally harbor memories of things that were unpleasant in their previous experience and expect that more of this unpleasantness will transpire in the future. The present day in which they live is robbed of all peace and joy. This so disturbs the mind that restful sleep is impossible. Such people seldom rise in the morning filled with buoyant hope, joyful anticipation, and the natural enthusiasm and zest for living that we all need if we are to get the most out of life.

Yesterday is forever past. We cannot relive it. No matter how we may regret what happened yesterday, it is impossible actually to live it over again; but too often in imagination, we do live it over again and again, and in so doing bring all the misery of yesterday into today. Learn to forget yesterday. After we have gone over it and learned by our mistakes, the thing to do is to correct those mistakes and forgive ourselves for anything we have done.

He that overcometh shall inherit all things; and I will be
his God, and he shall be my son. —REVELATION 21:7

It is easy enough to see how one who is surrounded by confusing situations
might feel inadequate to cope with them, and unconsciously might seek
some place of peace or retirement where nothing could bother him.

A completely integrated person is one who has learned to meet everything as it comes along and to make the best of it. When we say one should
make the best of things, we do not mean that one should grin and bear it, or
even suffer it to be so, for we know there is a way to meet every situation
through the use of the Power greater than ourselves. This is done by knowing that there is nothing to be afraid of, that we are One with an Infinite
Partner, and that there is nothing in the Universe designed to harm us.

Confidence and faith in a Power greater than ourselves must be gener-
ated. We must meet every situation as it comes with faith and trust. There is
nothing to be afraid of. Underneath are the everlasting arms.

In him we live, and move, and have our being. —ACTS 17:28

Life is activity, and when we stop being active we turn away from the newness of life. And the person who grows old in years without an inward expectation and assurance that he is going to live forever, somewhere, will find the last part of his life burdened with the thoughts of yesterday. Let us make up our minds that yesterday is gone. Tomorrow has not yet arrived. But today can be filled with wonder if we know that we stand on the threshold of that which is wonderful and new.

I have never yet met a single individual who maintained this attitude in the last part of his life unless he had faith. And I am talking about the kind of faith we all understand the meaning of—faith in Something bigger than ourselves, in a Power greater than ourselves, and a complete assurance that we are going to live forever, somewhere.

It is an interesting fact that, whether we know it and whether or not we like it, our lives are so tied in with God, the living Spirit, that we cannot remain young and enthusiastic unless we know that we are one with that which knows no age and no burdens.

Ye put on the new man, which after God is created
in righteousness and true holiness. —EPHESIANS 4:24

In all the kingdoms that exist, in all the planes that exist, and deep within
the self, hidden and yet felt, there is a High Priest ready to conduct us to the
sacred and secret chamber of the self, where God and man are One. The
search for union passes into the realization, not that we are just *with* or *in*,
but that we are *of* God. One *with*, or One *in*, implies separation. The great
realization is that we are *of* that which is; we are some part of it.

Many have found entrance to this door through deep spiritual meditation, some through high inspirational enlightenment, others just by sitting
still and letting something happen to them, as symbolized by the Descent of
the Holy Ghost.

The end, the aim, and the whole purpose of our study is not for the salvation of the individual life, because Life cannot be lost, but for the discovery of the Self, which the Scripture tells us is hid with Christ in God. The
aim of our search is to discover that the Universe is individualized in each
one of us and that individuality within each one of us has the possibility of
expanding to the universalization of the Self.

In the way of righteousness is life; and in the pathway
thereof there is no death. —PROVERBS 12:28

You and I should look across the new horizon of the greater possibility that
resides within us and meet the living God and feel the embrace of His Presence and come at last to know the infallibility of His Power. From out of the
great Mind that is God, the way of life is made perfect and straight and immediate. It is made happy and whole and prosperous.

We should awake to the living Presence of the Eternal God within each
one of us and enter into a realization of a new peace and joy. As we come to
surrender all littleness, and all fear and doubt, that great river of Life flowing from the Mind of God will renew our vigor, remake our strength, enno-
ble our being, heal our bodies, and bring peace to our hearts. As our
thoughts are cleared of all that is unlike Him who created us, they become
receptacles for the outpouring of all that is good, wonderful, and true.

God's Love always embraces us, His Wisdom is always within us, and
His Joy is ours to share. Abundance is everywhere.

All things were made by him; and without him
was not any thing made that was made. —JOHN 1:3

Every human being thrills at the thought of having dreams come true. The idea means different things to different people. To one it may mean physical health: the ability to walk, run, play, and engage in activity. To another, it may mean abundance: a home, a car, opulence. To yet another, dreams may mean education, the ability to get along with people, or to have a loving mate. Whatever your personal desires may be—as long as they do not hurt you or someone else—you have a right to attain them. And you can.

The ability to attain your goals—to control your experiences and have them result in happiness, prosperity, and success—lies in your own mind and the way you use it. This means you control your own experience—you are really in charge of your affairs and the way they are to develop.

If your thinking processes are under your personal control and if thought is acted upon by the creativity of Mind to produce results according to your belief, then you surely do have the power to become the master of your own affairs and to bring to pass those good conditions you desire.

Let us keep in mind that we not only have the God-given ability to do this kind of results-oriented thinking, but that we also have the right to do it. Every thought that is a negation should be changed to an affirmation. When we do so, the Power that constantly flows through us will respond by producing the new experience we have affirmed.

The Lord will perfect that which concerneth thee. —PSALM 138:8

The natural order of evolution has brought us to a place where there is a quickening of the spirit, a keener perception of the mind, a deeper intro-spection of the soul; the veil between Spirit and matter is thinning. We are emerging into a spiritual universe, proclaimed alike by the philosopher, the religionist, the scientist, and the idealist, and yet the nature of Reality or ul-timate Truth cannot have changed. Two and two were four a million years ago. The awakening is to the Mind and Spirit.

The passing of old orders of thought is but a proclamation of the inau-guration of new and higher orders. Modern psychology, metaphysics, and philosophy all announce a new birth of the Mind, a new discovery of the self, a new consciousness of the intimacy of the Mind with the subtle Spirit within each of us.

There appears to be one persistent purpose behind the great forward movement of evolution, namely, the expression of Intelligence, through creation, into higher, finer, and more complex forms. An insistent and in-telligent Urge in the Life-Principle impels it to express. Spirit is forever clothing itself in form. If we were to ask our imagination why this is so, the answer might be that God Himself would remain a nonentity unless He were expressed. Even to the Infinite, some form of creative action and ex-pression is necessary.

Delight thyself also in the Lord, and He shall give thee
the desires of thine heart. —PSALM 37:4

We do not change all of the patterns of our thought in a moment. Rather, it takes place little by little, until gradually the old thought patterns become transformed into new ones by some inner alchemy of the mind, the operation of which we do not see but the manifestation of which we do experience.

I know that all the Good there is belongs to me. God is Good. Good is God. I am surrounded by Good. I am enveloped in It. I feel Its presence.

There is nothing in me that can reject that Good. My whole inner feeling entertains It and experiences It. My whole expectation is one of joy and pleasurable anticipation. All the old thoughts of fear and doubt and uncertainty have vanished. Within me is the Secret Place of the Most High. Within me is the Presence and the Power and the Will to know and to do and to be.

There is nothing in me that can deny this statement or refuse to accept it. There is nothing in me that can limit me. My memory is one of happiness; my anticipation is one of joy; my experience is one of pleasure.

And Jesus said unto the centurion, Go thy way; and as thou
hast believed, so be it done unto thee. —MATTHEW 8:13

In releasing our word of affirmative prayer into the creative activity of
Mind, we do so with a glad and thankful heart. Giving thanks is a further
indication that we have fully released our prayer. It means that we are sure
of the completion of the creative process and that there are no lingering
doubts. The person who is still unconvinced does not rejoice—he waits until he sees if it is going to work. But if one has prayed with conviction, believing and trusting in a Creative Principle in and behind all that exists, he
will turn his back on that particular prayer of affirmation, give thanks for its
certainty, and rejoice in its fulfillment, even though he has not yet seen it
outwardly fulfilled.

The only time to make use of this Creative Principle is *now*. The real secret to its practical application lies not in how much we know, but in the use
of what we do know. The results, large or small, much or little, depend entirely on the degree of conscientious endeavor, enthusiasm and joy, conviction and faith that we can bring to bear on any particular situation. We have
to become quiet and, in the solitude of our own thought, discover for ourselves what it is we actually believe; and then proceed to put that faith into
creative action through patterns of thinking built around that faith.

If ye have faith, and doubt not, ye shall not only do this which is done
to the fig tree, but also if ye shall say unto this mountain, Be thou
removed, and be cast into the sea; it shall be done. —MATTHEW 21:21

Our activity of thought is actually a Divine compulsion of the One Mind in
us seeking an ever-increasing achievement and expression through us. The
forms and outlets for this self-conscious process of thought, which appear
as a unique creation of life in man, may manifest in many ways.

We each interpret and use the urge for greater expression. For some, the
fulfillment of this inner drive may be found in a new home, increased business activity, or better health, as well as in a desire for greater spiritual
awareness. All of these desires are urges of the indwelling Intelligence, and
we either can combat the urges we feel or we can give them expression. The
choice is ours to make. But we cannot stand still. We have to continue to express this action of Life within us because creativity is our Divine Essence.

Our lives and experiences may well be likened to a river. If we stand on
the bank of a river and watch it flow by, we become aware that the river
never changes but that its content is always new. By analogy, we might say
the purposeful dynamic quality of life within us never changes, but the content of our experience of living never remains the same.

I am Alpha and Omega, the beginning and the ending; saith the Lord,
which is, and which was, and that is to come,
the Almighty. —REVELATION 1:8

The Divine is the substance of all things and is the law of all things, and
there is everlasting motion and freedom. The Spirit is the stream of Life
throughout creation, forever purifying and renewing everything. Today I
cast out all limitation, and I am carried forward on the stream of Life. I now
release all hindrances to my good, and if new ones arise, I dismiss them with
finality.

God is my Source and Creator, and I accept His fullness and His gladness. I am a manifestation of God, possessing His Being and His Grace. I
bless God within me, and see myself as pure Spirit. I no longer need to accept ideas of human weakness or the necessary suffering of humanity. I live
today in an attitude of faith and Divine Love.

I am clear in mind and resolved to happiness. I am impelled toward my
good and decide now to be well instead of ill, joyful instead of sad. I accept
the perfect expressions of God with a whole heart. I accept the fulfillment of
love, the satisfaction of achievement. God is real in my life and in all that
concerns me. I have immediate access to the limitless Power and Energy of
the Universe Itself.

Many waters cannot quench love,
neither can the floods drown it. —SONG OF SOLOMON 8:7

We must have a firm conviction that all people live in God, and we must have a deep realization that we are all One in this Universal Spirit that is God.

There is a place where we begin and leave off physically, but there is no place where we begin and leave off mentally or spiritually. Our minds merge with the minds of others, and as they meet, some silent force within us attracts or repels automatically in accord with our accepted thought patterns.

If we do not merge with others in cooperation, in unity, and in happiness, we may be certain that there is something in us that feels it has been rebuffed or rejected. Here is where an adjustment has to be made.

If you want sunshine, step out into the sunshine. If you have locked yourself away in a dark closet, why not come out into the light? If you have been feeling that everything is against you and no one really cares for you, know that God is in everyone, and meet the God in others. See what happens. If you think that all the fears and failures and hurts you have been carrying around for years are something over which you have no control, come to realize that you are born out of Life. The thing that entered into you when you were born was God, the living Spirit. You are One with everything because you are One with God. Recognizing this truth, you can go forth to meet joy and love.

The kingdom of heaven is like unto treasure hid in a field; the which when a man hath found, he hideth, and for joy thereof goeth and selleth all that he hath, and buyeth that field. —MATTHEW 13:44

Because I am One with God, I am One with all people. Because I am One with Life, I am One with everything that lives. I feel my union with people and with nature. I feel that I belong to Life.

I love life and I enter into the joy of living. I enter into companionship with others, into cooperation with them. And I know that something within me reaches out and embraces the whole world. Something within me blesses everything it touches, brings life and happiness and joy to everyone. Something in me acts as a healing balm, restoring everything to its natural and native Perfection.

As I silently listen to the Spirit within me and think of Its Perfection, I know that I am being born into joy and hope and gladness, born into love and faith and assurance.

Silently I release every negative thought from my mind. I release it and let it go. And I, too, pray "that they all may be one; as thou, Father, art in me, and I in thee, that they also may be one in us."

O Lord, how manifold are thy works!
In wisdom hast thou made them all:
the earth is full of thy riches. —PSALM 104:24

May our minds be so open to the Infinite abundance of love and beauty, compassion and goodness, simplicity and sincerity, that it flows around the world, bringing back, as it must, the joy that is God. Let our song be full and all the weight and the burden fall away as we face the sun. Let us silence all fear, all doubt, all pain, and identify ourselves with the living Spirit.

Let us commune with that Presence and use that Power in the beauty and quiet of this moment. Breathe into us, O Eternal Spirit, everything that stands for beauty, everything that is meant by power, law and order, warmth and color, the artistry of life, and the certainty of love and friendship; impregnate our souls now with Thy Spirit.

Infinite God within and around us, we feel Thy Presence in our souls. There is One Life and that is God; there is One perfect Presence, which is Good. Infinite Spirit within us, Eternal Presence, "I am that which thou art, thou art that which I am."

Let us turn to that divine and radiant center of Life, the Light that lights every person's path, and consciously unify ourselves with the great love, wisdom, and power of the eternal One. "I am that which thou art, thou art that which I am."

And God shall wipe away all tears from their eyes; and there shall be no more death, neither sorrow, nor crying, neither shall there be any more pain. —REVELATION 21:4

How would it be if we all opened a spiritual account with the Bank of Life and, realizing that we drawing on the Infinite, each day deposited enough hope and happiness and faith to more than meet any emergency that might possibly arise? The wonderful part about this is that we know Life contains all these things and it wants to give them to us. It is intended by the Divine scheme of things that we should have them.

Why can we not think of it this way: God has already made the initial deposit—and a big one—for everyone who is ever born into this world, because God has given Himself to us. He has imparted His own Life and, in a mysterious way that is beyond our comprehension, has endowed us with the capacity to Love. If God is Love—and we sense deeply that this is so—and if each one of us has, as we must have, immediate access to the Love of God, then we earn the ability to draw on the Bank of Life in such degree as we become loving.

If you take the time to harmonize yourself with Love, you will find that, when some incident that seems hateful or discordant arises in your experience, you can draw on a Reserve Force. When some experience comes along that seems unloving, you are able to write a check from your Bank of Life that will cover every liability of unkindness. God is Love and all the Love there is is yours now.

According to your faith be it unto you. —MATTHEW 9:29

The Source of all things forever reveals Itself as Good. God is not only within me, He is also around me and is in my experience at all times. Deep within myself I know the Divine Presence. This knowing makes me receptive to Divine fulfillment. The truth about myself is not only perfect being but also perfect situation at all times. The good in me evolves out of the Spirit within me and concludes only in right action and greater good.

My consciousness is Life Itself, free of all impediment. The permanent Good of God resides in every situation. When circumstances seem to hide Reality, I let go and let God act for me. Deep within me is the answer to any question I might have. I let Divine Wisdom be my guide. As I turn from negativity and fear, my rightful place is shown to me. I not only have faith but I also have complete knowledge that all my prayers of affirmation are answered. As my consciousness accepts this truth, I am made free to accept my blessings. In back of me is the potential of the Universe. I declare new horizons will open for me, new ideas will flow to me, and a better world of joy and peace will be revealed.

Rejoice in the Lord always:
and again I say, Rejoice. —PHILIPPIANS 4:4

We perceive that the universe is a thing of beauty, of love. I believe that the impulsion of the universe is love and its propulsion is law, and one balances the other. It is inconceivable that it could be otherwise. One is personal; the other is impersonal. It seems to me that we are dealing with something that starts with pure intelligence. When the movement of this intelligence, which we call thought or contemplation, blends its specialization of law through a particular phase or mode of thought, it creates in a certain sense the law of its own being out of the law of all Being. This law, which we can consider to be the movement of intelligence and creativity, carries with it by the nature and constitution of its own being, and the Being of self-existence upon which it relies, everything necessary to impel and propel itself into action. For us it will be action through us. Therefore, the law set in motion produces the result.

I believe that no matter how much we love—and we do not enough for love is the impulsion—that love alone, as a mere sentiment, will not do anything. For instance, to say, "God is all there is" is a statement of conviction but it is only when we apply our conviction of the Allness and the Isness of the Beingness of this One Power that we become the instrument for that with which we have identified the mind. We have these two great realities: identification and instrumentality. All progress starts with thought, and we have no mind that belongs only to us, but we individualize a Universal Mind.

I will take sickness away from the midst of thee. —EXODUS 23:25

God is in and through His creation—the Universe—and all form is His Self-expression. My body is of God, the manifestation of a Perfect God. I am the beauty of God's work and the vehicle of His Consciousness. I allow the Divine Perfection to function through me as perfect health. My individuality does not imply frailty. I am created in God's image and I desire only His Perfection through me.

Today I increase my Divine experience and I recognize God's Consciousness in me. Each day my body is renewed. I am alive with Everlasting Life. This Life lives as me, and there is nothing else. Having discovered the Inner Reality, I turn to It with confidence. Easily the old doubts and negatives are dismissed. I let got of all thinking that would seem to keep me from the knowledge that I am perfect in all ways. By blessing my body and my mind, I acknowledge my Creator.

The joy of living circulates through me, warms me, and fills me with trust. I let go of any old fear of age or decline and only know with sure knowledge that I am forever growing better and stronger, that I am happier in mind and more perfect in body. I give thanks each day for my perfect health. My body is my temple, and my house is in order.

He shall call upon me, and I will answer him. —PSALM 91:15

All nature shows a Divine relatedness. I have but to contemplate the blade of grass, the growing leaf, or the solar system to see that He who has created me has shaped and arranged all things to prosper and to exist in harmony. The Spirit knows only harmony, and a similar harmony now exists in my world.

My thinking, in accord with the Good of God and acted upon by His creative activity, can displace nothing that is good and cannot subtract from the good of anyone. If there seems to be a difference of opinion, or a conflict of human will, I turn to the Divine Wisdom. Here, I find the answer that awaits me. It becomes clear to me how I may further the good of others and be free to accept my own good. I give up all impatience. I am in accord with Divine Activity and experience a perfect state of progress that cannot interfere with anyone else. I lay aside selfishness and fear. I know that the loving and bestowing Spirit gives of Itself to me and to all others.

There is no scarcity of good. My blessings are abundant, and by sharing them I add unto myself. With serenity, joy, and love, I now understand the true meaning of happiness. I see that no pain or sacrifice is entailed. There is only God's Wisdom bringing peace to all. I am happy and my world is made glad.

> If the Son therefore shall make you free,
> ye shall be free indeed. —JOHN 8:36

The Everlasting Now is my freedom in God. I am bound neither by false tradition nor human heritage. I have come from the One Source, God. I accept this gift, my own free will, and make the most of it. I refuse to be resigned to any limitation of life. I refuse to be tied to man-made ideas of God. I open my mind to Its own goodness and my heart to Its own steadfastness.

I am only of God—Perfect Substance, Perfect Form, and Perfect Life. I am guided correctly. I am lovingly inspired by Love Itself. If my will to be well or happy has been limited by timidity or laziness, I now resolve to get out of all emotional ruts. Today I achieve God's idea of me. Joy and well-being can be the only outcome, for God's work cannot be burdensome.

Nothing can stand in the way of my liberty. I now realize that I am spiritually entitled to success, affluence, and a happy disposition. I am free in my life, my work, my world, and my body. I am free to experience God's Love for me and to grow in God's Consciousness. God within me as me is All-Powerful, All-Good, and All there is.

> And they shall plant vineyards,
> and eat the fruit of them. —ISAIAH 65:21

Perfect work and perfect supply are mine. As I accept this truth, it is done. I refuse to look upon effects that have been brought about by my own limited thinking. I turn my mind to the Infinite, available everywhere to everyone, All-Loving and All-Powerful. I let go of all fear and open my hands to receive that which is mine.

Infinite Creativeness flows through every person. There is no reality of lack or limitation within me. I have talents and capacities that now become clearly known to me. I am guided by the Spirit to recognize my inner wealth. Divine Wisdom knows exactly what I can do and shows me how, when, and where to do it. The right ideas occur to me, and the right people and circumstances come into my life.

Each opportunity is better than the last, for God in me forever moves me onward. I move forward joyously now, accepting that which is my perfect environment, employment, and supply. I am prosperous in all things as I allow the Divine Nature of God to flow through me and to take form in my world.

The Lord is my light and my salvation. —PSALM 27:1

Of course, we all wish for salvation. We all want to be happy; we should like to be well. We want people to like us. We desire to love and be loved. And above everything else, we want and need an inward sense of security and peace of mind.

It is true that we all long for the Kingdom of God on Earth, and the great struggle of man is toward freedom, emancipation from want and fear and disease, and from everything that can hurt. We all long to return to our lost paradise. Man is put on Earth to enjoy life, and he is given the freedom to decide how he is to live; always there is placed before him the possibility of two things: to be or not to be.

Finally all real Power must rest on the side of Good, and finally evil will be vanquished by Good. This is the whole meaning of the story of the Savior, the lifting of the Life Principle on the Tree of Life—the coming to realize that we are One with God forever.

The story of the Garden of Eden is completed through the triumph of the cross. Jesus discovered the meaning of Life at the center of his own being and showed humanity, for all time, what can happen when someone lives as though God were real to him, as though Love were the final Power, and Good the final arbiter of fate.

What are we going to do with this greatest of all Truths—the relationships that we as individuals have to the Divine Spirit that is already Perfect and that desires only our good? If we are weary of our troubles, there is something we can do about it. We can begin to exalt the Life Principle within us.

I will praise thee, O Lord my God, with all my heart:
and I will glorify thy name for evermore. —PSALM 86:12

I turn my thought to Joy, which I know is vibrating through all Life.
Through my own being, in my innermost mind and heart, I reach deep into
Infinite Being, and hear the Song of Gladness that sings through all mani-
festations of life. I know that It also sings in me as I give It expression.

I feel the throb of life in all the harmony of form around me—in tree and
flower and grass, in blue sky and clouds, in the beauty of evening sunset—
wherever I look I hear and feel the underlying joyous note that Life sings
and that comes to its culmination in God's perfect Life.

Now, deep within my innermost being, I attune myself to this God-
conscious being, which I truly am. I permit God's perfect idea of me to be
manifest, to flow forth into expression. I know that I, God's perfect child,
cannot contain grief, sadness, inharmony. I know that in my true self I am
joy, for I am God-Life. My life is buoyant, vivacious, sparkling—free. It
contains all good. It is unity, perfection, love. And so I know that nothing
can make me—the Real Me—sad or dejected or heavy-hearted. The way is
made clear before me, and it is filled with joy and harmony. I am peace. I am
love. I am power. I am vitality and strength and All-Good.

MAY

JOY

Joy is the emotion excited by the expectancy of good. —ERNEST HOLMES

Joy has come to live with me. How can I be sad?
I do so love Thy presence, which is joy within me. —ERNEST HOLMES

> Be like the bird
> That, pausing in her flight
> Awhile on boughs too slight,
> Feels them give way
> Beneath her and yet sings,
> Knowing that she hath wings. —VICTOR HUGO

Happiness is a butterfly, which, when pursued, is always just beyond your grasp, but which if you will sit down quietly, may alight upon you.
—NATHANIEL HAWTHORNE

Joy is the realization of the truth of one-ness, the oneness of our soul with the supreme love. —RABINDRANATH TAGORE

In thy presence is fullness of joy; at thy right hand
there are pleasures for evermore. —PSALM 16:11

I turn my thought to Joy, which I know is vibrating through all Life. Through my own being, in my innermost mind and heart, I reach deep into Infinite Being, and hear the Song of Gladness that sings through all manifestations of life. I know that It also sings in me as I give It expression.

I feel the throb of life in all the harmony of form around me—in tree and flower and grass, in blue sky and clouds, in the beauty of evening sunset—wherever I look I hear and feel the underlying joyous note that Life sings and that comes to its culmination in Spirit made manifest through each human being.

Now, deep within my innermost being, I attune myself to the God-conscious being that I truly am. I permit God's perfect idea of me to manifest, to flow forth into expression. I know that I, God's perfect expression, cannot contain grief, sadness, inharmony. I know that in my true Self I am Joy, for I am God-Life. My Life is buoyant, vivacious, sparkling—free. It contains all good. It is Unity, Perfection, Love. And so I know that nothing can make me—the Real Me—sad or dejected or heavyhearted.

In the Lord put I my trust. —PSALM 11:1

The Kingdom of Heaven is at hand, and is within me. I am in constant contact with the indwelling Spirit. I am renewed, guided, and led, hour by hour, by the Almighty Power of Omnipresent Love.

I keep my vision focused on the Indwelling Harmony. I contemplate Perfection within me. Perfection manifests in my outer life. There is One Life in and through all. I consciously unify myself with my Source in Spirit. I look within and behold the Presence of God. This Presence of God, which is the Perfection within me, reflects Itself as perfection in my experience. I manifest that which I am. I am perfect in every part and harmonious in every action.

All power is given unto me from On High. Knowing this, I am strong with the strength of the all-vitalizing power of the Universe. I am sustained and healed by a divine stream of Spirit-Energy, which flows through me as radiant health and vitality. Every cell of my being responds to this spiritual flow. I stand revealed as the perfect child of the perfect Father.

I will praise thee, O Lord, with my whole heart;
I will show forth all thy marvelous works. —PSALM 9:1

The All-Intelligent Creative Presence is the souce of all that I am. I believe in the ability and the willingness of this great Source to sustain Its own creation.

The Kingdom and the Power and the Glory of God is expressed through me. I recognize myself to be a center through which this Intelligence and the power of this Universe find expression.

Infinite Mind, operating through me, now brings to me the manifestation of harmony, order, and the highest good. The consciousness of peace and plenty is established within me. All that is necessary to my happiness and well-being now comes into my experience. There is no belief in failure or mistake in the Divine Plan for me. There is no discouragement and no fear.

There can be neither limitation nor lack, for nothing has happened to the One Perfect Activity. It is in full operation for me. I am now free from any sense of bondage. Strength and courage are my divine birthright and I am now expressing my true self. All that the Father hath is mine. I draw from the spiritual treasure-house all that I need.

My lips shall not speak wickedness,
nor my tongue utter deceit. —JOB 27:4

I realize that I am formed in the spiritual image and likeness of God and that it is the desire of God to be manifested and expressed through me always. I know, too, that my spiritual body is now perfect, capable of perfect expression at all times—perfect expression of love, peace, poise, confidence, assurance, and power.

Now that I realize my true nature, every negative thought has left me. I have no fear, no dread, no feeling of inferiority, no feeling of tension. Every cell, tissue, organ, and function in my body is in complete harmony. Only good can be manifested through me.

I love everyone and know that everyone loves me and is interested in me and in the work I am doing. I go about my work with ease and relaxation. I work quietly, without strain. My nerves are strong, quick, steady, with abundant reserve power for any emergency.

All the Power of God is surging about me and through me in perfect peace and harmony. Perfect assurance is mine.

The Spirit of God hath made me, and the breath
of the Almighty hath given me life. —JOB 33:4

My body is the temple of the Living God. It is Spiritual Substance. Every part of my body is attuned to this Living Spirit within me. I have perfect confidence in my heart that God's life-giving Spirit is my life. Since God is my life and God is eternal, my life is eternal. Therefore I cannot be separated from God, from Good, or from Perfection.

The Perfect Life of God now is expressed through me, and every part of my body expresses its innate perfection and wholeness. As the sun dissolves mist, so does my knowledge of Truth dissolve all pain and discord. I know the Truth about myself as a child of God and that Truth makes me free. I am free because the Power of the Living Spirit is my power and It remolds and re-creates my body after the likeness of the perfect plan of God.

I accept, then, my own spiritual and physical perfection. I accept my privilege, as Its expression, of manifesting the Life, Love, Peace, Strength, Harmony, and Joy of God—the Almighty Presence who dwells within me and incarnates in me, as me.

I will fetch my knowledge from afar, and will
ascribe righteousness to my maker. —JOB 36:3

Today I consciously let go of every discord. I drop all sense of lack or limitation from my thought, and every belief that I have ever had in lack or fear. I now have a belief in success and faith. I permit the Spirit within me to express Itself in perfect freedom, bringing increasing joy into my experience.

I allow the Divine Wholeness to flow through me into ever-widening fields of activity. Every good that I have ever experienced is now increased tenfold. Every joy that I have ever experienced is now multiplied. There is a new influx of inspiration into my thought. I see more clearly than ever before that my Divine birthright is freedom, joy, and eternal goodness. I perceive this same birthright is bequeathed to all people.

As I look out into nature, it responds with a thousand joys of beauty and harmony. As I look deep into the souls of people I perceive the Divine Image implanted within them. Sorrow is now turned into joy, the belief in death into the certain knowledge of an eternal expansion.

The sun of hope rises, nevermore to set, and all power is delivered unto me. This power I use for my own and every other man's good. This Divine Presence interprets Itself to me in love and friendship, and peace, joy, and goodness are mine now and forever.

I will sing unto the Lord, because he hath
dealt bountifully with me. —PSALM 13:6

I am conscious that I daily enter into my Divine Inheritance, in my thought
and in the Spirit, I am entering into the realm of Absolute Causation. I completely believe that from this secret place of the Most High within me there
will be projected an objective manifestation of my every legitimate desire.

I know that all desires are legitimate so long as they do not harm any
other person. All desires are legitimate when they express life without hurt
to anyone. There is good enough to go around. Therefore I do not withhold
any good from myself or from others, but constantly proclaim that Good
belongs alike to each and all.

There is that within me that sees, knows, and understands this truth,
that completely accepts it, that remembers freedom, expresses freedom,
and anticipates freedom. There is that within me that is completely conscious of its unity with Good, of its oneness with all the Power there is and
all the Presence there is and all the Life there is. Upon this Power, Presence,
and Life I depend with implicit certainty, with complete confidence, and
with absolute assurance.

I am expecting more good; I am remembering only the good; I am experiencing good. In this memory of good, in this experience of good, and in
the expectation of more good, daily I know that I move and have my being
in an Infinite Sea of Perfect Life.

I will bless the Lord, who hath given me counsel. —PSALM 16:7

I know there is but One Power in the universe and that Power is God. That Power manifests in and through all form, all people, all conditions and so is at the very center of my being. This God-Power is me.

This Power is Life Itself, and Its nature is Love—All-Good. It contains all Wisdom, Peace, Joy, and Strength. At the center of my being I feel this Perfection in me. I know It is all around me. Everywhere I turn I behold It. It is my whole being. Every cell and atom of my being, my every thought and feeling, my every act is an expression of this God-Power.

The Intelligence within me is constantly guiding me. Clearly I see the right thing for me to do; I know the right thing for me to say in every circumstance. This Intelligence within me deals with every situation harmoniously. I find life thrilling, stimulating.

I know that Love protects Its own. I know that Love now makes clear the way before me, eliminating every seeming obstruction. I am guided into an ever-widening unfoldment of being, and I rest in perfect joy and peace. One with all Life, my every need is now fulfilled.

It is God that girdeth me with strength,
and maketh my way perfect. —PSALM 18:32

My body, and every part of it, is made of pure Substance—God. It cannot deteriorate. This instant this Infinite Substance within me, which is constantly flowing through me, takes form in the likeness of perfect, whole, and complete cells. Every cell of my lungs is strong and healthy, filled with life and vitality, strength and cleanliness.

I am now made vigorous and hardy. I have the stamina of the Infinite. I am sturdy and robust. I am fortified with God's perfection and right action. I am hale and able-bodied. All the life of the universe is my life. All of the strength of the universe is my strength. All of the power of the universe is my power.

Every breath I draw fills me with perfection, vitalizes, upbuilds, and renews every cell of my body. I am born in Spirit and of Spirit, and I am Spirit made manifest this instant. My body, Spirit in form, knows no time, knows no degree; it knows only to express fully, instantaneously.

I will call upon the Lord, who is worthy to be praised:
so shall I be saved from mine enemies. —PSALM 18:3

Now and always I recognize that I live, move, and have my being in God. I am part of Universal Mind. I am one with Universal Substance. All the qualities and all the wealth of good and desirable things that exist in Universal Mind are mine now. I perceive, accept, and experience them.

Daily I accept more joy, more happiness, more of the good things of life. Constantly my conviction deepens that a Divine Presence pervades my being, freeing me from loneliness and sadness. I turn to the Spirit within, knowing that It desires to manifest all good through me. The zest of learning to accept the good that is mine fills each day with interest and makes eternal life worthwhile.

I now lay aside all anxiety, all striving, and let the Law bring my good to me. I open every channel for Substance to flow through me and take form in my objective experience. I joyfully anticipate greater abundance, more success, and more joy.

Let the words of my mouth, and the meditation of my heart,
be acceptable in thy sight, O Lord,
my strength and my redeemer. —PSALM 19:14

There is only One Power and One Presence—God, the Good, all powerful and ever present. I am an individualized part of this Universal Presence and one with this Universal Power.

I am a perfect expression of Perfect Life now, and everything necessary to the fullness of that expression comes to me. Today I definitely claim as my inheritance Life, Love, Peace, Joy, Power, and an abundance of all Good. Running through me is the silent power of spiritual Wisdom harmoniously directing my thoughts and actions.

I am surrounded by an atmosphere of Love and I am guided and governed by the impulse of Love. This Love casts out all fear, for fear cannot abide in the same household with Love. I fill my consciousness with a sense of the Love of God, until my whole being is flooded with it. It blesses me, heals me, guides me, and sustains me forever.

The Life of God is my Life, self-existent and immortal. The Truth of God is my Truth, Unconditioned and Eternal. The Love of God is my Love, complete and perfect now.

I have set the Lord always before me: because he is at
my right hand I shall not be moved. —PSALM 16:8

As I attune myself to the Perfection of God; It flows through me; It dissipates all the obstructions of my everyday life, transforming all confusion into Love and Beauty.

I realize that I must bring this Perfection of Reality into expression, for the mind and heart of each human being are the only channels God has through which to manifest God's Infinite Mind and Perfect Love, which must be expressed continually that Life may evolve in greater and greater perfection.

As I permit this Reality to be expressed in me and through me, I am joyous in the assurance that I am bringing into being that much more of God-Perfection. I am transforming a part of Life, just as Nature passes through the beautiful transformation called spring.

I know I need only to realize the true state of Being, which is Love—that which I really am—to transform all that appears to be imperfect. Love is that which is Real—complete harmony. Love is the Great Harmonizing Agency.

I stand firm on the Rock of Reality, knowing all is well, knowing that there is but One and that One is Love.

The Lord is my shepherd; I shall not want. —PSALM 23:1

As my thought sinks deep into the quietude of my innermost Self, I am conscious of the perfect peace and love and strength of the One Universal Being, the One Divine Mind. It is like a tranquil pool—translucent, calm and beautiful—and as I contemplate It, I am refreshed. I realize that It is all-pervading—in all and through all—and that It is my true life, my true being. Now I am divinely confident of the Unity of Life.

There is but One Life, One Body of Love, and all are a part of it, one perfect Being. As I look at Nature I see how every part melts into another in a great transmutation—one part could not exist without the others. In human nature the fusion of love and thought makes us One. In the true meeting of hearts and minds there is scarcely even the need of words. I know that in the One Mind there cannot be misunderstanding, in the One Love all are included.

I have absolute faith in the Principle of Life, the Law of Love, and so I permit Love in its freedom to express through me, to radiate from me. Knowing that It transcends all other manifestations I am filled with Divine Confidence that the Laws of Life work just as accurately as the laws of mathematics. I use these Principles constantly, every hour of the day, in every situation, in every adjustment.

Mine eyes are ever toward the Lord; for he shall
pluck my feet out of the net. —PSALM 25:15

I now withdraw my thoughts from the world of confusion and realize that in the One Universal Mind, which is the Mind of God, there is quietude, peace, order. This is Reality.

It matters not that in the shadow world of form there is a sense of futility. I know that Life is real, worthwhile. I know that no effort toward unity with that which is Real, that which is True, is ever lost. I enter deeply into Peace and feel its strength and power.

I know that here, in this consciousness of Reality, is the supply for my every need—physical, mental, or spiritual—and I accept that supply in deepest gratitude. I am thankful that this is the way Life fulfills my needs, through the doorway of my inner self, and I am thankful that I know how to use this Perfect Law.

I come to this great Fountain of Supply, in the very center of my being, to absorb that for which I have need, mentally and physically, and I am filled with a joyous sense of the Reality of that which I desire. As I am filled with Reality I permit It to flow into my world of thought and action, knowing that It brings peace and harmony and order all around me. It flows out into the lives I touch. Where I am, there is peace, order, joy, harmony for I am One with Reality.

The Lord is my light and my salvation; whom shall I fear? The Lord
is the strength of my life; of whom shall I be afraid? —PSALM 27:1

I tune out all dull, negative ideas, and tune in with the Sunshine of Life,
with brightness and laughter, with the joyous Presence that is Life Itself.

I know that all the beauty of form around me is the Garment of God. I
know that that Presence that is manifested in my heart and mind is God expressing Himself within the Garment of Form. As I feel this Presence more
and more I hear the Song of Joy deep within. Always when I am still I hear
the Song of Life pouring through my consciousness. I have only to listen,
for It is always there.

With this knowledge, this assurance that that Loving Presence is always
here—"closer to me than breathing, nearer than hands and feet"—I have
nothing to fear. I feel this loving protection around me, and I know that it is
a bulwark of strength. I know that It is not only a Song of Joy, but a Song of
Love and Protection.

Knowing this, that I am the very Essence of God, Joy wells up within
my heart, and Life sings through me in radiant ecstasy.

Surely goodness and mercy shall follow me all the days of my life:
and I will dwell in the house of the Lord forever. —PSALM 23:6

I know that the Spirit of Truth is within me and that I contact this Spirit through my own self-recognition, belief, and expectancy.

I am not disturbed or confused by past occurrences, for I know that the Spirit of Truth ever guides me into perfect activity and complete self-expression. Within me is an ever-present beauty, a never-failing power, a perennial fountain of goodness. Today I expect more, greater, and better thoughts to be expressed through me. All my affairs prosper and quicken into radiant activity because of the indwelling Spirit.

I realize that no harm can befall me, because I "dwell in the secret place of the Most High" and "abide under the shadow of the Almighty." Perfect life is mine. Complete good is mine. Endless happiness is mine. Abundant supply and health are mine. Joy and peace are mine forevermore. Since I dwell in the shadow of the Almighty, no harm can come to me, no want, no lack, only joy and peace, confidence and trust.

There is, in the citadel of my soul, that which completes my life. This is God, the Complete and Perfect. In my realization of unity with this Central Self I link myself with enduring Power.

The Lord is my strength and my shield . . . therefore my heart greatly
rejoiceth; and with my song will I praise him. —PSALM 28:7

God could not withhold anything from me. That which God is, God has
given fully unto me to enjoy. The Life of God is perfect, it is eternal, it is the
essence of all things. That life is God's gift to me. Therefore, this fullness is
within me, ready to manifest through me as I partake of it, since I am self-
choosing, even though Divinely endowed. I partake of my Divinity only as
I let it through; I am always in the midst of plenty everywhere.

I now consciously begin to draw upon the life that is mine. I now begin
to reeducate myself definitely, by whatever steps I may, to a belief that there
is given unto me a fullness of life which is Divine in its origin, eternal in its
presence, and always fully available.

The Life of the Almighty is my life. The infinite richness of God is mine
to enjoy. The vital good health, the wisdom, the joy, the peace of God are
mine. All things that proceed from God may be mine. I now claim them.
The act of taking is my right and privilege. I exercise it now intelligently and
in full faith.

I will be glad and rejoice in thy mercy: for thou hast considered
my trouble; thou hast known my soul in adversities. —PSALM 31:7

I now realize that there is but One Mind, One Presence in the Universe.
This Presence is God—pure, absolute, unadulterated Spirit.

This Divine Presence being everywhere and filling all space must be in
me. It must be that which I really am. I recognize It is in me and It is that
which I am.

I let this recognition of my indwelling Divinity flow through my entire
consciousness. I let it reach down into the very depths of my being. I rejoice
in my Divinity.

Again I affirm that the Divine Presence fills all space, including myself.
I am full of God; therefore, I am filled with Light. Infinite Intelligence governs every move I make. An All-Wise Counselor accompanies me at all
times. The Spirit of the Almighty goes before me.

As the light dispels darkness, so this Truth, which I now affirm, dissipates all fear. It breaks down every doubt and casts out all uncertainty. It
looses every sense of bondage within my mind; stimulates my imagination
with the vision of peace, of joy, and of abundance; and directs my will
toward the accomplishment of my desires.

I will bless the Lord at all times: his praise
shall continually be in my mouth. —PSALM 34:1

Love is God and God is infinite, eternal, and omnipresent. Therefore, Love
is infinite, eternal, and omnipresent. I cannot escape Love. I exist in Love
and of It. I live by and through It. It motivates my every action. Everything
I see, I see with the eyes of Love. Everything I hear, I hear with the ears of
Love.

I can recognize nothing but Love at any time. Nothing but Love and
lovely things can come to me. I insist on seeing the Love in all things, the
Reality behind the seeming discord. To everyone I encounter, I definitely
and purposefully radiate Love. I love my work. I enjoy doing the things that
come to me to be done. I appreciate the good that has been expressed to me.

I do not want. I love into my experience the things I desire. I wrap their
expression to me in love so that they come harmoniously and with no strain.

People love me. They love to work with me and to be in my presence.
The God in them senses my loving nature. My office and my home are filled
with love and harmony. They draw love and lovely things and people to
them. Love enfolds me and mine at all times.

∽

I delight to do thy will, O my God:
yea, thy law is within my heart. —PSALM 40:8

I know that the Perfect Life of the Spirit is my life, and I now permit It to radiate through my world of thought and action—to express in my physical form.

Because my whole being is this perfect God-Life, I have nothing to fear. Every person I meet recognizes the perfect being that is my true Self, recognizes love and peace and wisdom and courage in me. Each person I contact feels our common bond, knows that we are part of the Perfect Whole, the harmonious centers of consciousness in the great Unity of Life, and so has faith in me.

No one could wish to harm or hurt me in any way. I, too, can know only love and understanding for my fellow beings. I am truly interested in each one I meet—interested in their hopes, their aspirations—and helpful to them.

I know, because I am God-Life, God in expression, that every circumstance I find myself in is right for me. Through my consciousness of Love, which is the very Essence of God-Life, I transform any seeming imperfection into the perfect idea of my True Self. God knows me only as a Perfect Idea, and that Perfection I now manifest.

As the hart panteth after the water brooks,
so panteth my soul after thee, O God. —PSALM 42:1

I realize that one of the reasons I may not have received a more definite answer to my prayer, more swift and specific manifestion from my spiritual treatment, is because I did not persist in my expectancy—I hoped for rather than had faith I would receive the good I desired. Now I realize that there must be a certain acceptance and expectancy that is built upon or sustained by faith. Because of faith I must accept the fact that my good is and persist in expecting its manifestation.

My faith sustains my expectancy at all times. Faith is an entirely individual and personal attitude. It flourishes within me. I realize that I may have as much faith as I will, regardless of anything and everything else. The only limit to what I may have is the faith I do have.

As is my faith, so is my acceptance; and as is my acceptance, so is my expectancy; and finally, as is my expectancy, so is my demonstration or experience. Through the broad avenues of expectancy created within me by my faith, all good comes to me.

> In God I have put my trust: I will not be afraid
> of what man can do unto me. —PSALM 56:11

There is a Power operating through me; a Presence, inspiring, guiding, and sustaining me. Upon this Power, I place my reliance. In this Presence, I feel myself to be an outlet of immeasurable Good. Because I am in this Divine Presence, and because It is in me, and because this Divine has all power, I know that my thought is made manifest in a perfect demonstration of health, of harmony, and of success.

I know the Creative Law of Good is infinite and has all power to accomplish. I know Its whole desire for me is freedom and joy. Therefore, I declare that this freedom and joy are mine today. This freedom and joy spontaneously express in my experience and there is nothing in me that can hinder this expression. Because this All-Good is mine and because it constitutes the only Presence there is in the Universe, I know freedom and joy cannot be separated from me, but remain in my presence, forever manifesting themselves.

I know the Infinite Creative Law is always bringing complete satisfaction into my experience. I am conscious that there is an Infinite Wisdom directing me. Whatever I should know, I will know. Whatever I should do, I will do. Whatever belongs to me, must come to me, and because of this Infinite Intelligence that is mine and that is within me now, I am compelled to recognize my Good, to see more, to understand and accept and express more.

I will abide in thy tabernacle for ever:
I will trust in the covert of thy wings. —PSALM 61:4

Realizing that the Spirit within me is God, the Living Spirit Almighty, and being fully conscious of this Divine Presence as the sustaining Principle of my life, I open my thought to Its influx. I open my consciousness to Its outpouring. I let that Mind be in me that was also in Christ Jesus. That is the Mind of Truth, the Mind of God, carrying with It all the power of the Infinite. I do decree and declare that every experience that I have partakes of the nature of harmony and peace.

I know and understand that Good alone is real. I know that silently I am drawing into my experience, today and every day, an ever-increasing measure of truth and beauty, of goodness, of joy, of harmony. Everything that I do, say, and think is quickened into right action, into productive action, into increased action. All there is is mine now; all there ever was or ever can be is mine now. Of this Divine Bounty I partake.

This same good I realize belongs to everyone else. I do not desire a good for myself that is greater than the good I desire for all people. Neither do I deny myself the good I affirm for all others. Since all are some part of the Divine, good belongs alike to all. I proclaim this good to be manifest among all people.

Create in me a clean heart, O God;
and renew a right spirit within me. —PSALM 51:10

I have within myself, as I sit here, the sense that though my body is real, tangible, with definite form and outline it is at the same time somehow made of a Living Stuff that is saturated with God-Life. I know that whatever the stuff is of which my body is made, though it is called material, it must really be made of the One Stuff and Essence of which all things are made. Therefore, I sense within the very cells and tissues of my body an eternality.

As I relax my body, consciously and definitely—which I am able to do by mentally relaxing and dropping all strain—I feel flowing through me a vital energy, a dynamic force, a great surge of living power.

The Spirit within me refreshes me daily. Right here and now I feel saturated with the Life Essence Itself. And I feel the same Life Essence flowing in and through me. I feel immersed in and saturated by a vital Essence of Perfection that brings me into tune with life. I feel myself to be a perfect instrument of Life's divine symphony, in tune with its harmony and perfection. My body is an instrument in, through, and upon which Life plays a divine and perfect harmony.

Truly my soul waiteth upon God:
from him cometh my salvation. —PSALM 62:1

I know that today, even now, Wisdom is available to me. There is no darkness in my mind, neither is there disease in my body because the Spirit of Wisdom, of Truth, has revealed my mental and physical perfection to me. The light of the Spirit shines from the very center of my being.

As a spark of God, I am illumined by the Spirit of Wisdom. I am free from the bondage of all false beliefs. The Spirit of Wisdom enables me to see all others as they are in reality—perfect expressions of God.

My thoughts are radiant with the light of Spirit, and the light of my consciousness shines to the very circumference of my world. There is no indecision in my mind. In Truth there is only one Power, only one God. I am directed by the Spirit of Wisdom and am assured of peace, joy, love, health, and plenty.

Every blessing attends my footsteps, because spiritual consciousness directs me in the way of my highest good. I know that I am guided onto right paths and that only good can come to me and mine, for the Spirit of Wisdom directs my steps this day.

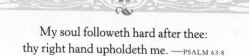

My soul followeth hard after thee:
thy right hand upholdeth me. —PSALM 63:8

I know that the Power of Good is an underlying Principle of the Universe, and that It is a manifestation of God. I know that God is All-Good. I know that Good underlies all manifestations of thought and form, because Good is harmony, complete balance. Good is at the root of all manifestion, regardless of its seeming absence.

I know that this Good is the basic principle of my existence. That which I am is Good, and I know that Good is the Law of my being. It is the vital, living Force that supports my every thought and deed that are in harmony with It. There is no other power, for God is Good and there cannot be God and something else. God is in all. God is all and God is Good.

I know there is nothing in me that could possibly obstruct or withhold the Divine Circuit of Life and Love, which Good is. My word dissolves every negative thought or impulse that could throw a shadow over my perfection. Good flows through me to all. Good shines through my thoughts and actions. Good harmonizes my body, so that it is revitalized and manifests perfection in every cell, in every organ, in every function. Good harmonizes my mind, so that Love sings joyously in my heart and I am completely conscious of All-Good in me, around me, and in all that is. I am in complete unity with my Good.

My flesh and my heart faileth: but God is the strength
of my heart, and my portion forever. —PSALM 73:26

I am conscious that the Life and the Intelligence within me is some part of the Universal Spirit. Therefore, I know that my mind is one with the Infinite Mind. Being one with the Infinite Mind, I am continuously guided and directed, and all my actions are controlled by the Spirit within me.

I know exactly what to do in every situation. Every idea necessary to successful living is brought to my attention. The doorway to ever-increasing opportunity for self-expression is ever open before me. I am continuously meeting new and larger experiences. Every day brings some greater good. Every day brings more blessings and greater self-expression. I prosper in everything I do. An abundance of good is mine today.

There is that within me that understands the Truth, that completely accepts It, that remembers freedom, expresses freedom, and anticipates freedom. There is that within me that is completely conscious of its unity with Good, of its oneness with all the Power there is, all the Presence there is, and all the Life there is.

Upon this Power, Presence, and Life I depend with complete certainty. I have absolute inner assurance that Divine Intelligence benefits me in everything I do.

My soul longeth, yea, even fainteth for the courts of the Lord: my heart and my flesh crieth out for the living God. —PSALM 84:2

As I center my consciousness in Infinite Being, I realize that Its Essence is Love and that this Love is in and through everything and everyone.

I know that this Love Essence, the very Substance of Life, the creative Principle back of everything, flows through my whole being—spiritual, emotional, mental, and physical. It flows in transcendent loveliness into my world of thought and form. I am conscious of this Divine Circuit, which Love is. I feel It as a golden stream of force flowing from God, through me, and out to all that my thought rests upon, and returning to God. I know that this force is ever flowing, ever renewing, vitalizing, bringing joy and harmony and blessings to everything and everyone it touches. It flows with power and purpose through everything I do as it leads me gently down the pathway of life.

Consciously I attune myself to this stream of Perfect Love. In Its flow I see It as an ever-widening spiral of continuous right action, bringing me into ever-widening fields of expression. I, who am Love, share myself—my Love—with all humanity. I know that in Love there can be no separation, for Love unites. Love sustains and protects Its own. I know that the Love I express blesses all who are in any way touched by it. It heals every condition, brings my own to me. I am immersed in Love.

Ask, and ye shall receive, that your joy may be full. — JOHN 16:24

Nothing in our thought about God should produce sadness or depression; rather, it should do quite the reverse, because our faith in and love of God should give us such a confidence and such a sense of security that we should indeed be able to say: "Joy to the world, the Lord has come."

We must come to realize that God is not in some far-off place, but instead that God is an inward, intimate Presence closer to us than our very breath. God is not nor can ever be separated from us, but too often we separate ourselves from God.

I now affirm that there is nothing in me that can doubt this Presence or limit the Power of Good in my life. There is nothing in me that can separate me from the Love of God, and I accept the joy of living in the very midst of It.

The Divine Presence leads me on the pathway of peace. It directs my thoughts, my words, and my actions into constructive channels of self-expression. It unites me with others in love, in kindness, and in consideration.

Today I accept this action gratefully and realize that it brings into my experience everything necessary for my joy and happiness. I affirm for others that which I accept for myself.

The fruit of the spirit is love, joy, peace. —GALATIANS 5:22

We should look across the new horizon of the greater possibility that resides within each of us and meet the living God and feel the embrace of God's Presence and come at last to know the infallibility of God's Power. From out of the great Mind that is God the way of life is made perfect and straight and immediate. It is made happy and whole and prosperous.

God's Love always embraces us, God's Wisdom is always within us, and God's Joy is ours to share. Just as surely as tomorrow will come and the sun will rise again across the darkness of the horizon and spill its beauty and warmth to awaken the valleys into fertility, so shall this be a new day in our life, bringing us into a greater joy of living because of a greater consciousness of the Almighty within our own souls.

I dwell in the house of Love. My dwelling place is filled with peace and eternal calm. Love attends me in my home of the Soul, and Joy awaits upon me in the "Secret Place of the Most High."

My sorrow is turned to gladness and my shame to rejoicing. My tears are wiped away and the sunlight of the Spirit shines through the clouds of depression and lights the way to Heaven.

I will say of the Lord, He is my refuge and my fortress:
my God, in him will I trust. —PSALM 91:2

At the center of my being is Peace—that peace that is felt in the coolness of early evening, after workers have turned from their labor, and the first star shines in the soft light of a translucent sky.

There is a freshness, a vitality, a power underlying this Peace. It broods over the earth quietly, tenderly, as a mother watches over her sleeping baby.

In this Peace that holds me so gently, I feel strength and a protection from all fear, all anxieties. It is the Peace of God, and, underneath it all, I feel the Love of the Holy Presence. As I become more conscious of this Love, all lack, all fear, all that is false slips away as mists fade in the morning sunshine. I am one with deep, abiding Peace. I know that all is well.

I know that as I permit this Peace to flow through my being, through my mind and heart, every problem is released. The way is made clear before me, and it is filled with joy and harmony.

I am Peace. I am Love. I am Power. I am Vitality and Strength and All-Good. Where I am—there is Peace.

JUNE
CREATIVITY

We are chemists in the laboratory of the Infinite. What, then, shall we create? —ERNEST HOLMES

We must say that all thought is creative, according to the nature, impulse, emotion, or conviction behind the thought. Thought creates a mold in the Subjective, in which the idea is accepted and poured, and sets power in motion in accordance with the thought. —ERNEST HOLMES

One principle must make the universe a single complex living creature, one from all. —PLOTINUS

To fall into a habit is to begin to cease to be. —MIGUEL DE UNAMUNO

That alone is truly real which abides unchanged. —ST. AUGUSTINE

My Word Does Accomplish

Since thought is a definite, dynamic, creative, consciously directed and intelligent energy, I know that a thought of Truth will definitely neutralize a negative argument. I am on guard to protect my own word by knowing that it is the activity of Spirit through me and as such cannot be denied. In effective prayer, I realize that a Power greater than myself consciously acts with creative intelligence upon my word. In this way, I free myself from a sense of personal responsibility, while, at the same time, remaining aware that even spiritual laws must be definitely used, if they are to provide tangible results in my experience.

I seek to believe with absolute conviction that my word will not return unto me void, and I do this when I realize that spirtual laws execute themselves, just as do other laws of nature. I know that my word penetrates every unbelief in my mind, casts out all fear, removes all doubt, clears away every obstacle, and permits that which is enduring, perfect, and true to be perceived by my mind. I provide faith, acceptance, and a joyous expectancy that all the statements I make in my affirmative prayers and treatments are not only true, but that they will be carried out as I have spoken. As my word is done with this sense of reliance upon the Law of Good, I know that "my word will not return unto me void," but "shall accomplish that whereunto it is sent."

Perfect Reality Is Manifesting in My Life

The Will of God for me is the will of a boundless life, flowing through me. It is the will of joy, of success, of happiness, of peace, of abundance. It is the will of the Kingdom of Heaven, not absent from this earth, but imperfectly seen. Nothing rewards or punishes me but the immutable law of cause and effect. There is no good that I cannot experience provided I first embody that good. There is no joy that I cannot reach provided I first clear my consciousness of anything that would limit this joy in myself or in others. I dispel any doubt in my mind as to whether or not God wishes me to have the best.

There is no judgment, no condemnation, no criticism. I know that any belief in a power that harms is false. Every such belief is eradicated. There is justice, knowledge, right guidance. Divine Intelligence operates through me without confusion, calmly moving forward, progressive, reaching outward. I am guided by Infinite Wisdom into that Light that is eternal. I accept the gift of Life for myself and for everyone else. God is right where I am. God is what I am. I enter into the conscious possession of this Divine Allness, this perfect Reality, today. I know that it is manifesting in my life.

Today I Meet My Good

Good is forever expressing Itself to me and all whom I love, which is everyone. I realize that this Good recognizes me and that I cannot depart from It. It presses against me and fills me with a great surge of life. I sense in the peaceful silence of the dawn a Divine Authority at the center of my being that announces Itself in every moment and event of my day. I have implicit confidence in that invisible part of me that is my share in the God-Nature, my partnership with the Infinite, my oneness with all that is, from the blade of grass to the glorious mountaintop. Today I accept my Good. Today I bless that Good and cause It to multiply in my experience.

I consciously receive this Good and loose it again into action, into everything I do. I know that my presence upholds and blesses everyone whom I contact and that healing power goes from me. I know that today I shall be able to help everyone whom I meet. There is a song at the center of my being that everyone hears, a joy that everyone feels, a strength that is imparted to all. I place upon everyone I meet the seamless robe of Christ, the garment of Truth, which is the unity of God and humankind.

The Infinite Law of Good Brings Me Complete Satisfaction

There is a Power operating through me, a Presence inspiring, guiding, and sustaining me. Upon this Power, I place my reliance. In this Presence, I feel myself to be an outlet of immeasurable good. Because I am in this Divine Presence and because it is in me, and because this Divine has all power, I know that my thought is made manifest in a perfect demonstration of health, of harmony, and of success.

I know that the Creative Law of Good is infinite and has all power to accomplish. I know Its whole desire for me is freedom and joy. Therefore, I declare that freedom and joy are mine today. This freedom and joy are expressed spontaneously in my experience, and there is nothing within me that can hinder this expression. Because this All-Good is mine, and because it constitutes the only Presence there is in the universe, I know that freedom and joy cannot be separated from me.

I am conscious that there is an Infinite Wisdom directing me. Whatever I should know, I will know. Whatever I should do, I will do. Whatever belongs to me must come to me and, because of this Infinite Intelligence that is mine and that is within me now, I am compelled to recognize my good, to see more, to understand and accept and express more. I know the Infinite Creative Law of Good is always bringing complete satisfaction into my life.

ᐁ

I Overcome Hate with Love

I know that there is but One Power in the universe and that Power is God. That Power manifests in and through all form, all people, all conditions, and so is at the very center of my being. This Power is Life Itself, and Its nature is Love—All-Good. I know that just as light dissipates darkness, just as heat warms the atmosphere, so a consciousness of good overcomes evil. I know that Good constitutes the only Power, Presence, and Law, and the knowledge of Good, which is the knowledge of Love, overcomes evil, dissipates it, obliterates it, blots it out.

I refuse to think of hate or any negation as a power, and I know that it will flee from me. Its dissolution is its flight . . . it disappears. Hate cannot exist where love is recognized. Knowing that Good alone is real, I turn the searchlight of Eternal Truth upon every so-called evil in my experience, and these dark places of imagination are instantly dissolved into light. The dissolution of evil is complete; the manifestation of good is perfect. I know that Love protects Its own, and now It makes clear the way before me, eliminating everything that looked like hate. I am guided into an ever-widening unfoldment of being, and my every thought, feeling, and act is an expression of the God-Nature—Love—through me. Continuously, I overcome hate with love.

Today I Meditate Upon My Divine Inheritance

The Kingdom of God is at hand. I inherit everything that belongs to this kingdom. The riches and the power and the glory of this kingdom are mine now. I do not rob anyone by entering into the fullness of the kingdom of power, of joy, and of abundance. I recognize that everyone inherits the same kingdom. There is no law of human heredity imposed upon me. Evil has no history. Limitation has no past. That which is opposed to good has no future. The eternal now is filled with perfection. I always have been and always will remain a complete, perfect, and whole expression of the Eternal Mind, which is God, the Living Spirit Almighty.

Today I enter into the limitless variations that the Divine Spirit has projected into my experience. I know that all things are good when rightly used. I perceive that all experience is a play of Life upon itself. I enter into the game of living, then, with joyful anticipation, with spontaneous enthusiasm, and with the determination to play the game well and to enjoy it. Today I enter into my Divine inheritance. I have shaken my thought loose from the belief that external conditions are imposed upon me by birth, through inherited tendencies or race belief. I proclaim the freedom of my Divine legacy of love, abundance, peace, and joy. I possess the Kingdom of Good today, in all of its fullness.

Today I Consciously Let Go of Every Discord

I drop all sense of lack or limitation from my thought and every belief that I have ever had in negation or fear. I now have a belief in success and faith. I permit the Spirit within me to express Itself in perfect freedom, bringing increasing joy into my experience. There is that within me that is completely conscious of its unity with good, of its oneness with all the Power there is and all the Presence there is and all the Life there is. Upon this Power, Presence, and Life I depend with implicit certainty, with complete confidence, and with absolute assurance.

I allow the Divine Wholeness to flow through me into ever-widening fields of activity. Every good I have ever experienced is now increased tenfold. Every joy I have ever experienced is now multiplied. There is a new influx of inspiration into my thought. I see more clearly than ever before that my Divine birthright is freedom, peace, joy, and eternal goodness. I perceive that this same birthright is bequeathed to all people. All power is delivered unto me and this power I use for my own and every other person's good. This Divine Presence interprets Itself to me in love. Friendship, peace, joy, and goodness are mine now and forever.

The Spirit of the Almighty Goes Before Me

I know that the Power of Good is an underlying principle of the universe and that it is a manifestation of Mother-Father God. I know that God is All-Good. I know that Good underlies all manifestation of thought and form because Good is harmony, complete balance. Good is at the root of all manifestation, regardless of its seeming absence. I know that this Good is the basic principle of my existence; that which I am is Good. It is the vital, living Force that supports my every thought and deed when they are in harmony with It.

Today I uncover the perfection within me. In its fullness I reveal the indwelling kingdom. I look out upon the world of my affairs, knowing that the Spirit within me makes my way both immediate and easy. I know there is nothing in me that could possibly obstruct or withhold the divine circuit of Life and Love, which Good is. My word dissolves every negative thought or impulse that could throw a shadow over my perfection. Good flows through me to all. Good shines through my thoughts and actions. Good harmonizes my body, so that it is revitalized and manifests perfection in every cell, in every organ, in every function. Good harmonizes my mind, so that Love sings joyously in my heart, and I am completely conscious of All-Good in me, around me, and in all that is. I am in complete unity with my Good.

I Demonstrate Through the Perfect Law

All laws are laws of God. Whatever Reality is, Its nature is One. If I wish to demonstrate my good I must faithfully and fervently declare that the Law of the Lord is perfect and that this Law is operating in my experience now. I believe that it is the nature of thought to externalize itself, to bring about conditions that exactly correspond to the thought. Therefore, I turn resolutely from every sense of lack, want, and limitation, knowing that even though I am dealing with an invisible Principle, the perfection of Spirit will be made manifest in my experience.

Today I declare that the Law of the Lord is perfect in everything I do. It will externalize happiness; it will bring every good thing to me. Today I am inwardly aware that there is a secret way of the soul, there is a secret pathway of peace, there is an invisible Presence forever externalizing Itself for me and through me. Today I believe in Divine Guidance. Today I believe that underneath are the everlasting arms. Today I rest in this divine assurance and this divine security. I know that not only is all well with my soul, my spirit, and my mind, but all is well with my affairs.

My Being Is Animated by the Divine Perfection

Chinese sages tell us that Tao, meaning Spirit, produces everything, nourishes everything, and maintains everything. It spreads Itself over everything. It flows through everything and is in all things. Indeed, being all that is, there can be nothing outside It. There is a mystical Presence that pervades the Universe, and this Presence, welling up in our consciousness, evermore proclaims Itself as the source and root of all. The enlightened of the ages have told us that it is this God within us that recognizes Itself in everything we are.

I know that as there is One Mind—and that Mind is God and that Mind is my mind—so also there is one Body, that Body is spiritual and that Body is my body. So, every organ, every function, every action and reaction of my body is in harmony with the Divine Creative Spirit. I have both "the mind of Christ" and the Body of God. I could not ask for more and greater could not be given. I now seek to realize the spiritual significance of the One Mind and the One Body. I live in the One Mind and act through the One Body, in accord with Divine harmony, perfection, and poise. Every organ of my body moves in accord with perfect harmony. The Divine circulates through me automatically, spontaneously, and perfectly. Every atom of my being is animated by the Divine Perfection.

Spiritual Substance Is My Supply

I know that Spirit fills all space and animates every form; therefore, Spirit is the true actor in everything. But I also know that Spirit can only act for me by acting through me. This means simply that God can only give me what I take. I am conscious that as I daily enter into my Divine inheritance, in my thought and in the Spirit, I am entering into the realm of Absolute Causation, and I completely believe that from this secret place of the Most High within me there shall be projected an objective manifestation of my every legitimate desire. Am I really accepting abundance? Is my thought really animating my experience with the idea of plenty? Am I affirming that Divine Substance is forever flowing to me as supply?

Today I praise the abundance in all things. I animate everything with the idea of abundance. I am remembering only the good; I am expecting more good; I am experiencing good. I acknowledge the good working everywhere. I give thanks that this good is flowing into my experience in ever-increasing volume. There is that within me that sees, knows, and understands this truth, that completely accepts it. There is good enough to go around. Therefore, I do not withhold that good from myself or others, but constantly proclaim Spiritual Substance is forever flowing to each and all as supply.

Right Action Is Operating in My Life Now

Right action means that every legitimate and constructive purpose I have in mind will be successfully executed. It means that I will know what to do, how to think, how to act, how to proceed. I definitely declare that since my word is in accord with the Divine Nature, it actually is the Law of God in my experience enforcing Itself. Hence, there is nothing in me or around me that can limit this word. The power of this Law is with me, and the action that results from this power produces harmony, peace, joy, and success.

I know that in this consciousness of Reality is the supply for my every need—physical, mental, or spiritual—and I accept that supply in deepest gratitude. I am thankful that this is the way Life fulfills my needs, through the doorway of my inner self, and I am thankful that I know how to use this perfect Law. I come to this great Fountain of Supply, in the very center of my being, to absorb that for which I have need, mentally and physically, and I am filled with the sense of the Reality of that which I desire. As I am filled with Reality I permit It to flow into my world of thought and action, knowing that It brings peace and harmony and order all around me. There arises within me limitless faith in the unconquerable Presence, the perfect Law and Divine Action.

I Recognize My Identity with Spirit

My knowledge that the great I Am is ever available gives me an increasing capacity to draw upon It and to become inwardly aware of the presence of Spirit. Through the quiet contemplation of the omni-action of Spirit, I learn to look quietly and calmly upon every false condition, seeing through it to the other side of the invisible Reality that molds conditions and re-creates all of my affairs after a more nearly Divine pattern. With a penetrating spiritual vision I can dissipate the obstruction, remove the obstacle, dissolve the wrong condition. Standing still I can watch the sure salvation of the Law.

I now claim health instead of sickness, wealth instead of poverty, happiness instead of misery. In such degree as I gain mastery over the sense of negation, whether it be pain or poverty, I am proving the Law of Good. Every thought of fear or limitation is removed from my consciousness. I know that my word transmutes every energy into constructive action, producing health, harmony, happiness, and success. I know there is something at the center of my being that is absolutely certain of itself. It has complete assurance and it gives me complete assurance that all is well. I maintain my position as a Divine Being, here and now.

Daily I Die to Everything That Is Unlike Good

The Talmud says that unhappy conditions arise when we mistake shadow for substance. Even the valley of the shadow of death causes no fear when we arrive at the consciousness of the Psalmist who, from the exaltation of his Divine deliverance, proclaimed, "thy rod and thy staff they comfort me." The rod and staff of Truth is the realization of the substantiality and the permanence of that which cannot change. We are ever renewed by the passage of the Divine light through our consciousness. The revitalizing, regenerative power of Spirit flows from the consciousness of wholeness into our physical organism and into every objective act when we give the realization of the Divine Presence free passage through our thought.

I know that every apparent death is a resurrection. Therefore, today, gladly I die to everything that is unlike the good. Joyfully I am resurrected into that which is beautiful, enduring, and true. Silently I pass from less to more, from isolation to inclusion, from separation into oneness. The perfect Law of Good is operating through me. Joyfully I accept it. Joyfully I permit its action in everything that I do. I know that my recognition of good is the substance of the good which I recognize, and I know that this good is ever taking form in my experience. It is impossible for me to be separated from my good.

Today I See God Reflected in Every Form

After long meditation and much deep reflection, having passed through the confusion of human experience, Job finally arrived at the conclusion that the Spirit of God was within him and that the breath of God was his life. We all have traveled this same pathway of experience, the journey of the soul to "the heights above," and always there has been a deep inquiry in our minds—What is it all about? Does life make sense? What is the meaning of birth, human experience, and the final transition, which we call death, from this plane? Somewhere along the line we too must exclaim with Job, "The spirit of God hath made me and the breath of the Almighty hath given me life." Nothing can be nearer to us than that which is the very essence of our own being. Our external search after Reality culminates in the greatest of all possible discoveries—Reality is at the center of our own being; life is from within out.

I feel that my search is over. I feel that I have discovered the Great Reality. I am not evolving into it, I am merely awakening to the realization of what it means. There is but one Life. This Life I am living. Today I speak this Reality into every experience I have. Today I see God reflected in every form, back of every countenance, moving in every act.

I Am Spirit Made Manifest This Instant

My body, and every part of it, is made of pure Substance—God. It cannot deteriorate. This instant this Infinite Substance within me, which is constantly flowing through me, takes form in the likeness of perfect, whole, complete cells. Every cell of my lungs is strong and healthy, filled with life and vitality, strength and cleanliness. My body, which is Spirit in form, knows no time, knows no degree; it knows only to express fully, instantaneously.

The Divine Presence, being everywhere and filling all space, must be in me. It must be that which I really am. I recognize It is within me and It is that which I am. I let this recognition of my indwelling Divinity flow through my entire consciousness. I let it reach down into the very depths of my being. I rejoice in my Divinity. I am now made vigorous and hardy. I have the stamina of the Infinite. I am sturdy and robust. I am fortified with God's perfection and right action. I am hale and able-bodied. All the life of the universe is my life. All the strength of the universe is my strength. All the power of the universe is my power. Every breath I draw fills me with perfection—vitalizes, energizes, and renews every cell of my body. I am born in Spirit and of Spirit, and I am Spirit made manifest this instant.

Today I Live

The wise Master Jesus taught that the knowledge of truth makes us free. All books of spiritual wisdom have said that it is not the one who makes the mistake whom we should seek to destroy; it is the mistake itself that must be erased. This means that evil has no existence in itself and has no history. No matter what the negations of yesterday may have been, the affirmations of today rise triumphant and transcendent over them. Thus, all the evils of our yesterdays disappear into their native nothingness. If we behold beauty instead of ugliness, then beauty will appear. If we persist in seeing the true rather than the false, then that which is true will appear. Let us, then, cease weeping over the shortcomings and mistakes and evils of our yesterdays and, steadfastly beholding the face of the great and the divine Reality, let us resolve to walk in the light wherein there is no darkness.

Definitely I know that every negative condition of the past is cleared away from my consciousness. I no longer think about it, see it, or believe in it. Nor do I believe that it has any effect whatsoever on my experience. Yesterday is not, tomorrow is not, but today, bright with hope and filled with promise, is mine. Today I live.

I Experience Complete Wholeness

I know that I am some part of the Divine Being, that the power and the presence of that Spirit is in the word I speak and that word infinitely and perfectly and permanently makes whole. I know that I represent an individualization of the Truth—the truth of Wholeness, the truth of Love, Reason and Sound Mind, the truth of Peace and Joy, the truth and the freedom of the circulation of the Divine in every atom, in every function, and every organ. I empty myself of any and every thought that denies this. I know that, silently but effectively, that Divine Power of the invisible Spirit is working here and now—this moment.

I take hold of this realization with complete certainty. I recognize that I am a perfect being, living under perfect conditons, knowing that Good alone is real. I also know that Good alone is the only thing that has any power either to act or to react. Everything that I do, say, or think today will be done, said, or thought from the spiritual viewpoint of God in everything. My recognition of the Power is sufficient to neutralize every false experience, make the crooked straight, and the rough places smooth. Definitely I know that this recognition establishes the Law of Harmony in my experience, the Law of Prosperity, the sense of happiness and health. I experience complete Wholeness.

Today I Am Redeemed

The larger part of our mental life is submerged. The habitual patterns of thought, which are subjective, automatically determine our physical and mental reactions. In this way, we are more or less hypnotized from the cradle to the grave. Inner impulsions of these subjective thought patterns are often stronger than the intellect, and willpower seems to have little effect on them. We must resort to imagination and feeling, to a deep conviction of, and an abiding faith in, something greater than our will, higher than our intellect. In this way we are redeemed. We stop using the Creative Power of the Universe to produce limitation in our life, and instead begin to awaken to our vast possibilities.

Today I realize that there is but One Power in the Universe and that my redemption is at hand. The Spirit within me refreshes me daily. I feel myself saturated with the Life Essence Itself; I feel the same Life Essence flowing in and through me. I feel myself to be a perfect instrument in Life's divine symphony, in tune with its harmony and perfection. My body is an instrument in, through, and upon which Life plays a divine and perfect harmony. I am not going out in search of another power, but am going to use the Power I know is already at the center of my own life. I know It heals every disharmony, overcomes every obstacle, breaks down every barrier, and frees me from every false condition. My redemption is assured.

I Partake of the Divine Bounty

Realizing that the Spirit within me is God, the Living Spirit Almighty, being fully conscious of this Divine Presence as the sustaining Principle of my life, I open my thought to Its influx. I open my consciousness to Its outpouring. I let that Mind be in me that was also in Christ Jesus. That is the Mind of Truth, the Mind of God, carrying with It all the power of the Infinite. I know and understand that Good alone is real. I know that silently I am drawing into my experience, today and every day, an ever-increasing measure of truth and beauty, of goodness, of harmony. Everything I do, say, and think is quickened into right action, into productive action, into increased action. My invisible good already exists. My faith, drawing upon this invisible good, causes that which was unseen to become visible. All there is is mine now; all there ever was or ever can be is mine now.

I Have Confidence in My Understanding of the Law

I believe that no matter what experience I am going through now, good will come of it. I believe that all poverty will be turned to riches; that all fear will be converted to faith. I believe that good will finally triumph over every evil and that love will finally heal all hate. I believe that I have a silent partnership with the Invisible; that this partnership has never been dissolved and never can be. I believe in the invisible Presence of Good in a universe peopled with perfect and eternal entities. I believe that all things are possible to him who does believe.

I have complete confidence in my knowledge and understanding of the Law of Good. I not only know what the Law is, I know how to use It. I know that I shall obtain definite results through the use of It. I realize that doubts about my ability to use this Law are things of thought. What thought has produced, thought can change. Knowing this, having confidence in my ability to use the Law, and using It daily for specific purposes, gradually I build up an unshakable faith, both in the Law and in the possibility of demonstrating It. There is no doubt in me, no uncertainty rising through me. My mind rejoices in certainty and in assurance. I confidently expect that my word shall not return unto me void.

I Rely Upon the One Perfect Activity of God

The all-intelligent, creative Presence is the source of all that I am. I believe in the ability and the willingness of this great Source to sustain its own creation. The kingdom and the Power and the Glory of God are expressed through me. I recognize myself to be a center through which the Intelligence and the Power of the universe find expression. Infinite Mind, operating through me, now brings to me the manifestation of harmony, order, and the highest good. The consciousness of peace and plenty is established within me. All that is necessary to my happiness and well-being now comes into my experience.

There can be neither limitation nor lack, for nothing ever restricts the One Perfect Activity. It is in full operation for me. I am now free from any sense of bondage. All Power is given unto me from On High. Knowing this, I am strong with the strength of the all-vitalizing power of the universe. I am sustained and healed by a divine stream of Spirit-Energy, which flows through me as radiant health and vitality. Every cell and atom of my being responds to this spiritual flow. I stand revealed as the perfect child of the Perfect God. Strength and courage are my divine birthright, and I am now expressing my true self. All that God has is mine. I draw from the spiritual treasure-house all that I need.

Today I Bestow the Essence of Love Upon Everything

We are made perfect when we enter into the communion of love with one another and with the invisible essence of Life. Love is the fulfillment of the Law, that is, we do not make the highest use of the Law unless that use is motivated by Love, by a sincere desire to express unity, harmony, and peace. As the soaring bird opens her wings to the sky's embrace, so we must open our hearts and minds to the influx of Spirit and receive Its Love that we may, in turn, express It to all whom we meet. We must embrace the essence of Love that we may transmit It, giving loveliness to all events.

Today I bestow the limitless Love flowing through me upon everything. Everyone will be lovely to me. My soul meets the soul of the universe in everyone. Nothing is ordinary; it is all beautiful, all meaningful. This love is a healing power that touches everything into wholeness, healing the wounds of experience with its divine balm. I know that this Love Essence, the very Substance of Life, the creative Principle back of everything, flows through my whole being, spiritual, emotional, mental, and physical. It flows in transcendent loveliness into my world of thought and form, ever renewing, vitalizing, bringing joy and harmony, and blessing everything and everyone it touches.

I Accept My Own Spiritual and Physical Perfection

My body is the temple of the Living God. It is Spiritual Substance. I have perfect confidence in my heart that God's life-giving Spirit is my life. Since God is my life and God is eternal, my life is eternal. Therefore, I cannot be separated from God, from Good, from Perfection. If I would renew body, mind, and affairs, I must first cause my imagination to rise above them. The supreme Ruler, omnipresent, therefore existing at the very center of my thought, the Christ within me, really has the power to make all things new.

The perfect Life of God now expresses Itself through me, and every part of my body expresses its innate perfection and wholeness. As the sun dissolves the mist, so does my knowledge of Truth dissolve all pain and discord. I know the Truth about myself as a child of God and that Truth makes me free. I am free because the Power of the Living Spirit is my power, and it remolds and re-creates my body after the likeness of the perfect pattern of God. I open wide the doorway of my consciousness to a greater influx from Almighty Spirit. I know that the all-conquering power of Spirit is with me. I accept my birthright, as a Divine being, of manifesting the Life, Love, Peace, Strength, Harmony, and Joy of God—the Infinite Life that dwells within and incarnates Itself in me, as me.

The Life of the Divine Is My Life

God does not withhold anything from me. All that It is has been given fully unto me to enjoy. The Life of God is perfect, it is eternal, it is the essence of all things. That life is God's gift to me. Therefore, this fullness is within me, ready to manifest through me as I partake of it. Since I am self-choosing, even though Divinely endowed, I partake of my Divinity only as I let it through; I am always, everywhere, in the midst of plenty. I know that I live in a changeless Reality. I am not disturbed by the passage of time, the movement around me, nor the variations of experience I go through. Something within me remains immovable and says, "Be still and know that I am God."

I now consciously begin to draw upon the life that is mine. I now begin to reeducate myself definitely, by whatever steps I may, to a belief that there is given unto me a fullness of life that is Divine in its origin, eternal in its presence, and always fully available. The life of the Father is my life. The infinite richness of the Father is mine to enjoy. The vital good health, the wisdom, the peace of the Father are mine. All things that proceed from Him may be mine. I now claim them. The act of taking is my right and privilege. I exercise it now intelligently and in full faith.

Life Sings Through Me in Radiant Ecstasy

Now and always I recognize that I live, move, and have my being in God. I am part of Universal Mind. I am one with Universal Substance. All the qualities and all the wealth of good and desirable things that exist in Universal Mind are mine now. I perceive, accept, and experience them. I know that all the beauty of form around me is the Garment of God. I know that the Presence that manifests in my heart and mind is God expressing within that garment of form. As I feel this Presence more and more I hear the Song of Joy deep within me. Always when I am still I hear the Song of Life pouring through my consciousness. I have only to listen, for it is always there.

With this knowledge comes the assurance that that loving Presence is always here—"closer to me than breathing, nearer than hands and feet." I have nothing to fear. I feel this loving embrace around me, and I know that it is not only a Song of Joy, but a Song of Love and Protection. I tune out all dull, negative ideas and tune in with the sunshine of life, with brightness and laughter, with the joyous Presence that is Life itself. I now lay aside all anxiety, all striving, and let the Law bring my good to me. I joyfully anticipate greater abundance, more success, more joy. Peace fills my heart and Life sings through me in radiant ecstasy.

I Will Fear No Evil

Today my heart is without fear, for I have implicit confidence in the good, the enduring, and the true. Fear is the only thing of which to be afraid. It is not the host encamped against us, nor the confusion around us, that we need to fear; it is the lack of confidence in the good that alone should concern us. Through inner spiritual vision, we know that evil is transitory, but good is permanent. We know that right finally dissolves everything opposed to it. The power of Spirit is supreme over every antagonist. Therefore, we should cherish no fear. When we neither fear nor hate, we come to understand the unity of life.

I realize that fear is not Godlike, since it contradicts the Divine Presence, repudiates limitless Love, and denies infinite Good. Therefore, I know that fear is a lie, a fraud. It is neither person, place, nor thing; it is merely an imposter that I have believed in. I have entertained it so long that it seems as if it really were something, and it attempts to make me believe that two and two are five, that the earth is flat, and that God is limited. Today I repudiate all fear. I renounce the belief in evil. I enter into conscious union with the Spirit. I accept the good as supreme, positive, and absolute. With joy I enter into the activities of the day, without regret I remember the events of yesterday, and with confidence I look forward to tomorrow, for today my heart is without fear.

The Law of God Is Written in My Heart

I know that the Perfect Life of the Spirit is my life, and I now permit It to radiate through my world of thought and action—to express in my physical form. As I relax my body, consciously and definitely—which I am able to do by mentally relaxing and dropping all strain—I feel flowing through me a vital energy, a dynamic force, a great surge of living Power. I feel immersed in and saturated by a vital Essence of Perfection, which brings me into tune with life.

Because my whole being is this perfect God-Life, I have nothing to fear. Every person I meet recognizes the love and peace and wisdom and courage within me. Each person I meet feels our common bond, knows that we are a part of the perfect Whole, harmonious centers in the great Unity of Life, and so has faith in me. No one could wish to harm or hurt me in any way. I, too, can know only love and understanding for my fellow beings. I know—because I am God-Life, God in expression—that every circumstance I find myself in is right for me. Through my consciousness of Love, which is the very Essence of God-Life, I transform any seeming imperfection into the perfect idea of my True Self. God knows me only as a Perfect Idea and that Perfection I now manifest. God's Law is written in my heart and I delight to do God's will.

I Have Dominion

I know that there is a God-Power at the center of every person's being, a Power that knows neither lack nor limitation, fear nor sickness, disquietude, nor imperfection. But out of my personal experience come the negative suggestions that arise from the race consciousness. If I permit them to, they act as a mesmeric or hypnotic power over my imagination. They bring up arguments from every person's experience, declaring that impoverishment and pain must necessarily accompany everyone through life.

But I know that there is a Presence, a Power, and a Law within me, irresistibly drawing everything that makes life worthwhile into my experience. I know that friendship, love, riches, health, harmony, and happiness are mine. I know that nothing but good can go out from me; therefore, the good that I receive is but the completion of a circle—the fulfillment of my desire for all. So, I refuse to judge according to appearances, either mental or physical, no matter what the thought says or what the appearance seems to be. There is always a higher Power. Upon this Power I rely with absolute confidence that it will never fail me. I have dominion over all apparent evil, which is merely a belief I no longer indulge in. I repudiate all its claims, cast out every fear accompanying the belief in it, and continuously exercise the dominion that rightfully belongs to me.

An Inspiration Within Me Guides Me Aright

The disciple John tells us that "God is a Spirit: and they that worship God must worship God in spirit and in truth." Wonderful indeed is this conception of the union of all life, which Jesus proclaimed in the ecstasy of his illumination, "I and the Father are one." All cause and all effect proceed from the invisible Spirit. Humankind is one with this Spirit and cannot be separated from It. Our word has power because our word is the action of God through our thought.

I now clarify my vision, purify my thought, so that it becomes a mirror reflecting inspiration direct from the secret place of the Most High, at the center of my own being. I do this by quiet contemplation, not through strenuous effort, but by learning to fast from all negation and to feast upon the affirmations of spiritual realization. I know that I need never break before the onslaught of any confusion that exists around me. Today I walk in the light of God's Love. Today I am guided and my guidance is multiplied. I know exactly what to do and exactly how to do it. There is an inspiration within me that governs every act, every thought, in certainty, with conviction and in peace. I know that the key that unlocks the treasure-house, the key to the Kingdom of God, is in my spiritual hand. This is the Kingdom of God's creation and is directly experienced by me today.

JULY
FREEDOM

Even the Spirit does not seek to control us, It lets us alone to discover ourselves. —ERNEST HOLMES

We have thought that outside things controlled us, when all the time we have had that within that could have changed everything and given us freedom from bondage. —ERNEST HOLMES

> To be, or not to be; that is the question;
> Whether 'tis nobler in the mind to suffer
> The slings and arrows of outrageous fortune,
> Or, to take arms against a sea of troubles,
> And by opposing end them. —SHAKESPEARE

Every new-born being indeed comes fresh and blithe into the new existence, and enjoys it as a free gift: but there is, and can be, nothing freely given. Its fresh existence is paid for by the old age and death of a worn-out existence which has perished, but which contained the indestructible seed out of which this new existence has arisen: they are one being.
—SCHOPENHAUER

Turn your face to the sun and the shadows fall behind you. —MAORI PROVERB

I Am Free with the Freedom of God

Stand fast therefore in the liberty wherewith Christ
hath made us free. —GALATIANS 5:1

We all wish to be free, but at the same time we should realize that liberty is not license. To say that we are free with the freedom of God does not mean that we are free to do that which contadicts the Divine nature. We are free only in that freedom that God is—the freedom to be alive, to enjoy living, to enter into the activities of everyday living with enthusiasm and interest. We are free to love and to be loved. We are free to give full and complete expression to every capacity we possess, provided this freedom harms no one and hurts no thing. This is freedom enough because if we were free to do that which is destructive we should ultimately destroy ourselves. And, in so doing, we would not only deny but would defame the nature of Divinity Itself. Therefore, we always pray, "Thy will be done," but within this Will we know there is scope enough for self-expression—plenty of room to move around and express life to its fullest.

I am free with the freedom of God. Today I manifest this freedom in joy. I think of it with deep gratitude to the Giver of all life and with a deep inward sense of my union with the Whole. In my own will and imagination I see myself free, complete, and perfect. I feel back to the center of my being, which is God, and affirm that His freedom is my freedom. And I include my own physical body in this freedom as well as every activity in which I am engaged. I expand my consciousness and invite new experiences, knowing that they shall be created for me by the same Power that makes everything. I enter into this freedom with complete abandonment, with the feeling that all things are working out well, and with the deep and sincere desire to live so that my freedom shall be imparted to others, that we all may feel that we are in partnership with the Infinite.

I Am Strong with the Power of God

Let every soul be subject unto the higher powers. For there is no power
but of God: the powers that be are ordained of God. —ROMANS 13:1

The Bible tells us that the powers that be are ordained of God. And since
God exists everywhere, the Power of God is wherever we recognize it—not
only all the Presence, but all the Power. We have no power of ourselves, as
if we were separate entities; therefore, we say with the Psalmist that our
strength cometh from the Lord who made heaven and earth. What we really
do is use a Power greater than ourselves, which Power is our strength, but
we are not that Power. Of ourselves we can do nothing; nor of ourselves do
we even hold our bodies in place. Rather, we rely on the power of gravita-
tional force that operates upon us. In just such a manner we are operated
upon by spiritual powers that become our strength when we use them. It is
in this sense that we are strong with the Power of God, the only Power
there is.

My strength cometh from the Lord who made heaven and earth. Recognizing this strength—which is perfect, complete, and everpresent with
me—I have implicit trust and confidence not only in its availability right
where I am, but in its action in and through everything I am doing. There is
a Power behind my every thought and word. There is a Power upholding
and sustaining me in everything I do. There is a Power going before me and
preparing my way. I rest in this Power in calm and serene confidence, with
perfect trust and faith. I know that this Power is good, it is constructive, it is
activated by love, it is directed by Divine Intelligence, and I use it even in
the simplest things in my life. Today, then, I accept that all the Power there
is belongs to me. In joy and in gladness I recognize and use this Power.
Therefore, today I am sustained and upheld by It, in peace, in joy, and in
wholenesss.

I Am Guided by the Wisdom of God

*Thus saith the Lord, Let not the wise man glory in his wisdom. . . .
But let him that glorieth, glory in this, that he understandeth
and knoweth me.* —JEREMIAH 9:23–24

Some universal and infinite Intelligence governs everything, holds everything in place, and directs the course of everything. The Intelligence that governs the planets in their course is the same Wisdom that is in the anthill or the beehive; this same Wisdom is in the bird that flies north in summer and south in winter and knows where to find its food. But that which is blind or instinctive knowing in the animal, should become conscious knowing and will in the human. In the animal kingdom it works as a blind force; in the human kingdom it works through blind force only in the automatic reactions of nature such as the involuntary functions of the human body. But the more personal use of it—whether or not we shall call upon the One Mind and Spirit to direct and govern our affairs—this depends upon our personal choice. This is what freedom and individuality mean.

Today I am guided by the Wisdom of God in everything I do, say, and think. Since there is nothing large or small in the Infinite and Divine Mind, I know that the same Wisdom that governs everything in the universe is brought to bear upon the little things in my personal life. I permit this Wisdom to direct me. I affirm the presence of this Wisdom and acknowledge Its action in everything in my life. Therefore, I know what to do under every circumstance. I know how to plan my life and direct my path because I recognize the Infinite Wisdom is doing this for me by doing it through me. There is no uncertainty or confusion in my life. The Divine Spirit always knows what to do, therefore I am never without guidance. There is one Wisdom, one Intelligence, one Mind. I live and move and have my being in this One. My every act, thought, and purpose is guided by this Wisdom.

I Am Held in the Goodness of God

And God, even our Father, which hath loved us . . . comfort your hearts,
and stablish you in every good word and work. —II THESSALONIANS 2:16–17

If we assume an all-powerful or infinite Presence and Power back of, within, and through everything—as we must—then we should realize that this Power or Presence, which is God, could not possibly operate against Itself without destroying Itself. We know of no energy in nature that can destroy itself. This means that the Power back of everything actually is good. We need not worry about this or wonder about it or ask questions about it. It is self-evident that goodness alone can endure forever. Good is a synonym for God. Good and God mean the same thing. Therefore, the final truth and absolute reality about all things is that God is good. And since God is the Divine Presence right where we are, good is right where we are and ever available to us. But we must recognize and claim this good if we are to use it.

Today I know that my good is at hand. I see this good in persons and places and things. Nothing but goodness can go from me, and nothing but goodness can return to me. There is nothing unlike goodness in my experience. There is nothing but kindness, nothing but generosity. My whole inner being responds to this goodness, recognizes it everywhere. Feeling it everywhere, seeing it everywhere, I am enveloped in it. And even as I draw this goodness to me and become saturated with it, it flows out in every direction, blessing everything it touches, helping everyone, bringing wholeness and happiness to everyone. "His goodness endureth forever," and I endure forever. In joy, then, I awake to every new day; in joy I rest in the eternal goodness, and evermore there is a song in my heart as it overflows with the acknowledgment of good.

I Share the Gifts of God

I will give unto him that is athirst of the fountain
of the water of life freely. —REVELATION 21:6

What a wonderful thought this is, that the very fountain of Life flows open
and free, that the gifts of heaven and earth are so bountifully bestowed upon
all who receive them. But there is another thought for us to consider. If
God, or Life, has already made the gift, then even God, the Supreme and
Perfect One, must wait for our acceptance of this gift. Perhaps we err in that
we do not expect to share the gifts of God. Perhaps we are bound by the
thought that we are not yet good enough to accept the gifts of the Kingdom
of Good or that we have not developed enough spiritually to appreciate
them. Too often we feel that these gifts are withheld, and so we do not live
in an enthusiastic and confident expectation of sharing with the Infinite.
What a wonderful thought it is that we actually share with the Infinite in the
boundless gifts of Life!

Today I consciously share in the gifts of Life. I open my whole thought
and my whole being to the Divine influx. I empty myself of everything that
denies this good I so fervently desire. I establish my mind in expectancy, a
feeling that all the good there is must belong to everyone who will take it. I
am receiving the Divine gift right now. I am entering into the spiritual inheritance that Life has willed that every person should possess. Today I am
seeing the gift of Life coming to me from every source, and even as it comes
into my outstretched hands, uplifted to receive it, I enjoy the gift and pass it
on. Freely I give everything I have, blessing the gift as it passes through me
to others, that it may be multiplied in their experience and in God's good
way come back again to me.

I Am Comforted by the Promises of God

Blessed by the Lord . . . there hath not failed
one word of His good promise. —I KINGS 8:56

The Bible is filled with Divine Promises, revealed through the spiritual intuition of great souls. We are promised long life and happiness, riches and
abundance, health and success. The Bible contains more promises than any
other book ever written and tells us to accept that these promises are not
vague, uncertain things. More particularly it tells us that these promises are
being fulfilled right now, in the day in which we live. "Beloved, now are we
the sons of God." We need not wait to enter into the fulfillment of these
promises. They are eternally given and wait only on our acceptance. This
acceptance is a mental as well as a spiritual act; it is the mind accepting its
highest hope in complete confidence, placing its entire reliance on a Power
greater than itself.

Today I accept the Divine Promises. I accept them with the simplicity
of a child, with the joy of one who receives his good in grateful acknowledgment of "the all-sustaining beauty." I accept Divine guidance watching
over me. I accept the enveloping presence of the Life that sustains me. I accept the beauty and the peace of this Presence. I accept happiness and success. I accept health and wholeness. I accept love and friendship. I realize
that what rightfully belongs to me also rightfully belongs to everyone else.
Therefore, I promise myself and all others to live as though the Kingdom of
God were at hand for all people. I accept a good beyond my fondest imagination, beyond my greatest dream, knowing that this good that I accept will
flow through me into complete expression. He shall give to me even more
abundantly than I have asked, for the promises of God are as certain as
life, as immutable as law, as personal as the air I breathe. Today I accept
my good.

I Am Rich with the Richness of God

Every beast of the forest is mine, and the cattle on a thousand hills . . .
for the world is mine, and the fulness thereof. —PSALM 50:10, 12

How beautiful was the thought of Jesus when he told us to "consider the
lilies of the field, how they grow; they toil not, neither do they spin; And yet
I say unto you, that even Solomon in all his glory was not arrayed like one of
these." Jesus was telling us to identify ourselves with the abundance of nature, the constant outpouring of the Divine Life in goodness, in riches, in
everything that makes for happiness and wholeness and success. God cannot fail. The Divine will never fail us if we have implicit confidence in It.
But we are so caught with fear and doubt and uncertainty that it becomes
necessary for us to take time every day to reaffirm our union with the great
out-flowing givingness of Life. This is the purpose of prayer and meditation. It is natural that we should wish for the more abundant life. It is right
that we should accept it. God has already made the gift; it is up to us to receive it.

Today I receive this goodness. Today everything that I am and have is
increased by it. I identify everything I do with success. I think affirmatively
and in all my prayers I accept abundance. Whatever I need, whenever I
need it, wherever I need it, for as long as I need it, will always be at hand. I
no longer see negation or delay or stagnation in my affairs, but rather, claim
that the action of the Living Spirit makes prosperous everything I do, increases every good I possess, and through me brings gladness and joy, happiness and success to everyone I meet. Everything I think about will be
animated by the Divine Presence, sustained by the Infinite Power, and multiplied by the Divine Goodness.

I Speak the Truth of God

He that speaketh truth sheweth forth righteousness . . . the lip
of truth shall be established forever. —PROVERBS 12:17, 19

We all wish to speak the Truth, but have we realized that every time we
make a claim about ourselves that is different from the claim we would
make about God, we are falling into the error of denying the Divine Presence in our experience? God is Truth and Truth is God. We also are included in this Divine and Perfect Unity. Therefore, every claim we make
about God, the Living Spirit, should equally be made about ourselves because we live and move and have our being in this infinite Truth or Presence. To say that we are poor or sick or weak or unhappy is to deny God.
God is not poor; God is not sick; God is not weak; God is not unhappy. We
must, then, make every endeavor, in simplicity and in truth, to identify our
personal lives with that One Life that forevermore proclaims: "I am that I
Am." There is nothing separate from this one I Am.

Today I say to myself: I am one with the Truth of God. I speak this
Truth and proclaim it to be the reality of my experience in what I call "little" and in what I call "big." In the simplest and the most complex things I
recognize the one Truth—changeless, permanent, and eternally manifesting Itself. Therefore, I know the Truth about myself. I know the Truth
about everything I do. I know the Truth about everyone I meet. I know the
Truth about every situation in which I find myself. This Truth is not only
perfection, it is also power. It is not only presence, it is also action. Therefore, the Truth and the Power and the Presence and the Action of the Living Spirit flow through everything I do, say, and think. I do know the Truth,
and the Truth I know frees me and keeps me free.

I Witness Everywhere the Beauty of God

And let the beauty of the Lord our God be upon us. —PSALM 90:17

I believe it was Plato who said that God is love, truth, and beauty. It has always seemed wonderful to me that one of the world's greatest thinkers should have included beauty as a necessary part of the Divine nature. How evident this beauty is everywhere we look! How wonderful is the landscape, the sunset, or the color of the desert at dawn. How beautiful is the daffodil in its sweet simplicity. And what majestic beauty and strength in the mountain and the wave. Everything is rooted in beauty. Beauty is harmony and right proportion. It is symmetry and charm and grace and loveliness. Surely we should identify ourselves with this terrific beauty that pours its warmth and color over everything and seems to be at the very root of our being.

Recognizing beauty in everything and knowing that God is the very essence of this beauty, I include myself, my personality, my individuality, my whole being, in this beauty. I am some part of an infinite harmony, a terrific loveliness, a universal flow of warmth and color and givingness. I claim all this as my own, not because of any particular merits I personally possess, but rather, because of the necessity of its being true. I shall no longer think of myself as separate from this beauty or different from it. Therefore, today, to love, to power, to order, I shall add this other thought—Divine Beauty is everywhere. In this beauty I am beautiful. In this infinite warmth and color I live and have my being. Its beauty flows through every act; its charm and grace manifest in every movement, in every thought, imparting itself in love to everyone I meet. Today I see beauty in others—the charm, the grace, the presence of the Living Spirit.

I Give Thanks for the Blessings of God

And he . . . took the five loaves, and two fishes, and looking up to heaven,
he blessed, and brake, and gave the loaves to his disciples,
and the disciples to the multitude. —MATTHEW 14:19

Have you and I had the faith to bless that which perhaps seemed so very small—a loaf of bread and a fish—and expect it to become multiplied in our experience to such an extent that it would not only bless us but also bless everyone around us? We cannot help but believe that as Jesus broke the bread and blessed it, in his own mind he saw it multiplied and growing and flowing out to those around him. This is an example we should follow—to bless what we have, recognizing that it flows from a limitless source; we are merely using it and distributing it. There is always more. The limitless resources of the Spirit are at our command. The power of the Infinite is at our disposal. We have as much to use as we know how to take. But the taking is a thing of the thought, the will, the imagination. It is a thing of an inward feeling or interior awareness in that place where the mind has unified itself with the Living Spirit.

Today I bless everything I have. I bless everyone around me. I bless the events that transpire in my life, the conditions and situations that surround me. I bless everything that goes out and everything that comes in. I acknowledge an increase of right action in everything I do, say, or think. I bless myself and others, for we are all partakers of the same Divine Nature, all living in the One Mind, all animated by the same Presence, all sustained by the One Power. "Bless the Lord, O my soul: and all that is within me." In joy and in love my blessing rests on everything. In confidence and in peace the blessing of God rests upon me.

I Am Radiant with the Health of God

Then shall thy light break forth as the morning,
and thine health shall spring forth speedily. —ISAIAH 58:8

Whatever we identify ourselves with we tend to become. Whatever we think about gradually becomes a subconscious pattern, always tending to manifest itself in our experience. Therefore, we should endeavor to identify our physical bodies with the spiritual Reality that is the very substance and essence of the physical being. We do not deny the physical body, but rather, affirm that every organ and action and function of the body is radiant with the perfection of God. There is an inner life of complete perfection that exists at the center of everything; otherwise, nothing could be. We should identify ourselves with this perfect pattern of our being, claiming its reality in our experience and continuously knowing that we are animated by the Living Spirit.

Today I identify my body with the action of God, the radiant Life of the Divine Being. Today I identify my physical body with my spiritual body, claiming that they are one and the same. Therefore, I see that every organ, every action, and every function of my body belongs to the rhythm of Life, is a part of the radiant Presence of the Living Spirit. There is one Divine Circulation flowing through everything—flowing through me right now. There is one infinite Rhythm at the center of everything. I am a part of this perfect Whole. There is perfect circulation, perfect assimilation, and perfect elimination. There is perfection in every part of my being, and wholeness and completeness. This physical body is a temple of the Living Spirit that animates it, sustains it, rebuilds it after the image of Its own perfection and keeps it in perfect health, in perfect harmony, in perfect wholeness.

I Express the Glory of God

Now is the Son of man glorified, and God is glorified in him. If God be
glorified in him, God shall also glorify him in himself. —JOHN 13:31–32

Perhaps this is one of the most profound thoughts Jesus ever gave to the
world, for it really tells us that when humanity is glorified in God, then God
is glorified in humanity. And it means exactly this: life is a mirror to each
one of us, and as we see the glory of God in this mirror, so shall this mirror
reflect back to us that same glory. For Jesus says that if God be glorified in
him, God shall also glorify him in Himself. So shall the image and its reflection become one even as the Father and the Son are one, in glory, in honor,
and in majesty and might. No more exalted concept of Divine Union could
possibly be given than this.

Today, then, I glorify myself in God and I glorify God in me. For I am
in Him and He is in me. And as He is glorified in me, so am I glorified in
Him. I do give thanks for this intimate and complete union of my soul with
its Center and its Source. And I do recognize in myself and in others the
glory of the incarnated God. Realizing the One Life without and within,
consciously uniting with It, I proclaim Its presence in everything. Knowing
that there is no great and no small, I proclaim Its presence in the smallest as
well as the greatest. All my affairs shall reflect the glory and the power and
the majesty and the might of the Infinite Spirit. And all that I do shall proclaim His love, His life, and His light. "Now is the Son of man glorified, and
God is glorified in him." I am that Person, and God is glorified in me today.

I Judge, and Am Judged, with the Justice of God

My judgment is just; because I seek not mine own will,
but the will of the Father which hath sent me. —JOHN 5:30

Jesus, the greatest of all the illumined, said, "Judge not that ye be not judged, for with what judgment ye judge ye shall be judged," by which he meant that we cannot judge others harshly without receiving back into our own consciousness and experience the very things we claim for others. While Jesus was the most compassionate of all people, he was also the most just, for he knew that our lives are governed by an exact and immutable law of cause and effect. He knew, and we all must learn, that it is impossible to wish something for someone else without at the same time willing it for ourselves. If we all were to follow this rule we should become more kind, if only for the purpose of self-preservation and personal happiness, for no one wishes to injure himself. Always, then, we are placed in this position—we dare not wish anything for anyone that we would be unwilling to accept for ourselves. If everyone were to live by this rule there would be no injustice in the world.

Infinite Spirit within me, which is God, cause me to think and act kindly; constrain my mind to gentleness and peace; guide my thoughts into loving kindness and eternal forgivingness; and cause me in all my ways to follow the path of truth and justice. I judge no person and am judged by none. It is my sincere desire that everything I do or say or think will come into harmony with universal truth and peace, with love and joy. Consciously I let go of everything that is unkind and seek to so enter into communion with the Eternal Spirit that I shall reflect to my environment and manifest in all that I do the spirit of kindness, of justice, and of compassion.

I Enjoy the Companionship of God

And I will pray the Father, and he shall give you another Comforter,
that he may abide with you for ever. —JOHN 14:16

Communion with the Spirit is one of the greatest privileges of life. By communion with God we do not mean telling the Infinite what to do or how to do it, for that is talking at God rather than communing with God. By communion we mean silently entering into Divine harmony and beauty until we feel that harmony and beauty in our own souls, in our own minds. For instance, if you find yourself distraught and mentally upset, and you follow the simple practice of communing with peace, you will find that peace enters into you. You do this by dropping all confusion from your mind and thinking about peace, by dwelling on its meaning and feeling that you are breathing it into yourself, until it floods your whole being with harmony. This is real communion—not telling peace what it ought to do or be, but entering into its spirit, silently, quietly, and alone. And so it is with love or joy or any other attribute of the Divine—we must commune by listening and feeling this Presence until the Presence is real to us. This is the very essence of communion.

God is my companion. It is impossible for me to be lonely or alone for wherever I go the One Presence will accompany me. I have an Infinite Companion who goes with me wherever I go. I have partnership with the Infinite that is steady and strong and certain. This same Presence I feel in everyone else—the One Companion of all. I am guided by this Presence; I am guarded by It; I am kept in the shadow of Its strength. I am fed by the bounty of Its love. I am guided by Its wisdom. This Presence is closer to me than my breath, nearer to me than my hands and feet. Therefore, I have no sense of aloneness, no feeling of isolation, because all the Presence there is is my companion. In this companionship there is love and beauty; there is peace and joy; there is happiness and success, today and forevermore.

I Am Supplied from the Substance of God

Every good gift . . . cometh down from the Father. —JAMES 1:11

We all have need of many things. We cannot believe that the Divine Spirit wishes to withhold any good from us. It is the nature of God to give, and it is our nature to receive. Back of every idea of supply, every need in our human lives, there is something that forever gives more of itself and takes the form of our experiences when we permit it to. Whether it be a house to live in, money that we have need of, or employment that furnishes the gratification of adequate self-expression—always there is the Giver flowing into these things. But the Divine has already given Its entire being to us. God has not failed humanity. But humanity has failed to accept the gift. It has failed to enter into the spirit and the nature of the Giver. It has even refused to believe that there is such a gift or such a Giver. How, then, can even God give us what we refuse to accept? This is why Jesus told us we must believe that we have really received the gift before we see its evidence. This is an active faith, but it should be a faith built on the sure knowledge, the certain foundation, the positive conviction, that there is something that responds to us, gladly, readily, willingly, joyously, and without limit.

Today I am living in the quiet and joyous expectation of good. God is not only my life, He is substance taking form in everything I do. God is not only the only Actor, He is acting through me now. God is not only the Giver, He is also the gift. This gift I receive in joy, with gratitude, and with a complete sense of security. I expect everything I do to prosper. I expect new and wonderful experiences to come to me. I am living in complete confidence that the Kingdom of Heaven is here and now and that I am prospered in everything I do.

I Am Endowed with the Perfection of God

Be ye therefore perfect, even as your Father
which is in heaven is perfect. —MATTHEW 5:48

When Jesus said, "Be ye therefore perfect, even as your Father which is in heaven is perfect," he was telling us that there is a Perfection at the center of all things, which, recognized, will spring into being. We must learn to identify ourselves with this Perfection, to so accept it that it is real to us and to so live that it may be expressed through us. Every organ, action, and function of our physical body is rooted in spiritual Perfection, from which it draws life. If this were not true we could not be here. No matter how imperfect, or painful or discordant, the appearance may be, there is still an underlying Perfection, an inner Wholeness, a complete and perfect Life, which is God.

Therefore, I say to my physical body: Be ye perfect, because you already are perfect in the Divine sight. There is One Life, that Life is God, that Life is your life now. This Life circulates through you. It animates your whole being. You are one with its peace and wholeness. There is no inaction in this Divine Life. There is no stoppage nor hindrance nor obstruction to it. And whatever may seem to be to the contrary is false, for I am identifying my physical body with the body of pure Spirit. I am opening my mind as a channel for the realization of the Divine Presence. I affirm it and accept it. There is nothing in me that can deny or reject it. Because God is perfect, I am perfect. Quietly I affirm and reaffirm these simple statements until they sink into my consciousness and become a habit pattern of thought that is no longer rejected. With complete conviction I accept the wholeness of the Spirit, and as I do so I identify myself and everything that I am with the harmony and the perfection and the wholeness of the Life of God.

I See with the Eyes of God

One thing I know, that, whereas I was blind, now I see. —JOHN 9:25

The ancients said that there is an "all-seeing eye" and that if we could cause our physical eyes to see with its vision we should be looking at things as they really are. But is it not true that too often we see with a blurred vision because we are so confused mentally? The all-seeing eye of God, by its very nature, being one and only, must forever see things as they really are. This is why Jesus said to judge not according to appearances but to judge righteously. We cannot expect to draw a pattern of this right seeing from the objective world of confusion or our inner thoughts of doubt and fear. Therefore, we are told to see and act according to "the pattern shewed to thee in the mount," that is, we are to look and think independently of the confusion around us. We are to view everything as we feel the Divine, Infinite, and Perfect Being must know and understand Its own creation to be. This is seeing with the eyes of God.

Today I am seeing with the eyes of the Divine. I am looking at things in a perfect and direct way. I am seeing through confusion to peace, through doubt to certainty, through fear to faith. Quietly, then, I review myself, those around me, and everything that occupies my attention, bringing to them all a broader vision, a deeper insight, a more complete perspective of the Infinite Harmony that I know is back of, in, and through everything that God has made. I am keeping my eye to this one truth—what God has done is good, therefore my experiences are good. What God has created is wonderful, therefore I am surrounded with good. In calm judgment, then, I sit quietly within myself and in my imagination look around and see everything according to the Divine Pattern. As I do this everything I look upon shall become transformed and reborn.

I Am Warmed by the Love of God

Behold what manner of love the Father hath bestowed upon us,
that we should be called the sons of God. —I JOHN 3:1

It has been truly said that love is the lodestone of life, the treasure of earth, and the highest gift of heaven. We all wish to feel that we are kept in the arms of love, protected by its shelter, and warmed by its feeling. But someone might ask, "How do we really know that 'the universe rests on the shoulders of love'?" The answer is simpler than it might appear. For instance, no one is ever harmed by love. The more love there is in our life, the better off we are. While the opposite to love, which is hate and dislike, can actually consume us mentally and destroy our health physically. If, then, love builds up while its opposite destroys, we may be certain that there is a universal Reality to it, that we actually are immersed in an Infinite Love as well as a Divine Wisdom. And we must learn to feel the presence of this Love and rely on it.

Therefore, let us say daily: I am one with the Love of God. I am one in the Love of God with all people. My love goes out to everyone and I know that it is returned from everyone. Overlooking everything that might seem to deny this Divine beneficence, I trust that Infinite Love will guide and protect me in everything. And I counsel my own soul to show forth this love in such a manner that it shall embrace and warm the heart of humanity, bringing confidence and trust and faith and hope to everyone it touches. Daily I affirm that love governs all of humanity into pathways of peace and joy. Daily I affirm that love goes before and makes the way plain and happy. And daily I affirm that my own love is renewed and rekindled by that great and vast Love in which I am immersed, that Love that is God.

I Am Governed by the Law of God

For I delight in the law of God. —ROMANS 7:22

This scriptural passage tells us first of all that we should have delight in living. All creation is a manifestation of the delight of God—God seeing Itself in form, God experiencing Itself in Its own actions, and God knowing Itself in us as us. For the highest God and the innermost God is one God, not two. But the passage also suggests that in addition to experiencing delight, the enjoyment of being alive and awake and aware, we should also recognize that we are subject to an exact law that must govern everything—the Law of the Lord that is perfect. We are, then, to combine our idea of delight with the concept of law, for Love and Law are the two great realities of life—Love as the outpouring of the Spirit, Law as Divine Government.

Let us, then, find delight in the Law of the Lord, which is perfect, as we say daily to ourselves: I am one with the Infinite Spirit of Love, one with the outpouring of the Divine Life. I am governed by the perfect Law of the inward man, made in the image and likeness of that which is pure, whole, and perfect. My whole life finds its impulsion in Love and all my actions are governed by the Law of Good. As I meditate upon this perfect Law of God, I realize that it is operating in my affairs, in my body, in my mind, and in my spirit. I know that the Law of Good is absolute; it is complete; it is operating in and through me now, bringing about everything that is happy. And since this Law must be perfect as well as exact, and since it must know how to bring everything about that is necessary to my good, I place my whole trust in it. And so I say today, and every day: The perfect Law of Good is governing everything I think or do and all my relationships with others. I delight in this Law and I delight in the Divinity within myself and all people.

I Honor the Presence of God

If I honour myself, my honour is nothing:
it is my Father that honoureth me. —JOHN 8:54

If I honor myself alone, not realizing that I am one with the Divine Presence, then I shall quickly exhaust the small portion of good that I, as a human being, can at any one moment contain. But if I honor the Presence of God in me, of God around and through me, of God in and through everything, then I am indeed honoring the Presence of God, for One Spirit is over all, in all and through all, and One Presence is all. There can be no separation from this Presence, no apartness, no division. It is one, complete and total, equally distributed and everywhere available. To feel this Presence in things, in people and in human events, and to sense that it is all-inclusive, is to honor God and to provide in one's own self a place where the Divine can go forth anew into creation.

Today I am honoring the Presence of God. I feel God's beauty in the rose-tinted dawn and in the glow of the evening sunset. In the flower I find the loveliness of God's beauty. In the mountains I see God's strength. In the quiet of eveningtime I feel God's Presence. And throughout the night I know that this Presence blankets me; therefore, I sleep in peace and wake in joy and live in a consciousness of good. Seeing God in others, I enter into companionship with the Divine in all people. In the outstretched hand, in the smile of recognition, and in the warm embrace of friends, I feel the One Presence, the One Power, and the One Life. And so I give thanks—with a song in my heart and with a joy unspeakable I give thanks to this Presence. May I evermore embrace and be embraced by the love, the beauty, and the goodness of God.

I Relax in the Peace of God

And the peace of God, which passeth all understanding, shall keep
your hearts and minds through Christ Jesus. —PHILIPPIANS 4:7

We often wonder if peace really exists anywhere. In a world distraught with
so much confusion and chaos we deeply need an inner, abiding sense of
calm and tranquility. Peace of mind really is what the world is searching after because without it we have only a sense of insecurity and loneliness.
Without peace, deep and abiding, there can be no happiness or contentment, no sense of security, no confidence. And yet Jesus said, "My peace I
give unto you," and the Apostle said, "The peace of God, which passeth all
understanding, shall keep your hearts and minds through Christ Jesus."
This means that in such degree as we attain peace, Christ, or the Anointed
of Heaven, the indwelling Presence, makes Itself known to us. For God is
not met through confusion, but only when the mind is tranquil, and, like an
unruffled body of water, reflects the Divine images of peace and perfection.

Today I enter into the Peace of God. My mind is stilled from all confusion, and I feel a deep and abiding inward poise. Christ, the Son of the living God, the One Son begotten of the only God, is real to me. I keep my
mind stayed on this Divine inner Presence, and, letting every thought of
discord slip away, I meet the Reality of myself, the eternal and changeless
Truth about me, which is that I am an expression of God, I am one with
God forevermore, there is no separation, there is no apartness. Here and
now, within me, there is a voice that says: Peace. Be still and know that I am
God; God in me, around me, and through me, the Divine forever incar-
nated and forever kept in the bosom of the Father. I glorify the name of
God; I exalt God's presence. "I am that which thou art; thou art that which
I am." And that which I am, and that which Thou art, is one and the same.

I Partake of the Nature of God

The Spirit of God hath made me, and the breath
of the Almighty hath given me life. —JOB 33:4

No one can doubt that God is perfect. But Jesus said, "Be ye therefore perfect, even as your Father which is in heaven is perfect." And he had already located heaven within. He also said, "Thy kingdom come. Thy will be done, in earth as it is in heaven," by which he meant that when we do the will of God, earth will be like heaven, that is, the without will be like the within, for the two really are one. Therefore, our claim, our affirmation, our prayer and our acceptance, our communion with the Infinite, should always be based on the realization that God is in and through His creation as well as around and about it. When we make this claim we are not speaking from the standpoint of the little, isolated ego that we appear to be, but rather we are acknowledging, accepting, and agreeing with a perfection that already exists. You and I had nothing to do with the creation of this perfection—we did not think it up or plan it out or cause it to be. For this we should be profoundly grateful. For the human mind is finite and limited. Our claim, rather, is one of identifying ourselves with the Divine, recognizing Its Presence, and accepting Its action in our lives.

Realizing that God is all there is, that God is perfect, and that God is right where I am, I gratefully acknowledge and accept my own perfection. Seeing and knowing myself as God must see and know me, I boldly claim the perfection of God to be my own perfection. There is nothing separate from the Divine. I am one with It. I am one in It. I am one of It. It flows through me and is my life. I am rooted in Its completion, Its wholeness. God is my life and my life is God—there is nothing else. Therefore, anything that claims to be something else I repudiate, I deny. I separate myself from everything that contradicts the nature of my being and simply and sincerely, and with complete relaxation, accept that which God has given me—myself.

I Am Happy in the Harmony of God

Now there are diversities of gifts, but the same Spirit . . .
and there are diversities of operations, but it is the same God
which worketh in all. —I CORINTHIANS 12:4, 6

We do not all have the same gifts because no two anythings are ever alike.
Nature never reproduces anything identically. And there are diversities of
operations. We are all engaged in different types and sorts of activities that
express the unique individualization that each one of us is. But it is the same
God working in all of us. This is one of the most terrific concepts we could
entertain, that out of all the variations of life, the infinite variety of color and
form and people—the rosebud, the elephant, the snow-capped mountain,
the tiny mouse in the field—one Power is working, one Life is being expressed, one Energy is animating, one Presence flowing through, and one
Law controlling. The one Mind is working in and through us now, not as
big or little, or hard or easy, but merely as spontaneous self-expression.
Back of our smallest act is the strength of the universe. Behind all our
thoughts is the Infinite Thinker. Diffused through every human activity is
the Divine Presence.

Today I am realizing that all my thoughts are formulated in the Divine
Mind; all of my actions are sustained by the Infinite Energy; all the Power
there is and all the Presence there is is right where I am. Therefore, I open
the channels of my thought to the influx of this Divine Presence that is now
doing something unique and different through me. I feel the impact of this
Presence in my own mind. I sense Its feeling and imagination in my own
thinking. I see It operating through all my actions. And since there is no big
or little, everything becomes important because everything is the self-
expression of That within me that doeth all things well. Therefore, I surrender myself completely to that one Power, that one All-knowing Mind, that
one Presence, which is beauty and love and peace and joy.

I Am Secure in the Everlasting Arms of God

The eternal God is thy refuge, and underneath
are the everlasting arms. —DEUTERONOMY 33:27

The everlasting arms suggest Divine protection, complete certainty, and the assurance that all is well with the soul. And how could it be otherwise, since the spirit of humankind is God. Therefore, when we say that we are secure in the everlasting arms of God, we are realizing that our spirit, being one with God and never separated from its Source, must be, and is, as secure as God. It is this inward sense of our union with the Whole that binds us back to the eternal Presence and gives us the joy of knowing that there is nothing to be afraid of, either out of the past, from the present, or in the future.

I am secure in the everlasting arms of God. I feel the Divine Presence in, around, and through me and all people. A great sense of calm and peace flows through my whole being, in confidence and in light. Realizing that there is no separation between the Spirit within me and the Spirit that God is and knowing that there is but one Spirit, which is God-in-me and God-in-everything, I feel confidence and safety and security in that Presence that evermore wraps itself around me and flows through me. I am indeed secure today in the everlasting arms of good, of peace, of joy, and of life. I am secure in the consciousness that today, and every day, I shall be guided and guarded and protected. And I am secure in the consciousness that all people are protected by the same Divine Presence, governed by the same Law of Good, and guided by the same Infinite Love. I am one with all, both visible and invisible; one with the seen and the Unseen; one with God and one with humankind. I bless this unity.

I Am Cleansed by the Purity of God

Thou art of purer eyes than to behold evil,
and canst not look on iniquity. —HABAKKUK 1:13

When the prophet said that God is too pure to behold evil and cannot look on iniquity, he was proclaiming one of the most profound concepts the human mind has ever entertained. For he was really saying that God, who is the originator of all things and the first principle of all life, can never experience evil, nor see it nor know it. "Thou art of purer eyes than to behold evil, and canst not look on iniquity." What could be plainer or more evident than what he was saying that God neither creates nor experiences evil, that we are cleansed by the purity of that which has never entered into impurity—we are cleansed by the purity of God. Suppose we liken this purity of God to a clear stream of water that knows no impurity and in which we bathe. The act of our entering the stream purifies us without contaminating the stream itself. And so it is in our relationship with the Divine, who is free from all evil, and the Law of Good that knows no limitation.

Today I enter into the stream of pure Life, knowing that as I bathe in the spiritual water of perfection, my whole being is cleansed, purified, and made whole. Today I turn from all evil, from every sense of limitation, of fear or uncertainty, and bathe in the waters of freedom, purifying myself from the belief or experience of want or need. Today, as I bathe in the waters of pure Spirit, I loose every negation of the past. I am cleansed of all fear of the future. I am purified from all uncertainty in the present. I enter a new, a complete, and a perfect Life, here and now. Today is God's day. I will rejoice in it. I will sing a song unto that which is beyond all evil.

I Live in the Life of God

It is the spirit that quickeneth. —JOHN 6:63

All life is One Life. Just as every physical substance known derives from one universal energy, so there is but one Life Principle, which is God, in which we all live and from which infinite Source our individual lives are drawn. If this one Life is present everywhere, It is also within us. To say that the Life of God is the only life there is, means that my life is not only in God and of God and from God—it is God, in and through me. If this were not true I would have a life separate from God, which is unthinkable and impossible. But if it is true that the Life of God is my life now, how wrongly I must have been thinking about this life. I have judged it falsely and condemned it unnecessarily and in every way, shape, and manner; in my ignorance, I have denied the very thing I should be affirming.

There is one Life, that Life is God, that Life is my life now. In God I live and move and have my being, and God lives in me and moves through me. I deny, then, that there is any life separate from Good, and I affirm that every organ, action, and function of my physical body is animated by the Divine Life that created and sustains it. It is this Life that is circulating through me now, in happiness, in harmony, and with perfect rhythm. I am one with the Whole; therefore, I say to my mind: You are to live and think and feel this truth until it is spontaneous and natural. And when you say, "God is my life," you are to know that the entire Life of the Divine and Perfect Presence is now flowing through you. I affirm this today—the Life of God is the only life there is, that Life is my life now, complete and perfect.

I Experience the Wholeness of God

For we know in part, and we prophesy in part, But when that
which is perfect is come, then that which is in part
shall be done away. —I CORINTHIANS 13:9–10

How true it is that we do see as through a glass, darkly, or only in part. But
to all of us there come fleeting moments when our inward vision is opened
and we seem to look out upon a newer and broader horizon. The Apostle
tells us that "when that which is perfect shall come, then that which is in
part shall be done away." What he really is saying is that we are all at a certain place in our evolution, but that there is a complete certainty before us.
We shall continuously expand and experience more and more of that Life
that already is perfect. But there is no reason why this awakening should not
come now. For we are not really waiting on God—God is waiting on us.
"Behold, I stand at the door and knock." All nature waits our recognition
and even the Divine Spirit must await our cooperation with It.

Today my eyes are open more widely and I look out upon a broader
horizon. Across all the experiences I may have had that were limited or unpleasant, I now see the rosy hue of a new dawn. Letting go of that which is
little, I now enter into a larger concept of life. Dropping all fear, I entertain
faith. Realizing that every form of uncertainty is seeing only in part, I open
my spiritual eyes to that which is wholeness. And even as I do this, the limitation, the fear, and the doubt slip away from my experience, taking their
departure in quietness and in peace as I turn to that which is greater and
better and fuller of eternal life, of happiness and of peace. Today my eyes are
open to the breadth and the height and the depth of Life that is God, Life
that is good, and Law that is perfect.

I Imbibe New Ideas from the Creativity of God

And greater works than these shall ye do also. —JOHN 14:12

Emerson tells us that the Ancient of Days is in the latest invention. In other words, since God is all there is, the only Presence, the only Power, and the only Mind or Intelligence, when we conceive a new idea we are thinking directly from the creativity of God. It is not our isolated, limited human personality that projects this new idea. We are merely the instrument through which this projection takes place. But we are in partnership with the Projector. God really is in the latest invention, in the newest song, in the latest novel, in the last picture that was painted, and in that feeling we have of new and greater and better things to come. For God is all there is—there is nothing else besides. God is both the inventor of the game and those who play in it, the author and actor, the singer and the song.

Today I imbibe new ideas from the creativity of God. My whole consciousness is alive and awake and aware. It is impregnated with Divine ideas and shall bear fruit after the image of the impression conceived within it and the Divine imprint made upon it. Today, then, I expect new ways of doing things; I expect to meet new people, form new friendships; I expect everything in my experience to enlarge and deepen and broaden. I expect more good than I have ever experienced before, and today I expect to give out more, to increase my love for others. Today I expect from myself a more gentle approach to life, a more kindly feeling, a more beneficent impulse. New thoughts, new ideas, new people, new situations, new ways of doing things, and a new influx of the Divine will make this day perfect, glad, and expressive of limitless bounty from the storehouse of the Infinite Good.

I Am Vitalized by the Strength of God

I shall be glorious in the eyes of the Lord,
and my God shall be my strength. —ISAIAH 49:5

If God is all the life that there is, then this life contains the only energy there is. If we are really hooked up with the eternal, everlasting, and perfect Energy, then we should never become weary at all. And when we have an enthusiastic and glad outlook on life we seldom do become weary. Therefore, we must convince ourselves that we are vitalized by the strength of God and we must do something to ourselves that makes it certain that this infinite Energy will increasingly flow through us. It is up to us to make the decision, to follow the course of affirmative thinking, prayer, and meditation that will continually keep this stream of Divine Energy flowing through our minds, our bodies, and our affairs, animating everything we do with the vitality that knows no weariness.

Today I am energized by the vitality of the living Spirit. All the Power there is, all the Energy and Vitality there is, is mine, and all the enthusiasm for life, the glad expectation of the more yet to be, and all the gratitude for what has been and now is is also mine. Every weight or burden of thought or feeling falls from me, and I am lifted up into the atmosphere of that Energy, that Vitality that knows only the joy of its own being and the strength of its own being. I am one with all this—vitalized, energized, and magnetized by the living Spirit. This Energy is never depleted; it is never lessened. All of it is present right where I am; all the enthusiasm for life is right where I am; and all the joy in living is right where I am. Everything within me, then, today and every day, responds to the thought that "I shall be glorious in the eyes of the Lord, and my God shall be my strength."

I Am Enriched by the Abundance of God

Prove me now herewith, saith the Lord of hosts, if I will not open you the windows of heaven, and pour you out a blessing, that there shall not be room enough to receive it. —MALACHI 3:10

What a promise this is! As though the Divine were issuing a challenge to each of us and saying, "Perhaps things are better than they appear to be. Have you ever really tried having confidence in the Spirit? Have you ever experimented with your own mind to see if you could come to a place where you really believe there is good enough to go around?" It is as though the prophet were telling us that even the Divine Bounty itself, lavish and extravagant as it must be, awaits our acceptance. Possibly we have been holding our bowl of acceptance and our chalice of life upside down so that even the fruit and the wine of the Spirit cannot be poured into it. Yet the windows of heaven must forever be open.

Today I open the windows of my own soul so that the windows of heaven may pour into my experience a blessing greater than I am able to receive. Nor would I withhold this blessing from others, for as surely as it comes to me, just as surely will it go forth multiplied and increased to heal and help, to bless and enrich and gladden others. Today my faith, my hope, my expectancy looks up and out and beholds a limitless abundance present everywhere, flowing through all things, a limitless love giving of itself to everything, an infinite peace enveloping all. And behind it all, and around it and through it, a joy forever singing a song of happiness and fulfillment. This is my day; this is my heaven; this is my life; this is my God. In Him will I put my trust.

I Am Joyful in the Joy of God

Thou hast made known to me in the ways of life; thou shalt
make me full of joy with thy countenance. —ACTS 2:28

Emerson says that prayer is the proclamation of a joyful and a beholding
soul. And throughout the Bible we find so many references to the joy of God
and the gladness that we should have in God's Presence. How can we help
being glad and filled with joy if we believe that the Presence and the Power
back of everything is one perfect Life, forever giving of Itself, forever imparting Itself to us, forever flowing through us in wondrous light and
power? Jesus said that if the multitude did not break forth in song, the very
stones would be compelled to, by which he meant that all nature is alive and
awake and aware with the Divine Presence, and that all nature and everything in life responds to the song of the heart.

Therefore, today I am filled with joy. I let every sense of depression or
heaviness depart from my mind and let my soul be lifted up in song to the
Giver of all life and to the joy of living. Joy shall accompany me like a companion, and happiness shall be to me as a comrade. There is a song in my
heart, singing unto the Creator of all things, and there is an invisible chorus
responding through everything in nature, through every person I meet, for
today I am meeting everything with joy and happiness, with song and
laughter, with gladness in my heart. I proclaim this day to be one of happiness, of thanksgiving and of praise to the Most High God, to the Divine
Presence that inhabits eternity and finds a dwelling place in my own soul.
Today I express joy and gratitude to this inner Presence, and this Presence
in which I am enveloped is one living Spirit of color and responsiveness—
the Author of joy and peace, of freedom and wholeness.

AUGUST
VITALITY

There is a vitality in our communion with the Infinite, which is productive of the highest good. —ERNEST HOLMES

The vitality of God is Self-Existent, Self-Propelling. As I become conscious of my Oneness with Good, I am filled with enthusiasm and a sense of energy and vitality. —ERNEST HOLMES

Only in prayer do we achieve that complete and harmonious assembly of body, mind, and spirit which gives the frail human reed its unshakable strength. —ALEXIS CARREL

To keep a lamp burning we have to keep putting oil in it. —MOTHER TERESA

> Know first, the heaven, the earth, the main,
> The moon's pale orb, the starry train,
> Are nourished by a soul,
> A bright intelligence, whose flame
> Glows in each member of the frame. —VIRGIL

I Am Vitalized by the Fullness of Life

You know that Life cannot withhold Itself from you. All that Life is and has is fully given to you to enjoy. The Life of God is perfect and eternal. It is the essence of everything that is. Life is God's gift to you. It is always ready to manifest Itself through you in Its entire fullness.

You are a self-choosing mind in a Divinity that permeates everything. You are always in the midst of Life, a Life that lives eternally and lives through you now. Therefore, you need not be disturbed by the passage of time, the movement around you, nor the variations of your experience. There is something within you that remains unmovable, that always speaks directly to you, saying, Be still and know that I am God.

Say: Consciously, I draw upon the Life that is mine. I know that the fullness of Life—which is Divine in Its origin, eternal in Its presence, and forever available—is mine. The Life of the eternal Spirit is my life. The infinite riches of Its being are mine to enjoy. The vitality, the wisdom and the peace of God are mine. I accept them in fullness, in joy, and in peace. My thought is a gateway to illumination; it is the secret place of the most High within me. Therefore, I revel in the fullness of life this moment. I accept life as a glorious experience, a spiritual adventure.

I Live Fully Today

The wisest man who ever lived said there is a truth that can set you free from fear, want, unhappiness, and death itself. He said that this truth is already within you. Suppose you accept this spiritual wisdom, since the one who gave it was able to prove his claims. Don't you think that this great and glorious person was telling you that the Kingdom of your Good is here today?

Now, this means that evil—no matter what face it wears, or what form it takes, or how many people believe it—is never a thing in itself. Jesus did not say that evil has no reality as an experience. He did say that you should not judge according to appearances. He said that you are to live as though the Kingdom were already yours. No matter what the negations of yesterday may have been, your affirmations of today may rise triumphant over them. Cease weeping over the mistakes of yesterday and, steadfastly beholding the face of the great and divine Reality, walk in that Light wherein there is no darkness.

Say: I know that every negative condition of the past is swept aside. I refuse to see it or to think about it. Yesterday is no longer here; tomorrow has not yet arrived. Today is God's day. God's day is my day. Today, bright with hope and filled with promise, is mine. I am alive, awake, and aware—today.

∾

I Sing Life's Song of Joy

You are part of the Universal Mind, one with the Universal Substance. You live, move, and have your being in pure Spirit. All the wealth, the power, and the goodness of this Spirit exist at the center of your being. You experience this good in such degree as you accept, believe in, and feel it. As you enter into life, feeling the Divine Presence in everything, more and more you will hear a Song of Joy singing at the center of your being. You have only to be still and listen to this Song of Life, for it is always there.

Say: Knowing that the loving Presence is always closer to me than my very breath, I have nothing to fear. I feel this loving protection around me. I know that the Song of Joy, of Love, and of Peace is forever chanting its hymn of praise and beauty at the center of my being; therefore, I tune out of my mind all unhappy and negative ideas.

I turn the dial of my thought into the sunshine of life, into brightness and laughter, into the joyous presence of radiant Spirit. I lay aside all anxiety, all striving, and let the law of Divine Love operate through me into my affairs. Joyfully I anticipate greater abundance, more success, and a deeper peace. Gratitude wells up within my heart for all the blessings I am now receiving.

God's Law Is Written in My Heart

Since the only life you can have is the life of the Spirit within you, you need but permit Its radiance to flow through your thought into self-expression. You are surrounded by a dynamic force, a great surge of living power. You are immersed in and saturated with the vital essence of Life. Its presence permeates everything, binding all together in one complete whole.

Say: Because my whole being is the Life of God in me, I have nothing to fear. Everyone I meet is part of the same Wholeness in which I live. Every person I meet is a center of the great unity of Life. It is this center of Life that I meet in all persons. It is this unity in and through all that I respond to. I cannot wish anyone harm, nor does anyone desire to harm me.

Through my consciousness of love, which is the very essence of goodness, I transform any apparent imperfection into the perfect idea of true being. I am knowing people as God knows them. I am seeing everything as God must see it. His Law is written in my mind and felt in my heart. I see God everywhere.

I Exercise My God-given Dominion

There is a God-Power at the center of your being, a Presence that knows neither lack nor limitation, fear nor sickness, disquiet nor imperfection. But because you are an individual, it is possible for you to build a wall of negative thought between yourself and this perfection. The wall that keeps you from the greater good is built of mental blocks, cemented together by fear and unbelief, mixed in the mortar of negative experience.

Now, you are to tear down this wall, to completely destroy it. The view that this wall obstructed is now seen in all its grandeur. The sun never really stopped shining and the River of Life forever flows. The experience of all people is an attempt to merge their own being with this eternal river, not to the loss of their identity, but to the discovery of that self that has never wholly left its heaven.

Say: I know that there is a Presence and perfect Law irresistibly drawing into my experience everything that makes life happy and worthwhile. The good I receive is but the completion of a circle, the fulfillment of my desire for all.

I have placed my reliance in the Power, the Presence, and the Perfection of God. Therefore, I have dominion over all apparent evil. I repudiate all its claims, cast out every fear of, or belief in, that which is not good, and I exercise the dominion that by divine right belongs to me.

I Live Eternally in the Household of God

You live in the house of God. The Household of God is a household of perfection. It is "the secret place of the most High" within you and within all people. The inhabitants of this household are all divine. They will become as divine to you as you permit. As you perceive them, that is how they perceive you, for this is the way of life. Everything responds to you at the level of your recognition of it.

In the Household of God there is no jealousy, no littleness nor meanness. It is a household of joy, a place of happiness and contentment. Here is warmth, color, and beauty. Seen in this light, your earthly house symbolizes the Kingdom of Divine Harmony in which no one is a stranger.

Say: Nothing is alien to me. Nothing enters into my experience but joy, integrity, and friendship. The good I would realize for myself I realize for all others. I cannot desire a good for myself other than the good I desire for everyone else. Neither do I deny myself the good I affirm for others. I know that in the household in which I live the host is God, the living Spirit Almighty, the guests are all people; the invitation has been eternally written for all to enter and dwell therein as the guests of this Eternal Host forever.

The Law of Good Brings Me Satisfaction

There is a Power operating through, a Presence inspiring, an Intelligence guiding, and a Law of Good sustaining you. Upon this Presence, this Power, and this Law you may place complete reliance. Because you live in this Divine Presence and because It is in you, you may know that the creative Law of Good, which is infinite and which has all power, can do for you or bring to you anything and everything necessary to your complete happiness. Its whole desire for you is one of freedom and joy.

Say: I know that freedom and joy are mine today. This freedom and joy spontaneously express themselves in my experience. There is nothing in me that can obstruct their passage. I permit them to flow through me in all their wonder and might. I am conscious of an Infinite Wisdom directing me. Whatever I ought to know I do know. Whatever I ought to do I shall do. Whatever belongs to me comes easily to me.

My every thought and decision is molded by intelligence and expressed through law and order in my experience. I not only think upon and realize the meaning of this truth, I am impelled to act upon it intelligently, creatively, without confusion, doubt, or hesitation. With joy I enter into the fulfillment of life.

The Protecting Power of the Infinite Sustains Me

As a child turns to its parents for comfort, so every one of us is relying on God, whether or not we realize it. This concept is so universal that it has been present in every age, with all people, and at all times. Jesus dared to place his hand serenely in the Hand of the Invisible. His works justified his words; his faith was manifest through his acts.

Nothing has happened to Reality since this glorious figure walked the highways of human experience. With equal confidence you should believe in the protecting Presence of the ever-available Spirit. Today you are to hold your thought steadfast in the realization that God withholds nothing from you. Therefore, prepare yourself for a life of joy, love, happiness, and well-being.

Say: I know that the Law of God surrounds me with love and friendship. I let it radiate in my environment, bless everything I touch, make whole that which is weak, turn fear into faith, and accomplish the miracle of healing through love. I welcome the opportunity to love fully, completely, and joyfully. I believe in myself because I believe in God. I accept life fully, completely, without reservation, holding to the conviction that good is the eternal Reality, that God is the everlasting Presence, that Christ within me is the eternal Guide, that my life is complete today.

I Experience Abiding Peace

Peace must exist at the center of everything or the universe itself would be chaos. You already know this and believe it; now you are going to act upon it. You are not only going to believe in it, you are going to act as though it were true, because it is true. There is peace at the center of your being—a peace that can be felt throughout the day and in the cool of the evening when the first star shines in the soft light of the sky. It spreads its comforting glow over all that exists.

Say: In this peace that holds me so gently I find strength and protection from all fear or anxiety. It is the peace of God in which I feel the love of a Holy Presence. I am so conscious of this love, this protection, that every sense of fear slips away from me as mist fades in the morning light. I see good in everything, God personified in all people, Life manifest in every event.

Spirit is not separate from persons or events; I see that It unites everything with Itself, vitalizing all with the energy of Its own being, creating everything through Its own divine imagination, surrounding everything with peace and quiet and calm. I am one with this deep, abiding peace. I know that all is well.

Divine Circulation Animates My Being

The Chinese sage said that Tao (meaning Spirit) "produces everything, nourishes everything, and maintains everything." It flows through and is in all things, being all that is. There is nothing outside it. There is a spiritual Presence pervading the universe, welling up in your consciousness, always proclaiming Itself to be the source of your being. The enlightened ones of the ages have told you that your recognition of Life is God within you recognizing Itself in everything you do.

Say: I know there is one Mind, one Spirit, and one Body—the Mind, the Spirit, and the Body of God—the Universal Wholeness, the ever-present Good, the all-sustaining Life. Every organ, every function, every action and reaction of my body is in harmony with the divine creative Spirit. I could not ask for more; greater could not be given.

I now seek to realize the significance of this one Mind and this one Body. I now become aware that the one Mind is acting through my body in accord with Its own divine perfection, peace, and harmony. The Divine circulates through me automatically, freely. Every atom of my being is animated by Its action. I know that at all times I have a silent, invisible Partner walking with me, talking with me, operating through me. Continuously, I keep my mind open to Its guidance, to Its inspiration and illumination.

I Bear the Eternal Stamp of Individuality

Life has set the stamp of individuality on your soul. You are different from any other person who ever lived. You are an individualized center in the Consciousness of God. You are an individualized activity in the Action of God. You are you, and you are eternal. Therefore, do not wait for immortality. The resurrection of life is today. Begin to live today as the immortal being you are and all thought of death, all fear of change will slip from you. You will step out of the tomb of uncertainty into the light of eternal day.

Say: I know that every apparent death is a resurrection; therefore, gladly I die to everything that is unlike the Good. Joyfully I am resurrected into that which is beautiful, enduring, and true. Silently I pass from less to more, from isolation into inclusion, from separation into oneness. Today, realizing that there is nothing in my past that can rise against me, nothing in my future that can menace the unfoldment of my experience, I know that life will be an eternal adventure.

I revel in the contemplation of the immeasurable future, the path of eternal progress, the everlastingness of my own being, the ongoingness of my soul, the daily renewed energy and action of that Divinity within me that has forever set the stamp of individualized Being on my mind.

I Am Spirit

There is a spiritual body that cannot deteriorate. This spiritual body is already within you; as much of it appears as is recognized. Spiritual perfection always responds to your consciousness, but it can respond only in such degree as you become aware of it. It is because this inward perfection is so insistent that you maintain a physical body, and because you are an individual with volition, you can, as it were, hang a curtain between your physical life and its spiritual cause.

Spiritual realization helps you withdraw this curtain. Every statement you make about your body or belief you hold about it that causes the mind to accept Spirit as the substance of the body tends to heal.

Say: I realize that there is a Divine Presence at the center of my being. I let this recognition flow through my entire consciousness. I let it reach down into the very depths of my being. I rejoice in this realization. I am now made vigorous and whole. I possess the vitality of the Infinite. I am strong and well. Every breath I draw is a breath of perfection, vitalizing, animating, and renewing every cell of my body. I am born of the Spirit. I am in the Spirit. I am the Spirit made manifest.

The Spirit Goes Before Me

Good is at the root of everything, regardless of its seeming absence. But this good must be recognized. Since there is but one Spirit and this Spirit is in you and in everything, then everywhere you go you will meet this Spirit. You meet this Spirit in people, in places, and in things. This one Spirit, which manifests Itself in and through all, including you, automatically adjusts parts to the whole. Therefore, you may accept with positive certainty that the Spirit within you goes before you and prepares your way. Your faith is placed in something as positive and certain as the laws of life, exact as the principle of mathematics; something ever present like the ethers of space, ever operating like the laws of nature.

Say: I know that the Spirit within me goes before me, making perfect, plain, straight, easy, and happy the pathways of my experience. There is nothing in me that can obstruct the Divine circuits of Life, of Love, of Beauty, and of Truth. My word dissolves every negative thought or impulse that would throw a shadow of unbelief across the threshold of my expectation.

I lift high my cup of acceptance, knowing that the Divine outpouring will fill it to the brim. I identify myself with the Living Spirit—with all the power, all the presence, and all the life there is.

Divine Power Is Mine to Use

Everything in nature is an individualization of one coordinating Life, one Law of Being, and one Presence. The mind has become so filled with that which contradicts this idea that even the Truth has to await our recognition. You must learn to become consciously aware of the Divine Presence and the Divine Power, the wholeness of Truth, of Love, of Reason, and of a sound mind. Instead of dwelling on negative thoughts, cause your mind to dwell on peace and joy. Know that the power of the invisible Spirit is working in and through you now, at this very moment. Lay hold of this realization with complete certainty.

Say: I know that I am a perfect being now, living under perfect conditions today. Knowing that good alone is real, I accept that there is one Power that acts and reacts in my experience, in my body and in my thought. I know that good alone has power either to act or react. I know that this recognition establishes the law of harmony in my experience, the law of prosperity, a sense of happiness, peace, health, and joy.

Today I hold a communion with this invisible Presence that peoples the world with the manifestations of Its life, Its light, and Its love. I withdraw the veil that hides my real self and draw close to the Spirit in everything and in everyone. I accept everything that belongs to this Spirit. I claim everything that partakes of Its nature.

I Open My Spiritual Eyes

The time has come to open your inward vision and look out upon a newer and broader horizon. You are at that place in your growth when there is complete certainty before you. You shall continuously expand and experience more and more of that Life that is already perfect. There is no reason why this awakending will not come now, for you are not waiting on God— God is waiting on you. All nature awaits your recognition and even the Divine Spirit must await your cooperation with It.

Realizing that you may, in your ignorance, have been using the power of your mind negatively, you are not going to condemn yourself or anyone else for this. If the light has come, the thing to do is to use it, forgetting the darkness. How can darkness have power over light?

Say: Today I realize that my good is at hand. In this breath I draw, in the eternal now and the everlasting here, I enter into a larger concept of life. I now see the rosy hue of a new dawn. The Spirit refreshes me. I am saturated with the essence of Life. My body is a vehicle for Its expression, my mind an instrument. My eyes are open to the breadth and heighth and the depth of that Life that is God. Today I will endeavor to feel this Presence as a living reality in my life. I will see It everywhere.

I Am Inspired from On High

Jesus, in utmost simplicity, proclaimed in the ecstasy of his illumination, "I and the Father are one." What do you suppose would happen if you believed his declaration, not as a mere intellectual concept, but with deep inward feeling and an expanding sense of its meaning? Would you not sell all that you possess for this single pearl of utmost worth, this drop of water taken from the ocean of being, this mountaintop of revelation? If the wisest person who ever lived proclaimed this truth, should you not accept it, simply, directly, sincerely?

Perhaps what Jesus taught seems too good to be true, and yet, all Nature is a living example, a continuous reminder, that there is a Spirit animating everything, a Presence diffused, a Law governing, a Unity sustaining, a coordinating Will binding all together, a unifying Principle holding everything in place.

Say: I cleanse the windows of my mind that it may become a mirror reflecting inspiration from the Most High. Today I walk in the pathway of inspiration. There is an inspiration within me that governs every act, every thought, with certainty, with conviction, and in peace. The key that unlocks the treasures of the Kingdom of Good is in my hand. I unlock the doorway of my consciousness and gently open it that the Divine Presence may flood my whole being with light, illumine my being with Its radiant glow, and direct my footsteps onto the pathway of peace and joy.

My Body Is a Temple of Spirit

Your body is a temple of the living Spirit. It is spiritual substance. Since the Spirit of God has entered your being, your life is spiritual. The Supreme Being, ever present, exists at the very center of your thought. This Presence within you has the power to make all things new.

The Perfect Life of God is in and through you, in every part of your being. As the sun dissolves the mist, so my acceptance of Life dissolves all pain and discord. You are free because the Spirit of Life in you is perfect. It remolds and re-creates your body after the likeness of the Divine pattern of body that exists in the Mind of God. Even now the living Spirit is flowing through you.

Say: I open wide the doorway of my consciousness to Its influx. I permit this physical body to receive the living Spirit in every action, function, cell, and organ. I know that my whole being manifests the life, love, peace, harmony, strength, and joy of the Spirit that dwells within me, that is incarnated in me, that is my entire being. I open my consciousness to the realization that all the Power and Presence there is clothes me in Its eternal embrace; the Spirit forever imparts Its life to me. I know that the Spirit within me is my strength and power.

My Word Accomplishes

You are either attracting or repelling according to your mental attitudes. You are either identifying yourself with lack or with abundance, with love and friendship or with indifference. You cannot keep from attracting into your experience that which corresponds to the sum total of your states of consciousness. This law of attraction and repulsion works automatically. It is like the law of reflection—the reflection corresponds to the image held before a mirror. Life is a mirror peopled with the forms of your own acceptance.

How careful, then, you should be to guard your thoughts, not only seeing to it that you keep them from doubt and fear—acccepting only the good—but, equally, you should consciously repel every thought that denies that good.

Say: I know that my word penetrates any unbelief in my mind, casts out fear, removes doubt, clears away obstacles, permitting that which is enduring, perfect, and true to be realized. I have complete faith and acceptance that all the statements I make will be carried out as I have believed. I do everything with a sense of reliance upon the Law of Good; therefore, I know that my word shall not return unto me void. I accept this word and rejoice in it. I expect complete and perfect results from it.

I Claim My Divine Inheritance

Your Kingdom of God is at hand. The riches, power, glory, and might of this kingdom are yours today. You do not rob others by entering into the fullness of your kingdom of joy, your kingdom of abundance. You recognize that all people belong to the same kingdom. You are merely claiming for yourself what you would that the Law of Good should do unto all.

There is no law of human heredity imposed upon you. Evil has no history. Limitation has no past. That which is opposed to good has no future. The eternal now is forever filled with the presence of perfect life. You always have been, and forever will remain, a complete and perfect expression of the Eternal Mind, which is God, the living Spirit Almighty.

Say: Today I enter into the limitless variations of self-expression that the Divine Spirit projects into my experience. Knowing that all experience is a play of Life upon Itself, the blossoming of love into self-expression, the coming forth of good into the joy of its own being, I enter into the game of living with joyful anticipation, with enthusiasm. Today I enter into my Divine inheritance, shaking my thought clear from the belief that external conditions are imposed upon me. I declare the freedom of my Divine nature.

Guidance and Wisdom Belong to Me

Realizing that all action starts in, and is a result of, consciousness, prepare your mind to receive the best that life has to offer. Become increasingly aware of the one Presence, the one Life, and the one Spirit, which is God. Try to drop all sense of lack or limitation from your thought. The Spirit works for you through your belief. All things are possible to this Spirit; therefore, everything is possible to you in such degree as you can believe in and accept the operation of Spirit in your life. There is something within you that is completely aware of its oneness with power, of its unity with life. Loose all thoughts of discord and fear and permit the true pattern to come to the surface.

Say: I allow the Divine Wholeness to flow through me in ever-widening circles of activity. Every good I have experienced is now increased. Every joy that has come into my life is now multiplied. There is a new influx of inspiration into my thought. I see more clearly than ever before that my divine birthright is freedom, joy, and eternal goodness. The Divine Presence interprets Itself to me through love and friendship, through peace and harmony. Knowing that life gives according to my faith, I lift my mind, I elevate my faith, I listen deeply to the song of my being.

My Faith Makes Me Whole

Faith is most certainly a mental attitude. A person approached Jesus and, from the inspiration of the occasion, standing in the light of one whose wick of life was ever kept trimmed and burning, feeling the warmth and color of its eternal glow, exclaimed, "I believe!" This was a simple, sincere, and enthusiastic response to the consciousness of one who had faith. But no sooner had he exclaimed, "I believe!" out of the enthusiasm of his will to believe, than old thought patterns arose to block his faith and he said, "Help thou mine unbelief."

Faith is more than an objective statement. Perfect faith cannot exist while there are subjective contradictions that deny the affirmation of the lips. It is only when the intellect is no longer obstructed by negative emotional reactions arising out of the experiences of doubt and fear that the word of the mouth can immediately bear fruit.

Say: I believe with a deep, inward calm that my word of faith is the execution of spiritual Law in my life. I have absolute reliance upon the Law of Good. I believe that the Law of Good will bring everything desirable into my experience. Today I proclaim my Divine inheritance. I am blessed with the richness of God; I am strong with the power of God; I am guided by the wisdom of God. I am held in the goodness of God, today.

I Partake of the Divine Bounty

Today you are to identify yourself with the more abundant life, to think of those things that make for peace, to dwell on the unity that underlies everything. As you consciously poise yourself in the realization that you live in pure Spirit, new power will be born within you. You will find yourself renewed by the Divine Life, led by Divine Intelligence, and guarded by Divine Love. Focus your inward vision on this indwelling harmony, knowing that as you contemplate its perfection you will see it manifest in everything you do.

Say: Realizing that the Spirit within me is God, the living Spirit Almighty, being fully conscious of this Divine Presence as the sustaining Principle of my life, I open my thought to Its influx; I open my consciousness to Its outpouring. I know and understand that Good alone is real. I know that silently I am drawing into my experience today, and every day, an ever-increasing measure of truth and beauty, of goodness and harmony.

Everything I do, say, and think is quickened into right action, into productive action, into increased action. My invisible good already exists; my faith, drawing upon this invisible good, causes that which was unseen to become visible. All there is is mine now; all there ever was or can be is mine now.

I Sense the Divine Presence Within Me

The Spirit of God is an undivided and indivisible Wholeness. It fills all time with Its presence and peoples all space with the activity of Its thought. Your endeavor, then, is not so much to find God as it is to realize His Presence and to understand that this Presence is always with you. Nothing can be nearer to you than that which is the very essence of your being. Your outward search for God culminates in the greatest of all possible discoveries—the finding of Him at the center of your own being. Life flows up from within you.

Say: I know that my search is over. I am consciously aware of the Presence of the Spirit. I have discovered the great Reality. I am awake to the realization of this Presence. There is but one Life. Today I see It reflected in every form, back of every countenance, moving through every act. Knowing that the Divine Presence is in everyone I meet, the Spirit in all people, I salute the good in everything.

I recognize the Life of God responding to me from every person I meet, in every event that transpires, in every circumstance in my experience. I feel the warmth and color of this Divine Presence forevermore pressing against me, forevermore welling up from within me—the well spring of Eternal Being present yesterday, today, tomorrow, and always.

The Essence of Love Expresses Through Me as Harmony

"The law of the Lord is perfect," and the law of the Lord is love. You are made perfect in the law when you enter into conscious communion with Love. It is only through love that the law can fulfill itself in your experience, because love harmonizes everything, unifies everything. You can never make the most perfect use of the law of your life unless that use is motivated by love. As the artist imbibes the essence of beauty, so you must drink in the love all around you. You must imbibe its spirit. This love is more than a sentiment. It is a deep sense of the underlying unity, beauty, and majesty of all life, the goodness running through everything, the givingness of Life to everything.

Say: Today I bestow the essence of Love upon everything. Everyone shall be lovely to me. My soul meets the soul of the universe in everyone. Everything is beautiful; everything is meaningful. This Love is a healing power touching everything into wholeness, healing the wounds of experience with its divine balm.

I know that this Love Essence is the very Substance of Life, the creative Principle back of everything, flowing through my whole being, spiritual, mental, and physical. It flows in transcendent loveliness into my world of thought and form, ever renewing, vitalizing, bringing joy, harmony, and blessings to everything and everyone it touches.

I Have Complete Confidence in the Law

The good in which you believe can triumph over every evil you have experienced. You have a silent partnership with the Infinite. This partnership has never been dissolved; it never can be. You are to have implicit confidence in your own ability, knowing that it is the nature of thought to externalize itself in your affairs, knowing that you are the thinker. You are going to turn resolutely from every sense of lack, want, and limitation, and declare that the perfect Law of God is operating in, for, and through you.

Say: I have complete confidence in my knowledge and understanding of the Law of Good. I not only know what the Law is, I know how to use it. I know that I shall obtain definite results through the use of it. Knowing this, having confidence in my ability to use the Law, and using It daily for specific purposes, gradually I build up an unshakable faith, both in the Law and the possibility of demonstrating It.

Therefore, today I declare that the Law of the Lord is perfect in everything I do. Today I believe in Divine Guidance. Today I believe that "underneath are the everlasting arms." Today I rest in this divine assurance and this divine security. I know not only that all is well with my soul, my spirit, and my mind—all is well with my affairs.

Spirit Permeates My Consciousness and Environment

It is only as you live affirmatively that you can be happy. Knowing that there is but one Spirit in which you live, move, and have your being, you are to feel this Spirit not only in your consciousness but in your affairs. You are united with all. You are one with the eternal Light Itself. The Presence of Spirit within you blesses everyone you meet, tends to heal everything you touch, brings gladness into the life of everyone you contact. Therefore, you are a blessing to yourself, to humankind, and to the day in which you live.

Say: Today I uncover the perfection within me. In its fullness I reveal the indwelling Presence. I look out upon the world of my affairs, knowing that the Spirit within me makes my way both immediate and easy. I know there is nothing in me that could possibly obstruct or withhold the Divine Circuit of Life and Love, which Good is.

My word dissolves every negative thought or impulse that could throw a shadow over my perfection. Good flows through me to all. Good shines through my thoughts and actions. Good harmonizes my body so that it is revitalized, manifesting perfection in every cell, organ, and function. Good harmonizes my mind so that Love sings joyously in my heart. I am in complete unity with Good.

I Am Bountifully Supplied from Divine Substance

Life fills all space and Spirit animates every form. But since you are an individual, even the Spirit cannot make the gift of Life unless you accept it. Life may have given everything to you but only that which you accept is yours to use.

Turning from every objective fact to the Divine Presence that dwells within you is turning from conditions to causes. It is turning from the relative to that realm of Absolute Being that, through self-knowingness, creates the forms It projects into the experience It creates. Thus the Spirit comes to self-fulfillment in everything. Through the manifestation of the power that is within you, you can project any objective experience you may legitimately desire. Be certain that you are accepting this truth, that you are living in joyous expectation of good, that you are accepting abundance.

Say: Today I recognize the abundance of life. I animate everything in my experience with this idea. I remember only the good. I accept only the good and expect only the good. I give thanks that this good is flowing in ever-increasing volume. I do not withhold good from myself or others, but proclaim that spiritual substance is forever flowing to each and all as daily supply.

I Receive Because I Ask in Faith

"Ask and ye shall receive." This is one of the most wonderful statements ever uttered. It implies that there is a Power that can and will honor your request. But it is only as you let go of the lesser that you can take hold of the greater, only as you drop confusion that you entertain peace, only as you transcend doubt and fear that you can be lifted up to the hilltops of the inner Life. In asking, you must identify yourself with the greatness of the Spirit. Permit your consciousness, through faith, to rise to a greater and broader realization of that Divine Presence that is always delivering Itself to you.

Say: Through the quiet contemplation of the omni-action of Spirit, I learn to look quietly and calmly upon every false condition, seeing through it to the other side of the invisible Reality that molds conditions and re-creates all of my affairs after a more nearly Divine pattern. I know that my word transmutes every energy into constructive action, producing health, harmony, happiness, and success.

I maintain my position as a Divine Being here and now. I know that in this consciousness of Reality is the supply for my every need—physical, mental, or spiritual—and I accept that supply in deepest gratitude. I permit a consciousness of Wholeness to flow into my world of thought and action, knowing that It brings peace, harmony, and order all around me. There arises within me limitless faith in the unconquerable Presence, the perfect Law, and Divine Action.

The Healing Christ Abides Within Me

The Christ Mind that abides within you is the incarnation of God in every individual. Not a person lives who does not at some time in his or her life sense this inward Presence, this vision of the Divine that presses against us. It is seeking entrance through our thoughts. We must open the door of our consciousness and permit It to enter. It is willingness, acceptance, and recognition that give entrance to the Divine Presence. It is faith and acknowledgment that permit Its creative power to flow through our word.

Say: Today I am opening my consciousness to a realization of the living, eternal Christ. I know that the Christ dwells in me and I know that there is an invisible Guide, a living Presence with me at all times. With complete simplicity and directness, I recognize my Divine center. Consciously, I unify myself with this pure Spirit in which I live, move, and have my being. I am strong with the strength of the all-vitalizing power of pure Spirit. I am sustained by Divine Energy, which flows through me as radiant health and vitality. Every atom of my being responds to this Divine Presence. I completely surrender myself to it.

I Overcome Hate by the Recognition of Love

There is but one Presence in the universe. Since It is in and through everything, It must be in and through you. This Presence manifests Itself in and through all forms, all people, all conditions. This Presence is Life Itself. Its nature is love and givingness.

Negation may be an experience and a fact; it can never be an ultimate truth. Life cannot operate against itself. Always the negative is overcome by the positive. Good cannot fail to overcome evil. Negative experiences may seem to exist for a brief moment, but Truth exists forever. The consciousness of Good must overcome the appearance of evil. Finally, Good will obliterate everything unlike Itself, even as the sun dissolves the mist.

Say: I refuse to contemplate evil as a power. I know that it will flee from me; it dissolves and disappears in the light of love. I know that hate cannot exist where love is recognized. I turn the searchlight of Truth upon every apparent evil in my experience. This light dissolves every image of evil. The manifestation of good is complete. Love makes the way clear before me. I am guided into an ever-widening experience of living. My every thought and act is an expression of the goodness that flows from Life.

I Accept Wholeness

See if you cannot let your faith soar and go into the mountain of the Lord, which is the secret place of the Most High within you, and let the whole harmony of your life flow from that perfect Spirit that is at the center of everything. Through a conscious acceptance of the fullness of the Presence of God there flows in and through you a joy, a love, and a wholeness that touches every part of your being.

You are one with God. Nothing can separate you from the Divine Presence within you. With complete faith in God's Power, know that all you are and do is the Divine within you expressing Itself through you.

Say: I am one with the infinite and perfect Spirit, the Giver of all good and perfect gifts. I open my mind and my heart to the inflow of this Divine Presence. I know that this living Presence is in every part of my being. There is no doubt or fear in my mind that rejects in any way all that God is, right here and right now. I decree that all I now bring into the scope of my thought is blessed and healed through the Presence of Good that is within me. I drink at the Fount of Life and am made whole.

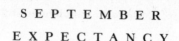

SEPTEMBER
EXPECTANCY

Our expectation looks for a more complete manifestation of our own inner divinity. Evolution will bring this about, as it does all things. We are an unfolding Principle of life, Truth, perfect law and action. We wait for a more complete unfolding of our inner life. —ERNEST HOLMES

Our work will best be done in quiet expectancy and in calm confidence. The results rest in the Eternal Law of Good. —ERNEST HOLMES

Belief in limitation is the one and only thing that causes limitation, because we thus impress limitation upon the creative principle; and in proportion as we lay that belief aside our boundaries will expand, and increasing life and more abundant blessing will be ours. —THOMAS TROWARD

The bounds of the soul thou shalt not find, though you travel every way. —HERACLITUS

> Ah, but a man's reach should
>   exceed his grasp,
> Or what's a heaven for? —ROBERT BROWNING

My High State of Consciousness Attracts Only Good to Me

Thou shalt make me full of joy. —ACTS 2:28

There is a law of attraction and repulsion that works automatically. It is like the law of reflection where the reflection corresponds with the image held in front of the mirror. Emerson said that we see what we animate and that we animate what we see. Jesus proclaimed that it is done unto us as we believe. This remarkable spiritual genius even went so far as to say that when we feel the need of anything, or desire it, we should pray for it and in the act of our prayer we should mentally receive the object of our desire as though it already exists.

This probably is the essence of that attraction that works automatically. How careful, then, we should be to guard our thoughts, not only to keep them straight, expecting only the good, but equally we should consciously expel every thought that denies good. This sometimes calls for long and difficult self-training. But if the principle is true, the reward will be certain. Nothing is more important than that we should consciously use this law of attraction with simplicity and in faith.

My prayer, today, then, is one of affirmation and acceptance. I lift my cup of acceptance, knowing there is Divine outpouring that fills it to the brim. If my cup appears to remain empty, I neither condemn myself nor lose confidence in Life. Rather I more carefully scrutinize my own thinking, turning away from that which denies my good.

I Prepare for That Which I Wish to Experience

And God is able to make all grace
abound toward you. —II CORINTHIANS 9:8

Realizing that all action starts with and is a result of consciousness, I prepare my mind to receive the best that life has to offer. Mentally I associate myself with that which is good, beautiful, and happy. I am increasingly aware of the One Presence, the One Life, and the One Spirit, which is God.

Believing that it is the Divine Intention for everyone to live an abundant life, I consciously align myself with the outpouring of Spirit. Accepting that all things are possible to the one who has faith, I daily increase my expectancy. I broaden my vision to include the greater good for myself and others. I cultivate faith, keeping my consciousness open to an increasing awareness of my union with good.

Today I expect an increase. Today I expect greater joy, more happiness, deeper peace, and a more complete sense of Divine Power. Today I meet everyone with the understanding that he or she is a part of the Divine Order. Today I gladly and joyfully enter into the inheritance of the Kingdom of Good.

I know that I have life, that I have intelligence, that I live by faith and am part of the One Divine Being. Therefore, I accept this life fully, without reservation. I hold the conviction that good is the eternal reality, that I live in this good now.

∾

God-Intelligence Governs My Daily Thoughts and Actions

Let this mind be in you, which was also in Christ Jesus. —PHILIPPIANS 2:5

Believing that the mind of God is ever-present, that Divine Intelligence is always available, I open my consciousness to Its guidance. Realizing that my attention must not be divided between believing and doubting, I carefully guard my mental reactions, seeking always to keep them affirmative, to keep them open to that which is constructive.

I keep my mind steadfast and loyal to the thought that I am governed by Divine Intelligence, which always knows what I ought to think and do and how I should do it. I feel that I am compelled to make right and constructive decisions, that I am impelled to right action, that there is something within me that always knows how to think and how to act.

Daily I reassure myself of this divine fact and affirm that the Intelligence that governs all things governs me; that the Life that flows through everything flows through me; that there is One Mind, which is God, that this Mind is my mind. I believe that this Mind is the source of inspiration as well as energy and action as well as illumination. Therefore, I know that at all times I have a silent, invisible partner walking with me, talking with me, cooperating with me. I keep my mind open to guidance. I let that Mind be in me that was also in Christ.

I Open the Door of My Consciousness and Welcome the Divine Guest

Behold, I stand at the door and knock. —REVELATION 3:20

The healing Christ comes with directness into the mind of all who receive Him. This Christ is the incarnation of God in the individual soul. Spirit has imparted Itself to all persons. This divine incarnation, this living Presence at the center of our being is Christ, the soul of every living person.

We do not will this Presence into existence, nor do we by declaration, affirmation, or demand command It. We do not court It by false humility nor engage Its attention merely by admiration. The Presence—the Power—is already there. It is willingness, acceptance, and recognition that gives entrance to the Divine Presence. It is faith and acknowledgment that permit Its creative power to flow through our word. Therefore, "I lift up mine eyes unto the hills [the Divine Presence within me] from whence cometh my strength."

I will look long and earnestly, sincerely and simply upon every object and every person until this Presence is revealed. I will wait at the doorway of my expectation until my acceptance grants my mind the privilege of "beholding God's face forevermore." But I will not wait too long, for today I expect to see God's shining Presence revealed. Today I expect to don the seamless robe of Divine union. Today the most High is revealed in my life.

Universal Law Is My Armor Against Negative Experiences

He that dwelleth in the secret place of the most High
shall abide under the shadow of the Almighty. — PSALM 9:1

We all seek the protecting power of some presence that we feel to be close enough to reach out and take hold of. As the child turns to its parents for comfort, and as in adulthood we turn to such laws as we have instituted for our protection, so intuitively we all seek divine protection. Every person is relying on God whether or not this is consciously recognized. The concept of a Supreme Presence is so universal that it is present in every age, with all people, and at all times.

It would be a mockery of faith to deny that such a Presence exists or that such a Power operates. Those who have wrought great and mighty works through faith have actually believed and have had complete confidence in divine protection.

To this Divine Presence, Jesus gave the name of "Our Father which art in heaven," which means the Spirit of Life—Divine Intelligence—within me, the protecting power of Spirit around me. Here was a man whose vision dared to penetrate the invisible, one who placed his hand serenely in the invisible Hand with implicit confidence. No one can doubt that his works justified his words, that his faith was manifest through his acts.

Nothing has happened to Reality since this glorious soul walked the highways of human experience. God, or Life, is the same yesterday, today, and forever. With equal confidence we should be able to believe in the protecting Presence and the ever-available Spirit.

Today, I put on the whole armor of faith. I wrap myself in the mantle of divine protection. I fear no evil, knowing that there is a Divine government of good, that there is a power available to me. I know that "underneath are the everlasting arms," the girders of divine protection.

My Mental House Is at Peace

I will fear no evil: for thou art with me. —PSALM 23:4

Fear is based on the supposition that evil is equal to good. The only thing that can adequately overcome fear is confidence and love. Love alone breaks down the barriers of fear and, through faith, discovers that there is an Eternal Heart. Emerson tells us that "the universe remains to the heart unhurt."

We must learn to turn from all of the little petty things that fret us, from the obstructions that seem so insurmountable, from the problems that seem too great to be solved. Realizing that "there is no fear in love; but perfect love casteth out fear," we should open our whole being to a love of everything, of everyone; for love to be real it must be all-inclusive.

Today my mental house is at peace, and I enter into a permanant and conscious relationship with the Divine Presence. I shall permit only that which is loving, kind, and true to find entrance or exit through my consciousness.

Realizing that I cannot ask for that which I refuse to give, I look upon all the earth as a dwelling place of Spirit. I love all creation and enter into conscious union with people, things, and events. Realizing that the kingdom of heaven is not far off but is ever at hand, I seek to become a worthy inhabitant of this kingdom, knowing that everyone is subject to the law of love, that everything is gradually being made perfect through that law.

I Receive Divine Strength into My Being

I will lift up mine eyes unto the hills,
from whence cometh my help. —PSALM 121:1

We tend to become like that with which we identify ourselves. It is only as we let go of the lesser than we can take hold of the greater, only as we drop confusion that we can entertain peace. If we would transcend doubt and fear we must lift up our thought unto the spiritual hills of the inner life.

It is said that Jesus went up to the mount to deliver the most famous sermon ever given to the world. We, too, must go up to the mount if we would rise above the little things that bother us. We must identify ourselves with the greatness of the Spirit if we would breathe in Its mighty power. Too long we have identified ourselves with that which is small, insecure, and uncertain. Now we must permit our consciousness, through faith, to rise to a greater and deeper realization of the divine Presence forever delivering Its nature to us. We must keep a watch in the tower of our minds. Consciously we must identify the self with Its Source.

Today I guard my thought and speech. I keep my consciousness steadfast with the realization that there is a spiritual power and strength upon which all men may call. If confusion enters, I shall repudiate it. I turn resolutely to that divine Source that knows no confusion, to that spiritual Center within me that knows no fear.

I Am Always Glad

I will be light-hearted as a bird and live with God. —EMERSON

I sing a song of joy today, of praise, and gratitude. I know that my health, my physical well-being, my mental poise and peace are drawn from the infinite Source. Today I know that the healing presence of Life is within me, forever restoring my mind and body.

Body and mind are one in Spirit. Physical health is a state of wholeness in mind, as well as in body. My body is a servant of the Spirit within me. My mind is an offspring of pure Spirit. There is a silent reaction going on between the Spirit within me, which is God, my mind, which receives impressions from this Divine Source, and my body, which is the servant of the Spirit.

Today I hold communion with the invisible Presence that peoples the world with the manifestation of Its Life, Its Light, and Its Love. I withdraw the veil that hides my real self and draw close to the Spirit in everything and in everyone. I anticipate everything that is worthy of the soul; I accept everything that belongs to the Spirit; I claim everything that partakes of the nature of the divine Reality.

The Immutable Law of God Sustains My Positive Acceptance of Perfect Faith

Thy faith hath saved thee; go in peace. —LUKE 7:50

Everyone believes that all things are possible to the person who has faith, but everyone has not taken the time to analyze exactly what faith is. Should we do this, we would at once see that faith is a definite mental attitude—or an attitude of the intellect, or the conscious mind—that is no longer denied by our subconscious reactions to life.

Faith is not perfect when we say, "I believe, help thou mine unbelief." The second part of this statement comes from the subjective reaction of doubt. Faith is perfect when we say, "I believe," and when there is nothing within us that says, "Help thou mine unbelief." Therefore, we see that faith is more than objective statement. We do not have perfect faith while subjective contradictions deny the affirmation of our lips. This is what the Bible means when it says that we must know in the heart. The heart symbolizes the innermost center of being. When the intellect is no longer contradicted by our emotional reactions, by unconscious doubts and fears, the word of our mouth will immediately bear fruit.

Today I have faith that my word shall not return unto me void. Today I surrender myself completely to this faith, for I know that there is a creative Spirit that gives substance to this faith and that will provide the evidence of this substance in actual fact. Therefore, I expect to meet my good, and I rejoice in the anticipation of this good. I know that my faith operates through an immutable Law and that there is no possibility whatsoever of Its failing.

I Stay Open to the Presence of Spirit Everywhere

The world is mine, and the fulness thereof. —PSALM 50:12

The Spirit of God, which is Life, is present everywhere. Like the air we breathe, It presses against us. On the mountaintop, in the valley, in the desert, and in the ocean—there is no place where Life is not. Therefore, in whatsoever direction we move, we move in God. In God we live, move, and have our being.

God is one undivided and indivisible Wholeness, one divine and spiritual Presence, one universal and all-encompassing Person. Perhaps it is a little difficult for us to understand the meaning of such an all-inclusive Person, but the very fact that we are personalities presupposes such a conclusion. Our endeavor, then, is not so much to find God, to discover the Divine Source of our personal being, as it is to become acquainted with God.

Today, I consciously commune with the Spirit. I know that it presses against me and flows through me. I endeavor to feel this Presence as a living reality in my life. Knowing that the Divine Presence is in everyone, I sense that the Spirit is in everyone I meet. I do my best to respond to this Spirit. Seeing It everywhere, I keep my consciousness open and alert that I may better understand the union of all life with its pure and perfect Source.

I Ask, Certain that I Shall Receive

Ask, and it shall be given you; seek, and ye shall find;
knock, and it shall be opened unto you. —MATTHEW 7:7

"Ask, and it shall be given unto you" is one of the greatest promises of the ages and has within it the greatest possibility ever experienced by the mind of man. Surely this implies that there is a power that can and will honor our request. But the same man said, "Ye ask and receive not, because ye ask amiss." These two sayings of Jesus are not contradictory, each implies that there is a Divine Givingness that withholds nothing from man but cannot contradict Its own nature. That is, God is good and we cannot expect evil from goodness; therefore, if we ask evil from goodness, goodness cannot honor that request. This would be "asking amiss."

Whatever we ask for in the name of Reality, that is, in the nature of that which is real, we shall most certainly receive. It is certain, however, that if we ask and have it given unto us, we must first seek and find, knock and have the door opened. What is this that we seek other than our true union with good? Where is the door that must be opened other than in our own consciousness? It is the door of acceptance, faith, and confidence. How can we receive that which the mind refuses to entertain?

I believe and I accept with thanksgiving. Therefore, today I ask and know that I shall receive. I seek and know that I shall find. Today I knock and know that it shall be opened unto me. I receive the gift of Life in all its fullness.

The Flow of Pure Spirit Always Pervades
My Consciousness and Environment

Now unto him that is able to do exceeding abundantly; above all that we ask or think, according to the power that worketh in us. —EPHESIANS 2:20

Today I hold my thought steadfast in the realization that Divine Life is flowing through me. I believe in the fullness of the bounty of God. There can be no lack in Spirit. Spirit now inspires me in everything I do, say, and think.

Realizing that God is the animating essence of all life, that God withholds nothing from me, I prepare myself for a life of joy, love, accomplishment, health, and well-being. I permit myself to believe in the divine freedom that is my birthright.

I know that the Law of Good keeps me in perfect activity, surrounds me with love and friendship, and causes me to experience the joy of living. It causes me to impart to everyone I meet an atmosphere of confidence and faith that uplifts and enlightens.

Today I permit the flow of pure Spirit to enter my consciousness, to radiate in my environment, to bless everything I touch, to make whole that which is weak, to turn fear into faith, and to accomplish the miracle of love.

Today—The Eternal Now—We Perfect Our Good

The eternal God is thy refuge and underneath
are the everlasting arms. —DEUTERONOMY 33:27

Today we say to ourselves, "Our experience is enriched by perfect faith; our affairs are in the keeping of Eternal Mind; we live in the Divine Presence; we are guided by infinite Wisdom and sustained by limitless Love." Today we say to ourselves, "We are part of Eternal Wholeness; we live, move, and have our being in this Spirit of God; we are consciously drawing upon this Spirit for inspiration. We are continuously receiving guidance from On High."

Today we remember that the Spirit is not far off but ever at hand, diffused through us. Today we remember that love is the great lodestone of life, that joy belongs to the Spirit, that the life more abundant is at hand. Today we carefully watch all our thinking, being certain that it sees in everyone it meets a reflection of the Divine Image, a copy of the Divine Pattern, a manifestation of the Life of the Spirit.

Whatsoever things are good, lovely, and true, these things I think upon, these thoughts I entertain in my mind. Deep within me there is a feeling nature that reaches up and out and grasps the full significance of the consciousness of good for myself and others.

I Recognize Physical Perfection as My Divine Birthright

Wither shall I flee from thy presence? —PSALM 139:7

There is One Life, that Life is God, that Life is my life now. It is only when we live affirmatively that we can be happy. It is only as we seek the good that we can find it. It is only as we mentally align our consciousness with abundance that it can seek us out.

We have been told to behold the face of God forevermore in everything. Now we know that we do not really see God anymore than we see life. No one has ever seen life, but everyone has experienced it through living. No one has ever seen God, but some people have experienced God's Presence so completely that their whole life has become a continual affirmation of peace, poise, and power. All persons have experienced this Presence to some degree. It is not entirely unknown to anyone.

Being told to behold God's face forevermore means that we should recognize life, poise, power, peace, joy, in and through everything and everyone. This has been called practicing the Presence of God. We can all do this with the certainty of splendid results.

Today I recognize the Divine Presence in everything. In the midst of darkness I see Light. At midnight I sing a song to the dawn, knowing that Eternal Light dissipates all darkness. Today I recognize beauty in the midst of ugliness, peace in the midst of confusion. Today I convert all doubt into certainty, all sorrow into joy, all fear into faith.

Daily I Contemplate My Importance in a Divine Plan

For we are laborers together with God: ye are God's field,
ye are God's building. —I CORINTHIANS 3:9

My thought is a gateway to illumination. I know that the Spirit within me is my strength and power. I approach life with a sense of security and well-being. I know that I have a secret source in God. I know that my thought is a gateway to illumination. It is the secret place of the most High within me from which comes inspiration, guidance, and wisdom. Therefore, I accept the fullness of this moment. I accept life as a glorious experience, a spiritual adventure.

I believe in myself because I first believe in God. I believe in my destiny because I believe that the law of good is operating through me. I have a calm confidence in the future, a keen and enthusiastic expectation of good things to come.

I open my whole consciousness to the realization that all the power and presence there is surrounds me in an eternal embrace, that the Spirit forever imparts Its own Life to me, forever flows through me into happiness, success, and well-being.

Knowing that I cannot live unto myself alone, but that I am a part of all Life, I gladly and enthusiastically unify with people, conditions, and events, flowing into them with the certain knowledge that I belong to the universe in which I live, that this universe belongs to me, that I am a part of it, necessary to it, one with it.

I Radiate the Fullness of Life, for I Fear Nothing

Ever follow that which is good. —I THESSALONIANS 5:15

In the name of good, I unify myself with the Divine Presence. Fear has no place in my being. God is not afraid of anything. The Divine Mind has no enemies. The Spirit knows no opposites. As I consciously draw close to this Divine Center and Source of all being, I feel the radiation of Its warmth and color.

I enter into that faith made perfect through love and confidence, that assurance made complete by the abandonment of myself to the Divine, acknowledging good in all my ways, desiring only the good for others, refusing to accept evil as a part of the Divine Kingdom. I rest in calm assurance.

Peace, poise, and power belong to my kingdom. Joy and love are gifts from On High, gifts that I gladly acknowledge and enthusiastically accept, knowing that the gift is not to me alone but is the gift of Life to all that lives. I gladly share my good, scattering it everywhere. Knowing that everything is love, I gladly give myself to life, to the joy of living.

Inspiration, Guidance, and Wisdom Belong to Me

Be ye doers of the word. —JAMES 1:22

Through Divine Intelligence I become an outstanding individual. The fullness of experience is mine. I have no fear of taking the initiative. I do not limit the possibility of my future to anything that has happened in the past. I realize that I exist at the standpoint of limitless opportunity for self-expression.

I am a center of consciousness in life. I am myself, an individual, a person, a reality. I am one with life, one with people, and one with events. I have no fear of expressing myself. I do not seek to imitate others or live from the resources of anything other than my own nature, because all wisdom, guidance, and power is mine now.

I welcome the opportunity to live fully, freely, and joyfully. I accept the fullness of life this moment. I believe in myself. Within me is the source of knowledge, of inspiration, and of guidance. I put myself and any cares I may have in the hands of Divine Intelligence. I release all sense of worry or anxiety.

All Things Are Made Out of Life

It is the Spirit that quickeneth. —JOHN 6:63

How wonderful to realize that from one formless and invisible Substance everything that is visible comes. This invisible essence of things is the spirit of Life Itself. Realizing this spirit at the center of people and things is silent communion with the Divine Presence.

There is but one Life. When we recognize life in others it is the life in us that is responding to them. As we unify with this life through people, it automatically unifies with us. As we agree with it, it agrees with us. From this recognition there comes a quickening of our own consciousness. It is written that, "It is the Spirit that quickeneth."

Today I know that my spirit is quickened as I recognize the same Spirit in others. Realizing the presence of life in all nature, I know that it responds to me. I am one with that which is alive, awake, and aware. There is nothing dead, nothing stagnant, nothing inactive. In all, through all, and around all, I realize One Presence. "There are diversities of things, but the same Spirit."

Divine Mind Pervades Every Atom of My Body

Spiritual Substance is my physical perfection. No one knows exactly what the mind is, but we certainly know that it is something within us that enables us to be conscious and aware. We are told to let the Mind be in us that was in Christ. What can this mean other than that each should recognize the Divine Incarnation in himself? It was this realization of His union with good, with life, with God, that endowed Jesus with his miraculous power.

There is One Mind, which all people use. Each one is an individual in It. It is individualized in and through each. The Mind of God in man is Christ. This Mind is not a far away presence, nor is It some future event toward which we travel. It is something that is already and forever established, that needs but to be recognized to spring forth into manifestation in our experience.

This recognition can come to anyone at any time. We need not move away from ourselves to discover ourselves. What we do is uncover and reveal that which is already concealed at the center of our being. Browning tells us that this is an act of loosing "the imprisoned splendor." To realize that there is but One Mind, which we all use is to understand the teachings of Buddha, Jesus, Plato, and Emerson, to enter consciously into communion with this Mind is the secret of spiritual and intellectual power, of intuitive perception and of Divine Guidance.

I Recognize That My Unity with All Humankind
Is of Divine Origin

I am the vine, ye are the branches. —JOHN 15:5

I believe there is but one Spirit in which everyone lives, moves, and has his being. In this Spirit I am directly unified with all people. I recognize this Spirit as individualized in everyone; therefore, I am learning to see every person I meet in the light of this divine and changeless truth.

There is one Spirit diffused through all humanity. With this Spirit in everyone I hold communion. In a handclasp I feel Its warmth and color. In the exchange of thought I feel the presence and the activity of the Divine Mind. In the blessing of friendship I sense Its love.

I am separated from none, united with all, and one with the Eternal Light Itself. As I go among people I know that the presence of pure Spirit within me, which I recognize, blesses everyone I meet, tends to heal everything I touch, brings gladness into the life of everyone I contact. Therefore, I am a blessing to myself, to humankind, and to every day in which I live.

I Live As an Immortal Being

For I am the Lord, I change not. —MALACHI 3:6

The stamp of individuality is eternal. Emerson said that nothing is dead; human beings feign themselves dead, and endure mock funerals and mournful obituaries, and there they stand looking out of a window, sound and well, in some new and strange disguise.

There exists in every person this hope, this belief in the immortality of his own being, and there is something about every living soul that knows he is made of immortal stuff, that there is no death. But eternity is not some far-off event—"Beloved, now are we the sons of God." It is today that I enter into a complete realization of my immortal being.

Today I sense that every person is as eternal as God. Today I know that all humanity is clothed with resurrection. Immortality is at hand and I must experience it. Therefore, I let go of every belief that would deny me the privilege of entering into my immortal state here and now. I live as an immortal Being.

Today, realizing there is nothing in my past that can rise against me, nothing in my future that can menace the unfoldment of my experience, life will be an eternal adventure, an unfolding experience of greater and better experiences. Evolution is onward, upward, forward, outward, expansive. Today I exult in this abundant life. I revel in the contemplation of the immeasurable future, the path of eternal progress, the everlastingness of my own being, the ongoingness of my soul, the daily renewed energy and action of that divinity within me, which has forever set the stamp of individualized Being on my mind.

I Am Sustained by the Truth

Tell me nothing but that which is true
in the name of the Lord. —I KINGS 22:16

Everyone believes that Truth alone can make us free. We all know that ignorance is the great mistake of the ages and that enlightenment alone can
save us from the thraldom of our own errors. Jesus, the wise, boldly proclaimed that the knowledge of Truth would automatically produce freedom. He also said that a knowledge of the Truth includes a realization of the
Presence of the Creative Spirit of life.

This teaching calls for a recognition of life in everything, of Spirit operating everywhere. He taught that we must recognize this Spirit in everyone,
that the Spirit of God is also the quickening life of the child. The entire
teaching of this most noble of all intellects, calls for a recognition of one infinite Life everywhere present, therefore at the center of our own being, and
an equal recognition that God and the child are One.

Today, I commune with the Truth that makes me free. I proclaim the
Presence of this Truth, active in everything I do. I rejoice in this recognition
and seek evermore to become consciously aware that I am sustained by the
Truth, that I am in it, of it, and one with it. This conscious union with life,
which Jesus called, "knowing the truth," frees us from the tyranny of fear
and the thraldom of fate. I daily practice the belief in this Truth, because I
believe there is but one supreme Actor.

I Have Faith in the Invisible

Now faith is the substance of things hoped for,
the evidence of things not seen. —HEBREWS 11:1

This passage from Hebrews means that faith rightly exercised will produce a definite evidence, or effect, molded from an invisible Cause that is the substance of all things. Faith produces evidence, therefore, faith creates fact. This is the sum and the substance of a spiritual life.

To teach this was the mission of Jesus. To illustrate or demonstrate it, He devoted His entire time and attention. What untold watching and waiting was His! What careful and painstaking control of His thought we do not know! In the desert, on the mountaintop, watching and waiting, believing and praying, asking and receiving, His faith produced an evidence of its reality. The facts that it produced substantiated the claims He made. But nothing has happened since this inspired and glorious soul walked the streets of His native towns, ministered to the sick, raised the dead, multiplied the loaves and fishes. Time is without beginning and end; experience alone can change. Truth or Reality, solid and substantial, is the foundation of sanity, and faith is available now.

I have faith in the substance of every legitimate desire, faith that there will be an evidence in fact, in actual experience, of my belief in the invisible law of good. I ponder these things deeply in my heart. I turn my whole attention to the thought that there is such an invisible Source, Substance, and Reality. My whole mind accepts the idea that "both riches, and honor come out of thee . . . and in thine hand it is to make great, and to give strength to all."

My Word Is Creative

Let every soul be subject unto the higher powers. For there is no power but of God: the powers that be, are ordained of God. —ROMANS 13:1

I identify myself with the more abundant life. I think of those things that make for peace. I dwell in the unity that underlies all life. Because I am at peace and poised in the realization that I live in pure Spirit, new power is born in me.

Realizing that all power is ordained of God and maintained by the Spirit and knowing that my word is the Law of Spirit in my life, I realize that my word is creative. Therefore, I speak that word in quiet confidence and with complete faith.

There is no need or want or lack in my life, for my consciousness places no limitation on the Divine Givingness. I know that all my needs are fulfilled from that Eternal Source, the Kingdom of God, which is ever present. My desire is now fulfilled and my experience enriched, and that which I have, I give.

The One Life within me is mighty to heal. I recognize that the Divine Spirit that flows through me is really the presence of Love. The words I speak, I speak from a consciousness of this indwelling Power. My thought is ever inspired from this Source of all inspiration, the Divine creative imagination of the Living Spirit. Daily I am renewed by the Divine Life, led by the Divine Intelligence, and guarded by Divine Love. I focus my vision on the indwelling harmony, knowing that as I contemplate this inward perfection, I shall manifest it in my life.

I Have Confidence in the Law

I will put my laws into their hearts, and in their minds
will I write them. —HEBREWS 10:16

Knowing that the Word of God is the Law of God, holding my consciousness high to the inspiration of the Spirit, I believe that, since the Law of the
Lord is perfect, my faith becomes this Law operating in my affairs.

The Divine Presence within me works for me, through me. Therefore,
whatsoever things I desire or have need of, that is done. Since all things are
possible to God, which is the universal Spirit, all things also must be possible to you and me, since we are individualized centers of this universal
Spirit.

I know that Life gives to me according to my faith. Therefore, I elevate
my faith. I lift up my mind. I engage the attention of the Spirit that It may
flow through me with inspiration. I listen deeply to that still, small voice
that evermore proclaims, "Behold I make all things new." Today I am made
glad in my recognition of the Divine Presence. I am made strong in my
recognition of the Divine Power. I am at peace in the recognition of the Divine Security.

I Release Every Tension of Mind and Body

Release and ye shall be released. —LUKE 6:37

Today I release all thoughts of fear from my mind. Today I lay down the burden of carrying the load of responsibility of life for myself or for others. Today I relax all sense of strain. I remember that Emerson said, "The universe remains at heart unhurt"; that Jesus said, "Let not your heart be troubled." I know that I live under the government of good and am guided by Spirit. Therefore, I lay all trouble aside, seeking to look through it, beyond it, above it; to detach it from the realm of Reality, to separate it from any consciousness that belongs to me or to anyone else, regardless of what any problem of the moment seems to be.

I align myself with the powers of goodness and of right action. I abide in perfect and complete faith in God as my ever-present good. I take up no arms to fight the negative. I turn from all fear; turn joyfully and resolutely to faith, realizing that light is immune to darkness, that the night has no power over the day, that dawn dissipates the shadows of midnight. I turn my attention to the Light Eternal, without struggle, realizing that that Light, shining through the dark places of my consciousness, will dissipate them and that I will walk in that Light in which there is no darkness. Not only will I walk in this Light, I will radiate it. I will impart it to others. I will remember the saying, "Let your light so shine before men that they, seeing your good works, shall glorify your Father which art in heaven." I will remember that the Father which art in heaven is in that heaven that is within me.

The Life Within Me Is God

Then shall thy light break forth. —ISAIAH 58:8

Whatever is true of God is true of our life, since our life and the Life of God are not two, but One. The enlightened have ever proclaimed this unity of good, this oneness of human beings with God. For this reason many have spoken of this Life within us as both personal and impersonal: impersonal from the standpoint that It is universal; personal from the standpoint that this Universal Life Principle is personified in us.

This Life within us, being God, did not begin and It cannot end; hence, we are immortal and eternal. We can never be less, but must forever be more ourselves as this Life within us unfolds through our experience, through our gathering of knowledge and our accumulating of wisdom. Evolution is the drawing out of the God-Principle already latent within us. It is this God-Principle within us to which Jesus referred when he said, "Before Abraham was, I am."

I believe that the Spirit with me, which is God, makes perfect and peaceful the way before me. In this faith and knowledge I discover a great peace of mind, a deep sense of belonging, a complete realization that God is right where I am. I put my whole trust in God and feel an intimate relationship with the Presence and Power that controls everything.

God Within Me Is Truth, Beauty, Harmony, and Wholeness

The spirit of God hath made me. —JOB 33:4

Divine Perfection is already within us. Being forever perfect and complete, we need no reunion with God, because God already is in our every act, every thought, every movement; God is in our every plan, purpose, and performance. The Divine Presence within us creates every circumstance and situation we have ever experienced. We have called these circumstances and situations things in themselves, but they have never been. They have been the fruition of our thought, and our thought has always been dominated by our beliefs.

By our use of the law of freedom, we create either bondage or liberty—not that bondage really exists, but the possibility of using freedom in a limited way exists. The restriction is not in the Principle, but in our use of it. If limitation were a thing in itself we could not change it, but since it is merely an experience, why not use our imagination to enlarge that experience? When we do this we will find the Life Principle within us responds just as quickly to a broader outline. Whatever we mentally see and spiritually comprehend, we may objectively experience, for the Divine Presence within us is not limited to any one experience. It is the Creator of all experience.

Today my eyes are open more widely and I look out upon a broader horizon. Across all the experiences I may have had that were limited or unpleasant I now see the rosy hue of a new dawn. Letting go of that which is little, I now enter into a larger concept of life. Dropping all fear, I entertain faith. Realizing that every form of uncertainty is seeing only in part, I open my spiritual eyes to that which is wholeness, which is greater and better.

The Mind in Me Is Also in All People

Be renewed in the spirit of your mind. —EPHESIANS 4:23

Emerson said there is One Mind common to all individual people, which means that the Mind of all human beings is the One Mind, which each uses. Therefore, the Mind you use is the Mind I use. It is the Mind everyone uses. It is the Mind of God, and because the Mind of God is a complete unity, It is omnipresent. Therefore, the Mind that you use and that is your mind is the God-Mind in you. This Mind is in all people, envelops all, and is at the center of everything.

This Mind, which is God, permeates every atom of your being. It is the governing Principle in every organ of your body. It is the Principle of Perfection within you. Your thought is the activity of this Principle. The Principle is perfect, complete, and limitless, but your thought circumscribes Its action and causes the very Mind of Freedom to create conditions of bondage. Your consciousness of the Divine Presence within you, like light, dissipates the darkness. This is your eternal and true self at the center of your being. It is the Mind of God manifesting Itself in you, as you. This you that It manifests is not separate from Itself, but is Itself.

Divine Mind within me is perfectly free. I am not merely a shadow of this Mind; I am the substance of it. I am this Mind in action. I project this Mind through my experience. Since the Mind within me is the Mind of God, and since the Mind of God not only created everything that has ever existed but also will create everything that is ever going to be, I have within me the ability to project new ideas, new thoughts, new inventions. Calling upon this Mind for an answer to a problem, I at once know the answer because the answer to every problem already is in the Mind I possess.

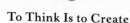
To Think Is to Create

With God all things are possible. —MATTHEW 19:26

The final creativeness of the universe is a movement of Intelligence within and upon Itself. This Intelligence already exists at the center of our own being. It really is our own being, and the very power of imagination that we exercise is this Intelligence functioning at the level of our comprehension of It. The Mind within us is the Mind of God. Since our mind is some part of the Mind of God, there is a place within us where we are universal, where we use Universal Power. To affirm the presence of good in our life is to use the Power within us for the creation of that good we affirm.

We have this possibility within us, for the Mind within us is God. We must accept our freedom, announce our liberty, and proclaim our Divine birthright. Whatever we believe to be true about God, we must declare to be the truth about ourself. We must know that the Power within us, which is God, is establishing right action in our life. In this way we will gain dominion and exercise authority.

I live in the world of my own creation. Knowing that thinking is creative opens the doorway to wisdom and power. That doorway is already within me. Somewhere within me the Mind of God reveals this truth, that I was born free and that the will of God for me is one of goodness, truth, and beauty. I rejoice that at last I am awakening to this realization of Truth. I have the power to use the Mind within me in any good way I see fit. I use my authority to create beauty, peace, and joy.

OCTOBER
FULFILLMENT

Whenever the Universe makes a demand upon Itself, out of that very demand is created its fulfillment. —ERNEST HOLMES

Every thought sets the fulfillment of its desire in motion in Mind, and Mind sees the thing as already done. —ERNEST HOLMES

You do not need to leave your room. Remain sitting at your table and listen. Do not even listen, simply wait. Do not even wait, be quite still and solitary. The world will freely offer itself to you to be unmasked, it has no choice, it will roll in ecstasy at your feet. —FRANZ KAFKA

The life of work is necessary and the life of contemplation is good. In service we gather the harvest that has been sown in contemplation.
—MEISTER ECKHART

Bring ye all the tithes into the storehouse, that there may be meat in mine house, and prove me now herewith, saith the Lord of hosts, if I will not open you the windows of heaven, and pour you out a blessing, that there shall not be room enough to receive it. —MALACHI 3:10

Every Worthy Desire of My Heart Is Fulfilled

When the dawn breaks and the shadows flee, when the hills are touched with the rosy glow of the sun's first rays, I wake to the thought that I am one with all life. I lift mine eyes to the Eastern sky and sing with the joy of one who beholds the Eternal Presence in everything. I permit my mind to become saturated with the Divine Ideal. In everything I do I sense the Divine Presence, sustaining, upholding, and guiding me. I rejoice in my unity with All-Power.

I know that I am not isolated from the All-Good, but am one with It. I know that there is a Divine Pilot steering my boat safely to a harbor of peace, to an environment of happiness, and to a haven of good. Therefore, I am not afraid, even when the billows roll and the wind sweeps by, for there is a Divine hand guiding my ship; there is an invisible Presence at the wheel. I lift the sails of faith and let the winds of love fill them with the mighty power of the Divine Presence. My boat rides upon a sea of Pure Spirit and finds safe anchorage everywhere, always.

I am guided by Divine Intelligence, which goes before me and makes perfect my way. I have a Divine Right to rise above fear, impoverishment, and limitation. Today I exercise dominion over my environment, over every circumstance and condition that I contact. The joy of life flows into my thought and work. Peace and harmony attend everything I do. Love and protection are ever present. Today I know that every worthy desire of my heart is fulfilled.

God Within Me Strengthens Me

"Fear thou not for I am with thee. . . . I will strengthen thee. . . . I will uphold thee. . . . I, the Lord thy God, will hold thy right hand." When we turn from all belief in separateness, we find the indwelling Spirit. When we have dismissed all fear, then we know that God is Love. When we have turned away from every sense of weakness, we know that God is Strength. This thought fills me with confidence and courage. Resting securely in this knowledge, I am renewed, guided, and led step by step by the power of an ever-present Love.

Today I permit the Divine Spirit to flow through me. Rejoicing in Its presence, I am free from fear. I live in perfect faith. There is but One Power and Presence in the universe, which is God, the living Spirit Almighty. Disregarding any appearance that seems to contradict this Divine fact, I press forward with the certain knowledge that I am forever one with the invisible Presence that is able, ready, and willing to direct all my ways. I know that "her ways are ways of pleasantness, and all her paths are peace."

Today I walk in these ways of pleasantness and "no wind can blow my bark astray." There is a Divine Authority at the center of my being that announces Itself in every act. I have implicit confidence in the invisible part of me, which is my share in the God-Nature, my partnership with the Infinite, my oneness with all that is. Today I accept my good. Today I bless that good and cause it to multiply in my experience. Today I shall not doubt nor fear. God within me strengthens me.

The Spirit of God Within Me Is Free

"Ye shall know the truth and the truth shall make you free." I am convinced that this truth, to which Jesus referred, is the reality of my own and of every other person's nature. The Spirit within me, being God, cannot be limited in any way. Today I drop every sense of bondage from my mind. Consciously I open my thought to the Divine Influx. In every act I seek to sense the freedom of Spirit flowing through me. Deliberately I loose every morbid thought of the past, and deliberately I expect every coming event to be fraught with gladness. Today I live in the complete conviction that the freedom of God is expressing itself through me. I reflect this freedom to every person I meet. I push the horizon of my thought further away and in every direction I look I expect something new, something bigger and better, to transpire.

I know that limitation and fear do not exist in God's kingdom. I know that even as the sun melts ice, so the Light of the Spirit within me dissolves every obstruction in my path, under the influence of Its divine ray. Everything unlike the perfect nature disappears. My entire thought, will, and imagination are saturated with the Divine Presence, which forever proclaims, "Behold, I make all things new."

Today I let nothing enter my thought that would contradict the all-ness and the goodness of the Spirit. The Divine Shepherd is ever with me, guiding, counseling, and leading me into pathways of peace, freedom, and security. My cup of joy runs over with the gifts of Life. Unhesitatingly, I accept them. The Spirit of God within me is free.

I Press Forward to Greater Accomplishment

Grateful for each success and each new accomplishment, I advance to new and greater revelations of Truth. Knowing that the Spirit within me is free, I am no longer bound by the patterns of yesterday. Freedom is made manifest through my thoughts, in my words and actions.

Becoming conscious of myself as I really exist in the Mind of God, I find that I am walking in pathways of peace, that something within me like a magnet attracts that which belongs to itself. This something is Love, the supreme impulsion of the universe. I know that I have no existence apart from this Love. As I grow in the knowledge that I am one with the Spirit, I know that I will grow in the ability to use the God-Power within me. Today I have complete confidence in the Law of Good. I have a complete sense of protection in the knowledge that good attends me. I experience the joy of knowing that this good permeates everything I do, say, and think.

I realize that this good recognizes me and that I cannot depart from it. Good is forever expressing itself to me and to everyone whom I love. It fills me with a great surge of life. I consciously receive this good and loose it into action. There is a song at the center of my being that everyone hears, a joy that everyone feels, a strength that is imparted to all. I press forward to greater accomplishment.

I Pray Without Ceasing Because I Live in Constant Faith

The secret power of faith is in a conscious union of the soul with the Over-Soul. Realizing that God is an ever-present reality, I know that I cannot escape my union with the Infinite. Therefore, I know that I am touched with the Spirit of Wholeness, filled with everything that the perfection of this Divine Spirit must contain. My being is so close to the Divine that there is no separation whatsoever. "If ye abide in me, and my words abide in you, ye shall ask what ye will, and it shall be done unto you."

I understand the meaning of the thought that no one can shut the doorways of my self-expression. I understand that there is no problem that cannot be solved. I realize that the Truth is already established and that the power of good is mine today, in all of its completion and perfection, in all of its purity and peace, in all of its wonder and joy.

Knowing that I abide in the Spirit of Truth and that the Spirit of Truth abides in me, today I open my consciousness to a greater acceptance of life. I realize that my entire being is in the hands of a higher Power, that my thought is molded by the Divine Will, that my mind responds completely to the indwelling Presence that is God. I fast from fear and feast upon faith, for I am certain that every good thing that God has intended for me exists right here where I am. Acknowledging my good, I enter into the banquet hall of Life. I recognize the Spirit as my Host. I recognize that all others are unified with me in the Spirit of Good. I pray without ceasing because I live in perfect faith.

I Acknowledge the Source of My True Self in God

"I will not leave thee nor forsake thee." Our divine nature never deserts us. Like the prodigal son, we may wander into far countries of despair, but the Divinity within us ever gently urges us back to the center of our true being; It ever reminds us of Its presence.

Today I acknowledge this True Self, knowing that It will instantly supply me with whatsoever things I need. Today I consciously reenter the kingdom of heaven within me. I sit at the table of the Lord and partake of the Divine Banquet, the wine of Spirit and the bread of Life. I know that the master at the table is my own indwelling Christ, that part of me that is perfect in God, that immortal Self that is birthless, deathless, and changeless. I know that my host is God, the living Spirit Almighty. I live, move, and have my being in this Divine Presence.

"In God there is life; in God there is peace; in God there is wholeness." There is no need for sorrow, no need for fear or regret. This is no occasion for anxiety or despair. In returning unto that which is whole, I am made whole. In returning unto that Power that contains all things, I realize that nothing can be lost. Today I keep my vision on this thought—there is One Power, One Presence, and One Reality from which I can never be separated. I am some part of this Divine Reality. I am dear to the heart of Being. I am one with God. I acknowledge the source of my true self in God.

I Consciously Enter into God's Presence Today

The Most High is enthroned in every soul; the Divine Spirit exists at the center of my being. Knowing that the Power of God, the Wisdom of God, and the Love of God are limitless and are available to me, today I have no fear. Knowing that Divine Power can accomplish anything and realizing that faith in this Divine Power draws It forth into my experience, today I exercise complete confidence in the Invisible.

I know that new and wonderful ideas will come into my consciousness today and that I will be compelled to act upon them intelligently. I am assured of Divine Guidance. I feel that it will be impossible for me to make any mistake, that even though I should start to move falsely, my movement will be corrected. I feel as though I am being constantly guarded and protected.

Since all things are possible to God, which is my true nature, I know that I have discovered the secret of life. I know that I have uncovered an inner spiritual reality that gives power to everything I do. I accept that Supreme Power is with me at all times. Since this Power cannot fail, I will not fail. Since this Divine Presence cannot be unwhole, my knowledge of my union with It makes me whole. Since this Supreme Intelligence cannot lack knowledge, I know that I am divinely guided. Since the Eternal Mind, which dwells within me, is forever at peace, I know that I am led onto pathways of peace. Since God is all there is, I know that I dwell in intimate union with the only Presence and the only Power that exists. Since God is everywhere, I realize that I consciously enter into God's presence today.

Today I Expect and Accept Only Good

Knowing the Truth leads me into a more abundant life. Today I affirm that with God all things are possible. I am conscious that the reality of my being is not separated from the Divine. I am not only one with God, God is also one with me and one in me. Deliberately I turn to this inner Self, knowing that it has no problems. It is never poor, sick, weak, or unhappy. Persistently I practice the Divine Presence. I enter the gates of Good with praise and thanksgiving, finding joy and fulfillment in everything I do.

Complete prosperity is mine. Good is forever flowing, eternally manifesting itself to me. My good flows to me from every source, because I recognize all sources as Divine. My hands open to receive and remain open that they may again give out and thus multiply the Divine Gifts.

Today the Truth leads me into the possession of everything necessary to my well-being here on earth. When I discover the inner kingdom, with its spiritual gifts, the material gifts that shadow forth this inner kingdom will also make their appearance. I now forget any wrong that may have appeared in my outer world and, turning with gratitude to that inner Light, I think upon those things that are good. I no longer contend against people or events. In doing this I become emancipated from my previous bondage. Today, everything in my experience is made new. Today, I expect and accept only good.

God Lives in Me and Enlarges My Life

This Life within me, being God, did not begin and It cannot end; hence, I am immortal and eternal. I can never be less, but must forever be more myself as this Life within me unfolds through my experience, through my gathering of knowledge and accumulation of wisdom. I recognize the omnipresent good. I acknowledge it. I prosper in all my affairs. Perfect success is mine.

All the mistakes I have ever made are wiped out, and today the business of living is the activity of God within me. Giving, I receive, and receiving, I give out again, thus increasing the Divine Bounty that meets me at every turn.

God within me creates every circumstance and situation I have ever experienced. They are the fruits of my thought. By my right thinking and right use of this law of liberty, I allow my imagination to enlarge my experience. The Life Principle within me responds with a greater abundance, harmony, and good flowing to me. Like a horizon where the earth and sky appear to meet, this apparent end continually opens up a wider expanse to me. This is my concept of God, the unlimited Creator of all experience. God lives in me and enlarges my life.

I Am One with All There Is

Truth, stated in the simplest manner, affirms that God is all there is. God never changes. God is in me. God is that which I am. God is in the universe. God is the universe. No mediator exists between myself and God but my own thought. I am the writer, the inspirer, and the thing written about. I am the creator of history and the One who experiences it. I am its record and its interpretation.

I Am is the thread of a unity running through all, binding all back to God. Because God is perfect Oneness, all of God exists everywhere. "Behold, I stand at the door and knock." This Divine Visitor, which is my true self, is both the one who stands at the door and knocks and the one who opens the door. It is the glory of this recognition that gives mastership.

There is but One Self, who needs no mediator. This Self is immediate, present, and available. Every cell of my body, every thought of my mind, every glory of my spirit dwells in the very center of the One. In the stillness of a new day, I know that I am one with all there is, now and always.

The Light of Spirit Shines Forth from Me

Today, I joyously proclaim a greater good. My thoughts are radiant with the Light of Spirit. There is no darkness in my mind. I am directed by the Spirit of Wisdom; I am guided into right action, into happiness and success, because the Light of Spirit shines from the very center of my being. This Light illuminates my path and makes straight the way before me. This Light is God, the living Spirit Almighty.

Gently I lay my burden and woes at the altar of my faith as I turn from the valley of my previous unhappiness. I make my ascent from appearance to Reality with a song on my lips and peace in my heart. The Light of Spirit shines forth from my soul. It is a beam of Eternal Radiance. In the Light there is no darkness. I close the door of my consciousness to everything that denies my good and affirm that all I need is at hand.

Today I accept a greater experience of Life's infinite bounty. Going within myself, I meet this Life and expect It to respond. I refuse to dwell in limitation. The Presence of the Spirit in me establishes in my life that which is good, beautiful, and true. All the Power there is flows through me as health, happiness, and success. The Light of Spirit shines forth from me.

Spirit Flows Through My Consciousness into Action

There is an eternal springtime in my soul. Always rising but never setting is the sun of my destiny. I refuse to worry about anything. I have complete confidence that the God who is always with me is able and willing to direct everything I do, to control my affairs, to lead me into the pathway of peace and happiness.

I release every sense of condemnation, either against myself or others. I loose every feeling of animosity. I now understand that there is a Principle and a Presence in every person gradually drawing that person into the Kingdom of Good. I know that the Kingdom of God is at hand, and I am resolved to enter it, to possess it, and to let it possess me.

I have a silent partner within me whose energy is inexhaustible and whose intelligence is without limit. It is Life Itself. I maintain close communion with my true Center, knowing that the Divine Spirit operates through me now. I know that I am not limited by anything that has happened or by anything that is now happening. I am entering into an entirely new set of conditions and circumstances. That which has no limit is flowing through my consciousness into action.

I Am on the Pathway of Endless Unfoldment

A universal and infinite Intelligence governs everything, holds everything in its place, and directs the course of everything. The Intelligence that governs the planets in their courses is the same Intelligence that is manifesting in me. The use I make of It to direct and govern my activities depends upon my personal choice.

Today I am governed by the Wisdom of God in everything I think, say, or do. Since there is nothing large or small to the Infinite, there is nothing in my experience beyond Its action. I affirm the presence of this Wisdom, accepting and acknowledging Its action in my every endeavor. I permit It to guide me in every circumstance. Today I free myself from all past mistakes and know that I shall receive full compensation for every right thought.

I now know how to plan my life and direct my path because God is doing this for me by doing it through me. There is no uncertainty or confusion. The Divine Spirit always knows what to do and how to do it, so I am never without guidance in the successful achievement of my good desires. My every thought, act, and purpose is guided by this Wisdom. I expect new and wonderful experiences to come to me. I live in complete confidence that I am on the pathway of endless unfoldment, walking in the Light of infinite Wisdom.

I Rejoice That My Spirit Is Free

I now allow the Living Presence of Spirit to flow through me in expanding circles of activity. Every past sense of limitation melts away and every good I have experienced is increased. Every joy that has come into my life is multiplied and there is a new influx of inspiration into my thought. I see more clearly than ever that my Divine birthright is freedom, joy, and good.

Spirit is not limited, so neither am I. I let go of all restricting ideas. Knowing that Life gives according to my faith, I lift my thought and elevate my faith. I accept the Divine Presence as now bountifully expressing peace and harmony in my life. Spirit will never fail me if I never fail to believe in Its goodness and Its responsiveness. Life becomes one grand song as I realize that since God is for me and within me, none can be against me. I will cease merely to exist; I will live.

In the awareness that God indwells my life, I know that my spirit is released from all lack and limitation. I understand and accept the truth about myself. My physical body and my objective affairs reflect the perfection that I feel, the wholeness of which I am certain, and the glorious freedom that rightfully belong to me. I rejoice that my spirit is forever free.

I Am Rich with the Richness of God

The Divine will never fail me so long as I have implicit faith in It. If I feel myself getting caught in fear and doubt, I take time to reaffirm my union with the great outflowing givingness of Life. I take time for prayer and meditation. In this way I am always receptive to the gift of abundance that God has already made.

Today I accept the gift of God's abundance. Everything that I am and that I have is increased by it. I identify everything I do with success. I think affirmatively and in all my prayers I accept abundance. Whatever I need, whenever I need it, wherever I need it, for as long as I need it, will always be at hand. I no longer see negation or delay or stagnation in my endeavors. The action of the living Spirit makes everything I do prosper, increases every good I possess, and brings success to me and everyone I meet.

Everything I think about and do is animated by the Divine Presence, sustained by the infinite Power, and multiplied by the Divine Goodness. "The world is mine, and the fulness thereof." Today I expect the more abundant life. I keep my thought open to new experiences and opportunities for greater expression. As I share and give of myself to life, the One Life pours its bounty upon me. As Life finds a fuller outlet through me, I discover a betterment in everything I do, a higher realization of the richness that is God.

I Am a Manifestation of Spirit

I commune with the invisible Presence within me until there comes a certainty that is beyond hope, something that enables me to see the future as clear-eyed as I see the past. I have the joy of knowing I will live forever. I am aware of the Divine within me. Peace, quiet, and confidence flow through my thought. I know that inspiration and guidance are mine. I permit myself to be moved upon by Divine Intelligence.

Laying aside every sense of burden or false responsibility, loosing all fear and uncertainty from my thought, I enter into my kingdom of good today. I know that this kingdom is accessible to all. I see through all apparent contradictions to the one Perfect Being in every person. I see through all confusion to the one Divine Presence at the center of everything. God's world is not a world of illusion, but of realities. All that exists is for the purpose of expressing Life. This includes everything—a tree, a rose, my own physical body.

Nothing can be excluded from this omnipresence. It was this Presence that Moses communed with through the burning bush, the Divine Flame that surrounded the bush with an aura of light and color. This flame of Divinity penetrates everything. God is ever flowing through me as perfect Life. I am a manifestation of the energy, the love, the peace, and the power of Spirit.

I Abide in the Realization of Divine Union

I always have been, and forever will remain, a complete and perfect expression of the Eternal Mind, which is God, the living Spirit Almighty. Today I enter into the limitless variations of self-expression that the Divine Spirit projects into my experience. Knowing that all experience is a play of Life upon itself, the blossoming of love into self-expression, the coming forth of good into the joy of its own being, I enter into life with joyful anticipation and with enthusiasm.

I know that God must be present in my every act, word, and thought. Therefore, I know that freedom and fulfillment are mine today, the freedom to think, to act, and to move in complete accord with the Divine Harmony. As I go forth into this new day, I rejoice in the good that comes to me and to all people.

Today I shake my thought clear from the belief that external conditions are imposed upon me. I declare the freedom of my Divine birthright, knowing that I possess the Kingdom of God in all its fullness. There is no bondage in God; therefore, there is no bondage in me. I have a great sense of joy in knowing this truth, since the burden of personal responsibility is lifted. Today I abide in the deep, calm realization of Divine Union.

I Accept the Fullness of Life

Today I cease weeping over the mistakes of yesterday and steadfastly behold the face of the great and divine Reality. I know that every negative condition of the past is swept aside. Yesterday is no longer here; tomorrow has not yet arrived. Today is God's day. Today is my day. Today, bright with hope and filled with promise, is mine. Today my heart is without fear. I have implicit confidence in the good, the enduring, and the true.

Today I keep my consciousness steadfast with the realization that there is a spiritual Power upon which I may rely. I turn resolutely to that Divine Source that knows no confusion, to that Spiritual Center that knows no fear. The Spirit is not afraid of anything; the Divine has no enemies; the Spirit knows no opposites. Consciously, I draw close to my Divine Center and feel the warmth of its presence.

I enter into a faith made perfect through love and confidence. Acknowledging good in all my ways, desiring only good for others, I rest in calm assurance. I open my consciousness to the realization that all the Power and Presence there is clothes me in Its eternal embrace, that the Spirit forever imparts Its Life to me. I believe in my destiny because I know that the Law of Good is operating through me. I have confidence in the future and enthusiastic expectation of good things to come. I accept the fullness of life this moment.

Today I Take Constructive Action

It is only as I let go of the lesser than I can take hold of the greater, only as I drop confusion that I can entertain peace, only as I transcend doubt and fear that I can be lifted up to the hilltops of the inner Life. I identify myself with the greatness of Spirit and breathe in Its Almighty Power. I allow my consciousness to rise to a broader and fuller realization of that Divine Presence that is always delivering Itself to me.

Believing that the Divine Mind is ever present, that Divine Intelligence is ever available, I open my consciousness to Its guidance. I keep my mind steadfast and loyal to the thought that I am governed by this Divine Intelligence. I feel that I am impelled to make right decisions, that I am compelled to act upon these decisions intelligently, knowing that the Power that is within me cannot desert me.

Through the quiet contemplation of the omni-action of Spirit, I look quietly and calmly upon every false condition, seeing through it to the other side of the invisible Reality that molds, conditions, and re-creates all of my affairs after a Divine pattern. With a penetrating spiritual vision I now dissipate the obstruction, remove the obstacle, dissolve the wrong condition. Every thought of fear or limitation is removed from my consciousness. Today I take constructive action, which leads me to health, happiness, and success.

I Have Limitless Faith

My knowledge that the great I Am is ever available gives me an increasing capacity to draw upon It and to become inwardly aware of the presence of Spirit. There is something at the center of my being that is absolutely certain of itself. It gives me complete assurance that all is well. I Am a Divine Being here and now. I know that in this consciousness of Reality is the supply for my every need—physical, mental, or spiritual—and I accept that supply in deepest gratitude.

I am thankful that this is the way Life fulfills my needs, through the doorway of my inner self, and I am thankful that I know how to use this perfect Law. I come to this great Fountain of supply, in the very center of my being, to absorb that for which I have need, mentally and physically, and I am filled with the sense of the Reality of that which I desire.

I know that Good is at the root of everything, regardless of its seeming absence. Since there is but one Spirit and this Spirit is in me and in everything, then everywhere I go I meet this Spirit. I meet It in all people, in all places, and in all things. There is a Divine Essence permeating everything, flowing through everything, becoming all things. I have limitless faith in this unconquerable Presence.

I Feast on the Idea of Abundance

The One Spirit manifests itself in and through all, including me. I accept with positive certainty that the Spirit within me goes before me and prepares my way, making perfect, plain, straight, easy, and happy the pathway of my experience. There is nothing in me that can obstruct the Divine circuits of Life, of Love, of Beauty and Truth. My word dissolves every negative thought or impulse that would throw a shadow of unbelief across the threshold of my expectation.

Today I have faith that my word shall not return unto me void. I surrender myself completely to this faith. My prayer, then, is one of affirmation and acceptance. I lift my cup of acceptance, knowing that the Divine outpouring will fill it to the brim. I identify myself with abundance and success. I identify myself with the Living Spirit—with all the Power, all the Presence, and all the Life there is.

Realizing that all action starts in and is a result of consciousness, I prepare my mind to receive the best that life has to offer. I see through all physical and mental obstructions to the one perfect Presence within me. I see through all apparent contradictions to the one perfect Being in every person. I see through all confusion to the one Divine Presence at the center of everything. I fast from all ideas of lack and feast on the idea of abundance.

I Rejoice in the Good of All

There is a Divine awareness within me that leads me upward and onward. I prepare myself for this ascent, filling my mental life with spiritual realization. My bread is manna from heaven, my meat the living word, my fruit the inspiration of hope, my wine the essence of joy. Laying aside all fear and uncertainty, I enter into my Good today.

Aware of my unity with Life, I loose all thoughts of discord and lack. I permit the true pattern of Wholeness to come to the surface. Tending only those thoughts of my Good with the fire of imagination and feeling, I refuse to think about anything unlike Wholeness. Knowing that Life gives according to my faith, I lift my mind, I elevate my faith, and I listen deeply to the song of my being.

Every good I have experienced is now increased. Every joy that has come into my life is now multiplied. There is a new influx of inspiration into my thought. I see more clearly than ever before that my divine birthright is freedom, joy, and eternal goodness. I realize that this same birthright is bequeathed to all people. The Divine Presence interprets Itself to all people through love and friendship, peace and harmony, joy and freedom. I rejoice in the good of all.

I Am Held in the Goodness of God

I know that there is no influence, either visible or invisible, other than the influence of pure Spirit, acting perfectly upon all people. I know that there is no presence but Love, and no power but the Creative Spirit, which has neither enemy nor opposite. Goodness, joy, and peace abide with me today.

I believe that every affirmation I make will immediately take effect in my life. I fill every statement with joy; therefore, I expect joyful happenings. I fill every statement with love; therefore, I anticipate love in all relationships. I fill every statement with kindness, with tolerance, and with divine understanding; therefore, I expect all of my relationships to be harmonious.

I believe with a deep, inward calm that my word of faith is the execution of spiritual Law in my life. I know that my word penetrates any and every unbelief in my thought; it casts out fear, removes doubts, and permits that which is enduring, perfect, and true to enter into my consciousness. I have complete conviction that my thoughts will be carried out in my experience with certainty. I have absolute reliance upon the Law of Good. I know that It will bring everything desirable into my experience. Today I proclaim my divine inheritance. I am rich with the richness of God. I am strong with the power of God. I am guided by the wisdom of God. I am held in the goodness of God, today.

My Faith Causes the Unseen to Become Visible

I know that the Spirit, which is Life, is present everywhere. Like the air I breathe, It presses against me, on the mountaintop, in the valley, in the desert, and on the ocean, It is ever present. There is peace at the center of my being, a peace that can be felt throughout the day and in the cool of the evening. I dwell on the unity that underlies everything.

As I consciously poise myself in the realization that I live in pure Spirit, new power is born within me. I find myself renewed by the Divine Life, led by Divine Intelligence, and guarded by Divine Love. I focus my inward vision on this indwelling Harmony, knowing that as I contemplate Its perfection I will see It manifest in everything I do. Realizing that the Spirit within me is God, the Living Spirit Almighty, I open my thought to Its influx. I open my consciousness to Its outpouring.

I know and understand that Good alone is real. I know that silently I am drawing into my experience today, and every day, an ever-increasing measure of truth and beauty, of goodness and harmony. Everything I do, say, and think is quickened into right and productive action. My faith causes that which was unseen to become visible.

I Realize the Presence of God

Expectancy speeds progress. Therefore, I live in a continual state of expectancy. No matter how much I am experiencing today, I expect greater good tomorrow. I expect to meet new friends. I expect to meet new and wonderful experiences. I know that when I live in harmony with the Divine Presence in and around me, I will be protected by Its power. No harm can come to me when I know that God is at the center of everything.

There is an inexhaustible reservoir of life, of imagination, energy, and will flowing through me into action. Divine Power exists everywhere and takes form for me through my ideas, my faith. Today and every day I expect good. I anticipate meeting new friends. I joyously anticipate contacting new situations that will increase my livingness. My life is an adventure. I know that wonderful things are going to happen to me. I know that everything I do will turn into good for me and for others.

Something within me today sings aloud as I marvel at the limitless opportunities for my self-expression. My Real Self is God, the eternal, perfect Self, the One undivided Self. There could not be a greater wholeness or a more complete oneness. It would be impossible for me to have any more faith than I now possess. I realize the perfect Presence of God in me.

My Soul Is at Peace

When a problem confronts me, I take it into the silence of my consciousness. Instead of thinking of the problem, I think of the answer. The Divine Presence guides, guards, and protects me. It counsels me with wisdom. It sustains and upholds me in everything I do. Having recognized the Divine Presence as my guiding star of hope, assurance, and certainty, I also recognize the Universal Law of Mind as my servant. My faith in this Law causes It to act upon my faith, bringing into my experience those things I accept.

I know that today I am free and unhindered. I feel the operation of Divine Love and Universal Law in my affairs. I know that everything I do is governed by Love and controlled through Law. I am conscious that I am one with all people. In complete reliance upon the Divine and with absolute faith in the goodness of God, I lay aside everything within me that contradicts the Divine and know that today peace, fulfillment, and happiness are mine. My soul is at peace, rejoicing in the eternal movement of Mind, of Spirit, and of God in all my affairs.

I Am Conscious of All-Good in Me

I hold conscious communion with Spirit. In a handclasp I can feel Its warmth. In the exchange of thought I feel the Presence of the Divine. I sense It in everything. It flows in transcendent loveliness into my world of thought and form, ever renewing, vitalizing, bringing joy, harmony, and blessings to everything and everyone It touches. I am united with all. I am one with the eternal Light Itself.

The Presence of Spirit within me blesses everyone I meet, heals everything It touches, brings gladness into the life of everyone I contact. I recognize all sources as Divine. Therefore, I am a blessing to myself, to humankind, and to the day in which I live.

Today I uncover the perfection within me. I look out upon the world of my affairs, knowing that the Spirit within me makes my way both immediate and easy. I know there is nothing in me that could possibly obstruct or withhold the divine circuit of Life and Love. God flows through me to all. Good harmonizes my mind, so that Love sings joyously in my heart. I am completely conscious of All-Good in me, around me, and in all that is.

I Am Renewed Daily

I am an individualized center in the Consciousness of God. I am an individualized activity in the Action of God. I am eternal. Therefore, I do not have to wait for immortality. The resurrection of life is today. Living today as though I were an immortal being, I allow all thought of death, all fear of change to slip from me. I step out of the tomb of uncertainty and into the light of eternal day. The nighttime of my soul has passed and the eternal light of everlasting day dawns as the great Reality in my life. Joyfully I am resurrected into that which is beautiful, enduring, and true. Silently I pass from less to more, from isolation into inclusion, from separation into oneness.

Today, realizing that there is nothing in my past that can rise against me, nothing in my future that can menace the unfoldment of my experience, I declare that life will be an eternal adventure of greater and better experiences. I revel in the contemplation of the immeasurable future, the path of eternal progress, the everlastingness of my own being. I am renewed daily by that Divinity within me that has forever set the stamp of individualized Being on my mind.

I Glorify in the Power of the Word

I have faith in the invisible because everything that is visible proclaims the invisible source of its being. I feel as though all things, even though they are temporary, are rooted in a changeless Reality. Today I enter into this divine play of Life upon Itself. Today I attend and witness the eternal birth of divine ideas. I recognize these ideas as supplying me with everything I need.

Today I have implicit faith that Substance is taking form in my affairs. This Substance takes the form of joy, friendship, and love. It takes the form of abundance and of perfect physical conditions. Everything is increased and multiplied, and the good that goes from me also is increased and multiplied. I believe in the power of my own word because I understand that it is not I but "the Father that dwelleth in me" that does the work.

I know that I individualize the Power of God. Through my spoken word, I exercise dominion over everything that comes into my experience. I do this without any sense of strain or compulsion, but rather with a joyous sense, a sense of the one who beholds that the works of God must be altogether good and perfect. I use my word and glorify in its power.

I Enter the Port of Attainment

I enter into my Divine Inheritance and know that all that my inward vision perceives will be mine. Like Moses, I stand on the mountaintop of spiritual perception. Now, free from all obstruction, the vista is perfect, the vision is sublime. There are no clouds in the sky. I look out across innumerable other mountain peaks and in each I recognize another Divine subject of the Heavenly Presence. The gates of my soul are lifted up and a flood tide of intuition flows through.

Confronted with discord, I will see harmony. Confronted with unhappiness, I will unmask it also by seeing through this false face to the true countenance of joy. It is written that "joy comes with the morning," and I know this morning is eternal. Confronted with a sense of lack, I will unmask this false sense and reveal the divine Horn of Plenty. I will lift up my bowl of acceptance that it may be filled with the divine gifts.

I embark upon the sea of today's experience, knowing that the heavenly Pilot is at the helm. I seek the bold adventure of discovering new lands, realizing that there is a place within me where thought springs spontaneous from the Infinite and where the idea and the thing merge into one. I permit the inspiration of the divine creative Genius of the universe to impart new ideas, to create new scenes, to enlarge all my horizons. I feel that the ocean beneath me is teeming with life, that the air is vibrant with invisible forces. My boat rides safe and sure, and even now I am entering the Port of Attainment.

Today I Rejoice in All Nature

Since happiness is the reason for my being, and since the Kingdom of Heaven is a joyous state of consciousness, and since the Kingdom of Heaven is here and now, today I consciously open my whole thought to the influx of the Divine Harmony. Today I realize that I am not a stranger on the shores of time, but am an honored guest in the Kingdom of Good.

Today I enter with joy into my kingdom, into the warmth and color of living. Today I enter into the peace and the calm and the poise that belong to the Kingdom of Good, to the Kingdom of Fulfillment, which is the Kingdom of God. Today I say to myself, "Behold, the Kingdom of God is at hand." This kingdom is my kingdom. My kingdom is here and now. My Host sits beside me, walks with me, gives me wise counsel. My Host advises and gently leads me down the corridors of time 'till all shadows are cast behind, and the golden rays of peace flood my whole being with eternal light.

Today, I will recognize the Divine in everything. I will realize that the ground upon which my feet tread is holy. The voice of Truth will rise from every form in nature, proclaiming the holiness, the wholeness of all that is. The sun will represent the warmth and color of the Infinite. Not only will the morning stars sing together, but I will chant my hymn of praise and with them I will rejoice in all nature.

NOVEMBER
GRATITUDE

An attitude of gratitude is most salutary, and bespeaks the realization that we are now in heaven. —ERNEST HOLMES

There is something in this attitude of thanksgiving that carries us beyond the field of doubt into one of perfect faith and acceptance, receptivity . . . realization. —ERNEST HOLMES

I awoke this morning with devout thanksgiving for my friends, the old and the new. Shall I not call God, the Beautiful, who daily showeth himself so to me in his gifts. —RALPH WALDO EMERSON

All of creation is a song of praise to God. —HILDEGARD OF BINGEN

If the only prayer you say in your entire life is "Thank You," that would suffice. —MEISTER ECKHART

Thanksgiving

O Lord, thou art my God; I will exalt thee, I will praise thy name;
thy kingdom is an everlasting kingdom . . . .
Hallowed be thy name. —ISAIAH 25:1

The attitudes of praise and thanksgiving are salutary. They not only lighten the consciousness, lifting it out of sadness and depression, they elevate consciousness to a point of acceptance. Praise and thanksgiving are really attitudes of recognition. They are affirmations of the Divine Presence, the Divine abundance, and the Divine givingness. It is only when we live affirmatively that we are happy. It is only when we recognize that the universe is built on affirmation that we can become happy.

Today, through praise and thanksgiving, I recognize the Divine Presence in everything. In the midst of darkness I will sing a song to the dawn, for I know that the Eternal Light dissipates all darkness. Today I will recognize the beautiful and the perfect in everything. I will call it forth with praise and thanksgiving, blessing the spiritual Reality back of all things.

Gratitude is one of the chief graces of human existence and is crowned in heaven with a consciousness of unity. —*THE SCIENCE OF MIND*, P. 497

2

Divinity

We all, with open face beholding as in a glass the glory of the Lord,
are changed into the same image from glory to glory . . .
by the Spirit of the Lord. —II CORINTHIANS 3:18

Beholding the image of Perfection in everything, to dominion we add glory.
This refers to the continual progression of the Soul. Since God is infinite,
our expansion is progressive and eternal. No matter how much good we experience today, the Infinite has more in store for us tomorrow. We should
joyfully look forward to this expansion with enthusiastic anticipation. The
march of life is not a funeral dirge, but a song of triumph.

The good that I experienced yesterday is going to be multiplied today. I
cast this good upon every wind of heaven, knowing that it goes out to bless.
I condition my mind to accept greater good for myself and for others. I wait
calmly, but with joy, for new experiences to come to me, for new opportunities for service. I expect my mind to be flooded with new ideas. I know that
the Spirit of the Lord is with me and that the glory of the Lord is around me.

There is that within every individual that partakes of the
nature of the Universal Wholeness and—in so far as it
operates—is God. —THE SCIENCE OF MIND, PP. 33–34

Humanity

Have we not all one Father?
Hath not one God created us? —MALACHI 2:10

Arthur Compton, in *The Freedom of Man,* tells us that science has discovered nothing that contradicts the idea of a Universal Mind, or Spirit, of which all people are offspring or emanations. It would be impossible to converse with each other unless there were a common medium or, as Emerson said, "one mind common to all people." It is impossible to depart from this Divine Presence, to be separated from this heavenly Father, which is the Parent Mind. Since God is everywhere, wherever we are, God is.

Today I know that there is one Spirit in every person I meet. Realizing that there is one Heavenly Father, I know that there is common bond among all humanity. There are no aliens, no strangers. The Divine Image in me cannot be separated from the Divine Image in others. I see God in everyone I meet, and the Spirit that is within me responds to the Spirit within them, for we have one Source.

The only way to know God is to be like God; and while this may seem discouraging in our present state of evolution, we should remember that we have but started on an eternal ladder that ever spirals upward. —*THE SCIENCE OF MIND,* P. 443

Peace

Peace be both to thee, and peace be to thine house,
and peace be unto all that thou hast. —I SAMUEL 25:6

Phillips Brooks said that "peace is the entire harmony between the nature of anything and its circumference." House is a symbol of the physical body and of "that house not made with hands eternal in the heavens." House is a symbol of any of the "vehicles, bodies, or habitations of the soul" on any or all planes. The Bible speaks of the House of Bondage and the House of Freedom. Symbolically, it tells us that we must come "out of the land of Egypt, out of the house of bondage," that we must be led by the Divine Spirit into that true home, which is heaven. Jesus said that "in my Father's house are many mansions."

Today I permit my mental house to be at peace. I know that my true home is heaven and that the Kingdom of Heaven is at hand. Today I enter into this permanent home. I consciously move in and make my dwelling place in this House of Peace and Gladness.

We cannot be in peace until we know that the Spirit is the only cause,
medium, and effect in our lives. There is no past, present,
and future to It. —THE SCIENCE OF MIND, P. 264

Right Action

Ye shall know the truth, and the truth shall make you free. —JOHN 8:32

Jesus implies that there is a truth, which known, automatically will demonstrate itself in our experience. What could this truth be other than a consciousness of our union with life? It is wonderful to contemplate this spiritual and exalted idea of truth—that truth which frees us from the tyranny of fear and the thraldom of fate.

It is neither in our stars nor in our environment that we should look to discover this pattern of truth. The truth that Jesus proclaimed would make us free lies only in the conscious communion of the soul with its Source, the conscious union of each individual with God, the conscious union of the heart's desire with the Source of its Being.

Today I commune with the spiritual truth in everything. Today I know that the truth makes me free from fear, doubt, or uncertainty. Today there is a song in my heart, as I gladly proclaim that truth which is the revelation of Divinity through humanity.

In mental work, we must realize that there is One Infinite Mind, which is consciously directing our destiny. —*THE SCIENCE OF MIND, P. 290*

Protection

He that dwelleth in the secret place of the Most High
shall abide under the shadow of the Almighty. —PSALM 91:1

This is a song of hope, a psalm of praise, the acknowledgment of an over-shadowing Presence—the Most High Good, to which Jesus gave the name "Our Father which art in heaven." We have a right to know that, in so far as we live in accord with the Divine, we are protected by Its omnipotent Law. "His truth shall be thy shield and buckler." The knowledge of truth will ward off the darts of evil, for evil is as night before the onrushing day; it is as darkness dissipated by the rising sun; it is as a fire extinguished by the waters of Spirit.

Today I put on the whole armor of faith. I place before me the shield of Divine Wisdom. I surround myself with the conscious knowledge of the overshadowing Presence. Therefore, I fear no evil, for thou art with me.

We are to demonstrate that spiritual thought force has power
over all apparent material resistance, and this cannot be done
unless we have abounding confidence in the
Principle that we approach. —THE SCIENCE OF MIND, P. 159

Forgiveness

I have blotted out, as a thick cloud, thy transgressions. . . .
For, behold, I create new heavens and a new earth: and the former
shall not be remembered, nor come into mind. —ISAIAH 44:22

Whatever the mistakes of yesterday may have been, today is a new creation.
Turning from the errors of the past, and no longer carrying with us the sorrows and mistakes of yesterday, today we may enter into a new experience.
But it is only when we forgive everyone that we may feel certain that the
weight of condemnation is lifted from our own consciousness. We should
refuse to carry the negations of yesterday into the positive atmosphere of today, for today the world is made new in our experience.

Today I loose all condemnation. I judge not, and I am judged only by
the Law of Good. There is no animosity, no criticism, no hatred. I shall behold the face of love, of beauty, and of peace in everyone I meet. I know that
every right motive has the blessing of the Spirit and that there is nothing
that opposes this blessing or denies this Divine givingness.

The mind that condemns, understands not the truth of being, and the
heart that would shut the door of its bosom to one who is mistaken,
strangles its own life. —*THE SCIENCE OF MIND*, PP. 457–58

Attraction

What things soever ye desire, when ye pray, believe that
ye receive them, and ye shall have them. —MARK 11:24

How simply Jesus tells us that whatever we need we shall receive, if we believe that we have it! Is it so hard, then, for us to believe that the divine gift
is forever made? Prayer is a sincere desire of the intellect to enter into conscious union with the Divine Presence and to receive direct from It every
good thing that makes life worthwhile.

My prayer today is one of affirmation. It incorporates a complete acceptance of the Divine beneficence and the eternal givingness of the Spirit.
Today I lift high my cup of acceptance, knowing that the universal Horn of
Plenty fills it to overflowing. This shall include everything I need, whether
it be health, happiness, or wisdom. Today my mind is open and my consciousness receives the Kingdom into itself.

Every business, every place, every person, every thing has a certain
mental atmosphere of its own. This atmosphere decides
what is to be drawn to it. —THE SCIENCE OF MIND, P. 296

Love

There is no fear in love; but perfect love casteth out fear . . .
[for] God is love. —I JOHN 4:18, 16

There is no fear in love, and there is no liberation from fear without love. Fear is always based on the supposition that we are unprotected, rejected, friendless. If the fearful mind would entertain love, and the harmony and peace that go with it, it must turn from everything that denies this love and, trusting in Divine Guidance, open its being to the influx of love—not just love of God, but love of everything, for love is an all-inclusive conception.

"I will fear no evil for thou art with me." Today Divine love and infinite tenderness sustain me. In order that I shall not separate myself from this love, I endeavor to see it reflected in everyone and everything. I shall permit only that which is loving, kind, and true to find entrance to or to exit from my consciousness. Thus shall I be assured that I am bathed in the warm glow of that Love that casteth out all fear.

Love is the self-givingness of the Spirit through the desire of Life
to express Itself in terms of creation. —*THE SCIENCE OF MIND*, P. 608

Mind

Let this mind be in you, which was also in Christ Jesus. —PHILIPPIANS 2:5

This scriptural passage means that we should recognize the Divine Incarnation, universal in essence, but individualized in personal experience. The spiritual genius of Jesus enabled him to see that each is a unique representation, an individualized expression of One Mind. The Mind of God in us is the Mind of Christ. At the center of every man's being the Eternal Christ waits, knocking at the door of his intellect for admission. This is not a faraway Presence, nor a future advent. The recognition of Christ can come to anyone at any time, and under any circumstance. The consciousness that walked over the troubled waters of human experience, the inner calm that stilled the tempest, is accessible to everyone.

I know that the Christ in me is always triumphant. I know that Christ in me is one with God; there is no separation, no isolation, no aloneness. There is a Divine Companion who walks with me and in whose Light I see the Light.

Mind is potential energy, while thought is the dynamic force that produces the activity for manifestation. —*THE SCIENCE OF MIND*, P. 612

Spirit

Now there are diversities of gifts, but the same Spirit. . . .
It is the Spirit that quickeneth. —I CORINTHIANS 12:4 AND JOHN 6:63

Out of unity comes variety. All things are made from one formless Substance. The invisible essence of everything is pure Spirit. It is a realization of this Spirit at the center of everything that enables us to see God in everyone. "It is the Spirit that quickeneth." When we recognize the Spirit in anything or anyone, there is an equal reaction from the Spirit back to us, and we are made more alive through the divine influx that follows our recognition.

Today I am resolved to see the Spirit in everything; therefore, today I know that my own spirit is quickened. I know that there is an inner Presence in everything I will contact and that will respond to me. I know that everything is alive, awake, and aware with this Presence; that in all the changing scenes of my experience I will be contacting this one Presence. Therefore, I go forth to meet the Divine, to enjoy His bounty, and consciously live in His house forevermore.

Spirit is the active and Self-Conscious Principle. Spirit is
First Cause or God—the Absolute Essence of all that is.
It is the Great or Universal I Am. —*THE SCIENCE OF MIND*, P. 81

Body

Know ye not that your body is the temple of the Holy Ghost
which is in you? —I CORINTHIANS 6:19

Emerson said that "God builds His temple in the heart," and Seneca said that "God is to be consecrated in the breast of each." St. Augustine said that "the pure mind is a holy temple for God." To realize that God is in us, with us, and for us, is the first step toward understanding that we are the temple of the Holy Ghost. Bishop Wilberforce tells us that "the conscious mind . . . is the temple of the Christ Mind." We must so control the conscious mind that the Christ Mind may function through it. We must permit the Spirit to control the intellect.

Today I realize that my body is the temple of God, that there is the divine pattern of perfection at the center of my being. I will not think of my physical body as being separated from this spiritual Presence. The Presence is the Cause, the body is the effect, and the two are one. Therefore, I, too, will exclaim: "In my flesh shall I see God."

The Universe has been called the Great Trinity, or Triune Unity
of Spirit, Soul, and Body—the Body being the result, the effect,
the objectification of Spirit. —*THE SCIENCE OF MIND*, P. 98

Communion

His delight is in the law of the Lord; and in his law
doth he meditate day and night. —PSALM 1:2

There is always a silent communion going on between the individual soul and the invisible Presence. This communion should become a conscious union of the self with the Over-self, of the mind with the Spirit, of the personal with the Impersonal.

As the artist communes with the essence of beauty, and gives birth to form through this communion, so our minds should commune with the Presence of God. This communion should arise from an awareness of the Divine Presence.

Today I commune with the Spirit. In nature I see the Spirit manifest, and in everyone I meet I shall commune with the living Christ, the Divine Presence in him, sensing its perfection, realizing its beauty, and being consciously aware of its love. Today I hold silent communion with that invisible Presence that peoples the world with the manifestation of Its life, Its light, and Its love.

The greater the consciousness of God, the more complete must be the realization of the True Self—the Divine Reality. —*THE SCIENCE OF MIND*, P. 343

Christ

*Till we all come in the unity of the faith, and of the knowledge
of the Sons of God, unto a perfect man, unto the measure
of the stature of the fullness of Christ.* —EPHESIANS 4:13

The Bible tells us the real self of each of us is Christ. This Christ is the perfect, invisible Presence back of, in, and through every living soul. Just as there is but one God, or First Cause, so there is but one Person, the manifestion of the Divine Spirit, in and through all people. Throughout the ages this Christ has come with some degree of clarity to those who have meditated long and earnestly upon the nature of the Divinity that is in everything.

Today I permit Christ to be born in my consciousness. Today I realize that Christ is the universal Person, appearing through every deed of goodness, truth, or love. As I unveil the Christ in my own nature, I know that the countenance of the same Christ will be revealed to me through others. I enter into my Divine inheritance through the recognition of my union with the supreme Spirit.

*We must understand the Christ is not a person, but a principle. . . .
As the human gives way to the Divine in all people,
they become the Christ.* —THE SCIENCE OF MIND, P. 359

Understanding

Wisdom is the principal thing; therefore get wisdom:
and with all thy getting get understanding. —PROVERBS 4:7

As all scriptures tell us, true understanding comes from a spiritual perception of the Divine Unity back of all things. Knowledge is of the intellect; wisdom and understanding are of the heart. Those who have had true spiritual understanding have always taught us of the unity of good, that we are one in essence with the Spirit. They have told us that the unreal never has been, that the Real never has ceased to be.

Today I permit my spiritual understanding to penetrate everything that seems opposed to good. Back of all variety, I perceive the One Cause, the One Presence, and the One Purpose. Today I consciously align myself with this Divine Presence that runs through everything. I open the gates of my consciousness and with enthusiasm, through recognition and acknowledgment, permit the Spirit of Wholeness, the Spirit of Oneness, to flow through me. I know there is One God, one Spiritual Self, one perfect Law, and one eternal Life.

We should expand our thought until it realizes all good, and then cut
right through all that appears to be and use this Almighty Power
for definite purposes. —*THE SCIENCE OF MIND*, P. 148

Abundance

Commit thy way unto the Lord; trust also in him;
and he shall bring it to pass. —PSALM 37:5

It is written that the Law of the Lord is perfect; therefore, when we commit our ways unto the Lord, we are automatically using this perfect Law, even in the most trivial things of life. To this Law, there is neither great nor small. It is always responding to us by corresponding with our mental attitude toward It. Our mental attitudes can be consciously controlled; therefore, we can always make conscious use of the Law of Good.

Today I have faith in the Law of Good. Today I guard my thinking, consciously endeavoring to think affirmatively and with faith. I believe that the Law of the Lord will bring every good and perfect thing to me and will bless everyone whom I hold in consciousness. Knowing that the Law of Good operates through my word, I speak this word with implicit confidence, with complete acceptance, and with absolute abandonment to good.

Such is the power of right thinking that it cancels and erases everything
unlike itself. It answers every question, solves all problems,
is the solution to every difficulty. —THE SCIENCE OF MIND, P. 188

Sympathy

My little children, let us not love in word, neither in tongue;
but in deed and in truth. —I JOHN 3:18

Humanity and Divinity will be identical when we recognize Divinity in humanity. We must learn to see through the apparent, to not judge according to appearances, and to realize that at the center of every person's soul God is enthroned. Sympathy and compassion are the ties that bind us together in mutual understanding and in the unified attempt to uncover the Divinity in each other. Sympathy is the most gentle of all human virtues, for it is the outpouring of the Divine givingness through humanity.

Today I extend the hand of sympathy to everyone I meet. I permit my inward vision to penetrate every apparent obstruction, every obstinate attempt to cover up the Divine, every ignorant misuse of the Law of Good. I withdraw the veil that hides my real self, and in so doing unveil the Reality in others. Today I love as never before. I draw close to the Spirit in everything and in everyone.

Whatever is true of the Universe as a Whole must also be true of the
individual as some part of this Whole. —*THE SCIENCE OF MIND*, P. 106

Faith

Now faith is the substance of things hoped for,
the evidence of things not seen. —HEBREWS 11:1

Faith is more than objective statement. We do not have perfect faith while any subjective contradictions deny the affirmations of our lips. This is why the Bible tells us that we must know in our heart. Heart symbolizes the innermost center of the being.

When the intellect is no longer contradicted by our emotional reactions, by unconscious doubts and fears, then the word of our mouth will immediately bear fruit.

Today I have faith that my word shall not return unto me void. Today I surrender myself completely to this faith, for I know that there is a creative Spirit that gives substance to this faith and that will provide the evidence of this substance in actual fact. I expect, then, to meet my good, and I rejoice in the anticipation of this good. I know that my faith operates through an immutable Law and that there is no possibility whatsoever of its failing.

It is this science of faith we are seeking to uncover—a definite technique
that will conduct our minds through a process of thought, if necessary,
to that place that the sublime minds of all ages have reached
by direct intuition. —THE SCIENCE OF MIND, P. 160

Divine Guidance

Be strong and of a good courage . . . for the Lord thy God,
he it is that doth go with thee; he will not fail thee,
nor forsake thee. —DEUTERONOMY 31:6

We all wish to know that the Divine Presence goes before us, and we all
have a right to feel this assurance. Every person is a unique presentation of
the Divine Mind, a separate, without being a separated, entity in the universal Spirit. Every person is, as Emerson said, "dear to the heart of God."
We should all develop an increasing consciousness that we are protected
and guided in everything we do, say, or think.

Today I know that the Spirit goes before me, making plain my way. I feel
that everything I do shall be prospered, and I fully accept that I am in partnership with the Infinite. It is my desire that only good will go from me:
therefore, I have a right to expect that only good will return to me. I live under the government of Good and am guided by the Spirit of God. This I affirm; this I accept.

The practice of the Science of Mind calls for a positive understanding
of the Spirit of Truth; a willingness to let this inner Spirit guide us,
with the perfect knowledge that "The law of the Lord
is perfect." —THE SCIENCE OF MIND, P. 54

Success

They that seek the Lord shall not want any good thing. —PSALM 34:10

Success does not mean the accumulation of wealth, the maintenance of position, or a supremacy of power. Success means a life free from the burden of anxiety, liberated from fear. There is no successful life without peace or without that inner spiritual certainty that knows that the soul is on the pathway of good, forever expanding into the conscious union of God with humanity.

Today I expect every good thing to come to me. Everything that is worthy of the soul, I anticipate. Everything that belongs to the Spirit, I accept. Everything that partakes of the nature of the Divine Reality, I claim as my own. Today I identify myself with abundance and success. I know that my destiny is divine, that my destination is certain, that the Kingdom of Heaven is at hand. I know that this Kingdom contains everything necessary to my well-being. In gratitude and with joy, I receive this Kingdom into myself.

Only remember we are surrounded by a Universal Subjectivity . . . that is receptive, neutral, impersonal, always receiving the impress of our thought and that has no alternative other than to operate directly upon it, thus creating the things that we think. —THE SCIENCE OF MIND, P. 278

Identity

> Be ye therefore perfect, even as your Father
> which is in heaven is perfect. —MATTHEW 5:48

There is a pattern of perfection at the center of everything. This, the saints and sages of the ages have told us. There is, as the Platonists taught, a prototype of perfection at the center of every form. It is this spiritual prototype with which the mind should identify itself, for this is the Father in heaven within us. Nothing has ever violated the integrity of this inner kingdom. It exists forever in the bosom of God, and we are in God, even as God is in us.

Today I consciously identify myself with the Supreme Presence that inhabits eternity and finds a dwelling place at the center of my soul. By some deep inner spiritual realization, I penetrate the mask of separation and discover the unity of all life. I identify myself with this unity, finding Christ within and knowing that "Christ is God's." I recognize my union with all the Power, all the Presence, and all the Life that there is.

> Healing is not creating a perfect idea or a perfect body; it is revealing
> an idea that is already perfect. —*THE SCIENCE OF MIND,* P. 212

Joy

Sorrow is turned into joy before him. . . . Thou hast put gladness in my heart. . . . Thou hast turned for me my mourning into dancing; thou hast put off my sackcloth, and girded me with gladness. —JOB 41:22; PSALMS 4:7, 30:11

We cannot conceive of the Spirit as being sad or depressed. There is ever a song at the center of everything. This song is reflected in all nature, turning "mourning into dancing." To put off sackcloth means the turning of the personality to a complete reliance upon the Divine. To be girded with gladness means to cover ourselves with the threefold nature of good. This is a symbol of Divine protection. Turning the mind to God and recognizing the omnipresence of Love causes us to rejoice, as we recognize that in pure Spirit we live, move, and have our being.

Today I deliberately turn from everything that depresses and sing a song of praise, of gratitude, and of joy. I am going forth to meet joy, singing the song of the triumph of Spirit over all apparent negation.

We are to rejoice evermore. There is no sadness in the Spirit. It is happy and free, for It knows neither depression nor confusion, and we belong to It, are in and of It. —*THE SCIENCE OF MIND*, P. 496

Receiving

Ask, and it shall be given you; seek, and ye shall find;
knock, and it shall be opened unto you. —MATTHEW 7:7

How can we receive that which the mind refuses to entertain? Should we
not, then, consciously develop the ability to receive more? We make life little and mean, and limit our own possibilities when we refuse to accept the
whole gift of God. We should open our consciousness to a receptivity of the
Divine. There will never be any point of saturation, because God is infinite.
We cannot contract the Infinite, but we can expand the finite.

Today I ask and know that I shall receive. Today I seek and know that I
shall find. Today I knock and know that it shall be opened unto me. But
what is it that I ask for? What is it that I really seek? It is to discover God in
everything, to see the Divine manifest in everyone, to come into close and
conscious communion with Life. Today, then, I receive the gift of God in its
fullness, unstinted, complete.

As God cares for the birds, who do not gather into barns, so shall we
be cared for if we trust and do not doubt. —THE SCIENCE OF MIND, P. 432

Intuition

Before they call I will answer; and while they are yet
speaking I will hear. —ISAIAH 65:24

Dr. Alexis Carrel tells us that intuition is not a product of the intellect, nor
is it something that is developed in the process of our evolution. It is, then,
a thing in itself. That which is instinct in the animal, blindly, unerringly
leading it to food, water, and shelter, becomes intuition in man, consciously
perceived. Instinct is intuition acting unconsciously; intuition is instinct el-
evated to the point of self-awareness. They are identical. Intuition is Omniscience acting omnipresently; therefore, whether or not we believe it, it is
ever present with us.

Today I know that intuition, which is the presence of the Divine Mind
in me, will guide me aright. It will set me on the path of right action. It will
direct my footsteps. It will counsel my mind. Today I am aware that there is
a light that dispels ignorance, fear, superstition, and doubt, and sets me,
safe and sane, on the pathway of Truth.

The mind that we discover within us is the Mind that
governs everything. —THE SCIENCE OF MIND, P. 34

25

Power

> So God created man in his own image. . . . And God blessed them and God said unto them . . . replenish the earth, and subdue it; and have dominion over the fish of the sea, and over the fowl of the air, and over every living thing that moveth upon the earth. —GENESIS 1:27–28

It is because the Spirit of God is incarnated in us that we have dominion over the world of effects. This dominion is exercised in such degree as we sense its true meaning. It is written that we have dominion over evil, not that we have dominion in or through evil. Spiritual dominion is exercised only as we rise above that which denies the Divine Goodness.

Today I exercise my spiritual dominion through the recognition that good alone is real, that God is the only presence, and Love the only power. Today I rise above the sense of separation into a consciousness of my union with Good. Today I understand that the power of God flows through me to everything I contact.

> We all use the creative power of the Universal Mind every time we use our own mind. —*THE SCIENCE OF MIND*, P. 30

Companionship

I am a companion of them that fear thee,
and of them that keep thy precepts. —PSALM 119:63

We all long for intimate relationships; we wish to feel that we are one with people. This yearning, which every normal person has, emanates from an unconscious, but spiritual, perception that we all are one with Life itself. Where there is no sense of rejection there will be no loneliness.

I no longer reject myself. Knowing that I am one with all people in the Spirit, I receive everyone as a friend. I establish a close and intimate relationship with everyone I meet—something goes out from me and becomes unified with them. I include all and exclude none. Higher than all differences is that union of the soul with its Source; beyond all differentiation, the Infinite Person is enshrined in the sanctuary of my own consciousness. One with all people, I enjoy this Divine companionship. I embrace the Infinite in everyone and in turn am embraced by It.

One of the first things to do is to love everybody. If you have not
done this, begin to do so at once. —*THE SCIENCE OF MIND*, P. 298

Health

The Lord will take away from thee all sickness. . . . I am
the Lord that healeth thee. —DEUTERONOMY 7:15; EXODUS 15:26

Health is a state of wholeness in mind and in body. The body is the servant
of the mind, and the mind is the offspring of pure Spirit. Thus the Bible tells
us that we are spirit, soul (or mind), and body. These three are really one and
are supposed to work in perfect unison with one another. This can be done
only when the mind lifts its countenance to the Spirit, permitting Its flow of
harmony, unity, and beauty a clear passageway. The body will always reflect
this inner poise.

Today I know that my health, my physical well-being, as well as my
mental poise and peace, are drawn from an infinite Source of perfection. Today I know that the Lord, the Law of Good, is the healing Presence of life,
forever restoring my mind and my physical being. I pray to, or commune
with, this Spirit within me. Thus I am made whole.

When the prayer of faith penetrates the subjective thought
and neutralizes false images, then the sick
are raised into health. —*THE SCIENCE OF MIND*, P. 501

Unity

Hear, O Israel; The Lord our God is one Lord. . . .
I and my Father are one. . . .
Who hath seen me hath seen the Father. —DEUTERONOMY 6:4; JOHN 10:30

Perhaps the most difficult thing for us to perceive is that there is one Life running through everything, one Presence manifest in everything, and one Person individualized through everyone. The perception of unity sees through all differences to one universal sameness. But unity does not mean uniformity. We do not all have to be alike, think alike, or act alike, but the world is learning that we must all act in unison. The Infinite One manifests in infinite variations, each rooted in the One, but each divinely unique in its own right. Good, bad; high, low; across, above, and beneath—are all one to the Infinite Mind.

Today I seek my union with Life. Today my imagination reaches back through all differences to the universal sameness. Today I know that I am in God, God is in me, we are One. Today, as never before, I shall seek to sense this Divine union of the soul with its Source and of all people with the Infinite.

If we would come to the Universal Wholeness, we must approach it
through the law of its own nature. This means that we must give
our undivided attention to the spiritual unity back
of all things. —*THE SCIENCE OF MIND*, P. 447

Illumination

Lift up your heads, O ye gates; and be lifted up, ye everlasting doors;
and the King of glory shall come in. —PSALM 24:7

The gates that we have to open represent the place in our consciousness where the Divine flows into the human. The light that the saintly artists of medieval times painted around people—particularly the halo—represents the lifting up of these gates. Illumination or cosmic consciousness is a reality. This is what Jesus referred to when he said, "Let your light so shine before men, that they may see your good works, and glorify your Father which is in heaven."

Today I lift up my consciousness to the light, and I know the King of Glory will come in. Today I keep this inner light, this Candle of the Lord, trimmed and burning, for I know that the bridegroom, who is Christ, my true Self, will enter my consciousness. I know that there is a Divine radiance emanating from everything. I know that in this light, which emanates from the very center of everything, there is no darkness at all. In this light I shall see the light.

There can and does descend into our minds—embody and personify in
our person—a Divinity, a Unity, the Spirit of God, the direct incarnation
of the Original Thing, in us—the mystical presentation
of Christ. —*THE SCIENCE OF MIND, P. 341*

Giving

Give, and it shall be given unto you; good measure, pressed down,
and shaken together, and running over. —LUKE 6:38

We all wish to receive, but how many of us desire to give? If, as Jesus inti-
mated, receiving is the other end of giving, then the more we give, the more
we shall receive. "Who loses his life shall find it." We should give the best
that we have to one another and to the world. This gift of Life is made without effort. It is a complete abandonment of the self to Life—a conscious letting go of all the tight strings of our being, a loosening of the Divine gifts
within us. Only when we have learned to give all will we be in a position to
receive all.

Today I give myself unstintingly to Life. I unloose the wellsprings of my
being and make a complete deliverance of the self to Life. This I do spontaneously and with joy, withholding nothing. I will not do this with any hope
of reward, but in the glad joy for the opportunity to increase my own livingness. Everything that I have belongs to the world. Giving, I will receive the
world back into my own consciousness.

Today is good, tomorrow will be even better, and that vista of tomorrows
that stretches down the bright eternities of an endless future will all be
good, for the nature of Reality cannot change. —THE SCIENCE OF MIND, P. 471

DECEMBER

LIGHT

A new light is coming into the world. We are on the borderline of a new experience. The veil between Spirit and matter is very thin. —ERNEST HOLMES

Then shall thy light break forth. —ISAIAH 58:8

The knowledge that there is a central chamber of the soul, blazing with the light of divine love and wisdom, has come, in the course of history, to multitudes of human beings. —ALDOUS HUXLEY

In the world as it is, the richness of the outer stirs us all to the wonder of the inner whose greatness is displayed in acts so splendid. —PLOTINUS

The wonderful ordering of the sun, the planets and the comets cannot but be the work of an intelligent, all-powerful Being. —ISAAC NEWTON

I can see that in the midst of darkness light persists. Hence I gather that God is Life, Truth, Light. God is Love. God is the Supreme Good.
—GANDHI

In moments of deepest realization, the great mystics have sensed that One Life flows through all and that all are some part of that Life. They have also seen Substance, a fine, white, brilliant stuff, forever falling into everything; a Substance indestructible and eternal. It is at such times of complete realization that they have been blinded by the Light of which we have been speaking. —ERNEST HOLMES

I Am Resolved to See the Good In Everyone and in Every Event

For what fellowship hath righteousness with unrighteousness? and what communion hath light with darkness? —II CORINTHIANS 6:14

Not God but ye yourselves, are the creators and supporters of moral evils. —THE TALMUD

Light can have no union with darkness; evil has no affinity with good. If good is the great Reality, while evil is the great negation or denial of Reality, then it follows that we should see the good in everything and recognize the apparent evil merely as a theoretical opposite of good. There is not God and something else. The Divine Spirit inhabits eternity; overshadows everything, including human events; dwells within our own soul; and is released through our own act. To see good as evil is to becloud our vision, to obstruct the pathway of our progress, and to cast a shadow across the sun of righteousness. This Spiritual Sun was the Guiding Star that led the Magi of old to the place where the little child lay, that is, to the place of good in our soul, to the Presence of God at the center of every person's being. The humility of the manger is the common place in every person's life. It is here, in the common place, that we must find the good and, finding it here, we shall also discover that the larger issues of our experience are overshadowed by this same good that we have discovered in the common place.

I am resolved today to see the good in everyone and in every event. I will call upon the good and will refuse to accept that anything other than good can come into my experience. In this way I will be praying to the good through meditating upon it.

Today Nothing Emanates from My Consciousness Other Than That Which Will Bless and Heal

But if ye bite and devour one another, take heed that ye be not consumed one of another. —GALATIANS 5:15

I destroy the ignorance-born darkness by the shining lamp of wisdom. —THE BHAGAVAD-GITA

This lesson teaches us the Law of Cause and Effect, the plaything of the soul. Sages have always taught that our thoughts and acts ride on a return circuit and that they never fail to react upon us until we have transcended the negative causation set in motion by such acts. This is why we are taught that we should do to others what we would like them to do to us. It is the old law of the returning circle. In this law alone can we find exact justice, and through understanding this law come to realize with Robert Browning, "All's love, yet all's law." The universe imposes neither evil nor limitation upon us, nor can we impose evil or limitation upon it. However, being free agents, we may and must experience, at least temporarily, the result of our own acts. As the Bhagavad-Gita tells us, the lamp of wisdom shining in the darkness of ignorance alone can free us.

Realizing that the universe has bestowed upon me the Divine right to be affected by my own act, today I guard all of my thoughts, seeing to it that nothing emanates from my consciousness other than that which blesses and heals. If nothing goes forth from me that can hurt, then nothing can return to me that can harm. The knowledge of this truth makes me wise. The consciousness of good at the center of my being is my sanctuary. Faith in the justice of the universe is my altar. Upon this altar I lay my offering of peace, of joy, and of prosperity for the whole world.

Today I Live

And God shall wipe away all tears from their eyes; and there shall be
no more death, neither sorrow, nor crying, neither shall there
be any more pain. —REVELATION 21:4

Pray not that sinners may perish, but that the sin itself
may disappear. —THE TALMUD

The wisest man who ever lived told us that the knowledge of Truth shall
make us free. All books of spiritual wisdom have taught us that it is not the
one who makes the mistake whom we should seek to destroy; it is the mistake itself which must be erased. Now, this means that evil has no existence
in itself and has no history. No matter what the negations of yesterday may
have been, the affirmations of today rise triumphant and transcendent over
them. Thus all the evils of our yesterdays disappear into their native nothingness. If we behold beauty instead of ugliness, then beauty will appear. If
we persist in seeing the true rather than the false, then that which is true will
appear. Where is the false, the untrue, and the evil when the knowledge of
Truth has made us free? Its days are as though they had never been; its
cause is neutralized; hence it leaves no effect. Let us, then, cease weeping
over the shortcomings and mistakes and evils of our yesterdays and, steadfastly beholding the face of the great and the divine Reality, let us resolve to
walk in that light wherein there is no darkness.

Definitely I know that every negative condition of the past is cleared
away from my consciousness. I no longer think about it, see it, or believe in
it. Nor do I believe that it has any effect whatsoever in my experience. Today I express perfect life here and now. Today I live.

Divine Intelligence Directs My Faith and Makes
Perfect and Plain the Way Before Me

But we speak the wisdom of God in a mystery, even the hidden wisdom,
which God ordained before the world unto our glory. —I CORINTHIANS 2:7–8

The person who is happy within, who rejoiceth within, who is illumined
within, that Yogi, becoming the Eternal, goeth to the Peace of
the Eternal. —THE BHAGAVAD-GITA

The hidden wisdom of God is the knowledge that we are one with the Divine Being. This wisdom, which is hidden from us until we perceive our fundamental unity with Reality, is clearly revealed when we seek the Eternal in everything. The masters who have penetrated the mystery of life that so often eludes the intellect are those who with utmost simplicity have found direct approach to the Supreme Reality at the center of their own soul. The Bhagavad-Gita tells us that we must become the Eternal if we wish to enter into the peace of the Eternal. This has an identical meaning with the saying of Jesus that we must be perfect even as God in us is perfect. This calls for the recognition of the Spirit as an indwelling Presence, as well as overshadowing Power. The road to self-discovery often calls for the clearing away of the underbrush of ignorance, fear, superstition, and a sense of isolation that has made us feel that we were unworthy, unholy, and lost. In the divine providence of good, salvation is unnecessary but self-discovery is essential. We do not save that which was lost; we merely discover that which needs to be found.

I know that God is within me and I know that this Divine Spirit is perfect. I enter into Its peace and am secure in a sense of Its protection. Love will guide and Intelligence will direct me. The power of the Infinite will sustain and uphold, as well as direct. The unerring judgment of Divine Intelligence directs my faith and makes perfect and plain the way before me.

Today I Consciously Live in the Eternal Presence

But seek ye first the kingdom of God, and his righteousness;
and all these things shall be added unto you. —MATTHEW 6:33

Fix your mind on Me. Give Me your whole heart. —THE BHAGAVAD-GITA

Since the Kingdom of God is a Kingdom of righteousness, and since it is a Kingdom that contains everything, then it becomes of prime importance to seek this Kingdom, which Jesus so plainly stated is to be found within the self; that Self upon which is set the stamp of the Eternal—the God-Self. The real Self is inseparable from God, thus in discovering the self, we also discover God, the Cause of the self. Everything is included within the Divine, and since we are in It and It is in us, true self-discovery is the key to the mysteries of life. Hermes tells us that God has everything within Itself as thought, that the whole cosmos itself is a thing of consciousness. This is the true City of God—the city of right thoughts and right actions, the city that is four square, the length and breadth and thickness of which are equal. This is the city that Saint Augustine so beautifully depicts in his great essay on the relationship of the individual soul to the Universal Spirit. All the sages have plainly told us that we already walk the streets of this city, but, like the slaves of Plato, our vision is blurred by shadows cast on the wall of human experience. Evil deals with shadows; Truth deals with light, which dispels the shadows. We are of the Truth. Evil is neither person, place, nor thing.

Today I consciously live in the Eternal Presence. The Kingdom of Heaven is within me and I live in the City of God. I am one with all other citizens who inhabit this celestial metropolis. Here, in a true communion of Spirit, I find unity, peace, and joy.

I Stand on the Mountaintop of My Soul and Cause My Spiritual Vision to Encompass More

For as he thinketh in his heart, so is he. —PROVERBS 23:7

As far as mind extends, so far extends heaven. —THE UPANISHADS

My soul hath built for me a habitation. —BOOK OF THE DEAD

Note that Proverbs does not say that we are as we think we are—quite the contrary. It says we are as we think. Here is a vast difference. We might imagine ourselves to be very clever while remaining quite dull, but if our thoughts are brilliant we also will be brilliant. As we think in our heart so are we. The heart stands for the center of consciousness, the point from which everything that we are circulates. It is said that Moses was led by the Divine Spirit into a high mountain and told that all the land that his vision could encompass his feet could tread upon. This high mountain stands for an exalted place in consciousness. As consciousness extends its vision it extends the possibility of its objective experience. This means that objectively we possess that which subjectively we encompass. Our soul is always building a habitation for us, because consciousness is forever dealing with First Cause, with the Causeless Cause, with That which plays with cause and effect as children play ball. Emerson tells us to stay at home with the cause, to build a habitation and therein to dwell. It is wonderful to realize that our true home is not made with hands but is eternal in the heavens.

Today I stand on the mountaintop of my soul and cause my spiritual vision to encompass more. I will push out the horizons of my previous experiences in order that I may have more room. My soul will look out and see that all is well. I am filled with peace, with joy, and with contentment.

The Changeless Abides with Me. I Am Calm and Peaceful in the Midst of Confusion

I am the Lord, I change not. —MALACHI 3:6

The Tao, considered as unchanging, has no name. —TEXT OF TAOISM

We should realize that all the great scriptures have taught one identical message—the unity of good. All the sacred books have been inspired by the one Mind. Each in its own tongue has told the story of Reality. "I am the Lord, I change not," was revealed to the Hebrew mystic. To the great Chinese sage came the same message, "The Tao cannot change, it has no name," and to Hermes, God is in Itself, by Itself, full and perfect. If we can bring to this glorified conception the realization that this Divine Being is the breath of our breath, omnipresent, forever within us, then we shall realize that we live in one eternal and perfect Mind. An excerpt from the sacred books on the attributes of God says, "There is no variableness in God since God is eternal, immortal, and infinite. Nevertheless God is that from which every transformation arises." This means that, while we live in the Eternal, which does not change, we are forever drawing from It the possibility of the manifold expressions that give variety to existence and that make living interesting.

I know that the Changeless abides with me. I am calm and peaceful in the midst of confusion. I know that nothing moves the soul. Peace, infinite peace, is at the center of my being. I live, move, and have my being in that which is perfect, complete within Itself. That Self is my self.

Today I Feel That I Merge with the Infinite

Canst thou by searching find out God? Canst thou find out the Almighty unto perfection? It is high as heaven. . . . The measure thereof is larger than the earth, and broader than the sea. —JOB 11:7–9

The Tao cannot be heard; what can be heard is not It. The Tao cannot be seen; what can be seen is not It. The Tao cannot be expressed in words; what can be expressed in words is not It. Do we know the Formless which gives form to form? In the same way the Tao does not admit of being. —KWANG-TZE

Realize that thou are "that"—Brahma, which is the cessation of all differentiation, which never changes its nature and is as unmoved as a waveless ocean, eternally unconditioned and undivided. —RAJA YOGA

Job asks us if we can find God by searching. He means that since God is everywhere, and since the subtle essence of the Infinite is invisible, we do not have to search out the Divine Spirit, but, rather, we should recognize It as the center of all life. That which we see is merely a reflection of this invisible Presence. The Spirit Itself cannot be seen, but It is felt, just as we do not see God but we do feel the Divine in everything. The Creator is revealed in Its creation. The Formless gives rise to the formed. We should consciously unite ourselves with this invisible Essence that pervades everything, that which our lesson says is eternally unconditioned and undivided. To do this is to find wholeness.

Today I feel that I merge with the Infinite. While there seems to be a beginning and an end to each particular experience, there is neither beginning nor end to myself. My real spirit is omnipresent in God, secure in Good, and perfect in Divine Being.

I Have a Spiritual Vision Within Me that Beholds a Perfect Universe

I am Alpha and Omega, the beginning and the ending, saith the Lord,
which is, and which was, and which is to come,
the Almighty. —REVELATION 1:8

But verily thou art not able to behold Me with these thine eyes;
the divine eye I give unto thee. —THE BHAGAVAD-GITA

There is but one Brahma which is Truth's Self. It is from ignorance of that
One that god-heads have been conceived to be diverse. —THE MAHABHARATA

Spirit as Absolute Cause is the beginning and end of everything. If we place complete reliance upon this Spirit as being the adequate Cause, then we may as certainly place complete reliance upon It as producing the desired effect. When we give a spiritual mind treatment we are using this Absolute Cause, which is the Alpha. From It automatically proceeds the effect, which is the Omega. Thus the treatment contains the potential possibility of its own answer. Jesus said, "The words that I speak unto you, they are spirit, and they are life." He knew that because he consciously dealt with First Cause, there would be no question about the effect. Our lesson says that a lack of the realization that there is but one final Power has given rise to the belief in many gods. Some of these gods we call evil, lack, want, limitation, pain, death. These false gods must be deserted for there is but One, which is Truth's Self. We are told that while we cannot behold the invisible Presence with these physical eyes, "The divine eye I give unto thee." This has an identical meaning with the saying of Jesus that spiritual things must be spiritually discerned.

I have a spiritual vision within me that beholds a perfect universe. Daily this vision guides me to success, happiness, prosperity, physical and mental well-being. My spiritual vision is open—I am awake to the greater possibility.

I Know That My Spirit Is Free from All Limitation

I am the Almighty God; walk before me, and be thou perfect. —GENESIS 17:1

Whoever knows the God who is without commencement, without end, who within this impervious [world] is the creator of the universe, who is of an infinite form, the one penetrator of the universe, becomes liberated from all bonds. —THE UPANISHADS

Thus it is that the Tao produces [all things], nourishes them, brings them to their full growth, nurses them, completes them, matures them, maintains them, and overspreads them. —TAO TE CHING

Our Chinese text tells us that the Tao, which means Spirit, produces everything, nourishes everything, and maintains everything. It spreads Itself over everything, It flows through everything and is in all things. Indeed, being all that is, there can be nothing outside It. Our Hindu text tells us that in such degree as we understand God, who is the one penetrator of the universe, in such degree we become liberated. And the Hebrew text says, "Walk before me and be thou perfect." We are to recognize the Divine in everything, to speak to the Divine in everything, to see It everywhere— "Lift the stone and you will find me, cleave the wood for there am I." There is a mystical Presence that pervades the universe. The fragrance of the rose, the beauty of the dewdrop glistening in the sun are manifestations of Its Presence and activity. This mystical Presence welling up in our consciousness evermore proclaims Itself as the source and root of all. This Source, Hermes tells us, forevermore proclaims Itself as "the Oneness, being source and root of all, is in all things as the root and source." And the Christian scriptures tell us, "I am over all, in all, and through all." The enlightened of the ages have told us that it is this God within us that recognizes Itself in everything we are.

I know that my spirit is free from all limitation. I know that my mind understands the truth about myself. I know that my physical body and my objective affairs reflect and manifest the perfection that I feel, the wholeness that I am certain of, and the prosperity that rightfully belongs to me.

Today I Will Walk in the Light and My Consciousness Will Be Illuminated

The sun shall no more go down; neither shall thy moon withdraw itself:
for the Lord shall be thine everlasting light, and the days
of thy mourning shall be ended. —ISAIAH 60:20

Who uses well his light, Reverting to its [source so] bright,
Will from his body ward all blight. —TAO TE CHING

There are so many illustrations in the sacred texts of the world relating to the Light. The Spirit is thought of as being the essence of light. People are spoken of as being the "candles of the Lord." "The light shines in the darkness and the darkness comprehendeth it not." That is, the darkness has no power over light; light will overcome darkness, but darkness cannot overcome light. When Isaiah said that "the Lord shall be thy everlasting light," he meant that there is a light within us, the light of Truth, of Spirit, of God, that cannot set, cannot become obliterated, cannot be blown out. The "candle of the Lord" burns forever because its wick is sunk deep in the wellsprings of Reality—that light, that spring, that substance—to which Jesus referred when he told the woman at the well that if ever she drank from it she would never thirst again. It is no wonder that the woman asked him to give her of this water that she might no longer be compelled laboriously to draw from the fountain that can become depleted.

Today I will walk in the light and my consciousness will be illuminated. My thoughts will be guided and my way guarded, for I know that in my light there is no darkness. In this Divine Light there are no shadows.

I Know That the Truth Is in Me, Perfect and Complete

I have not written unto you because ye know not the truth, but
because ye know it, and no lie is of the truth. —I JOHN 2:21

This is God your Lord: All power is His: But the gods ye call on beside
Him have no power over the husk of a date stone! —THE KORAN

However anxious you may be, you will
not save [yourself]. —TEXT OF TAOISM

There is no power, presence, or person outside the Divine. God not only is,
It is also One. Our lesson from the Koran says that a belief in any opposite
to the One has no power, even as darkness has no power over light. God is
Light, and in God there is no darkness. To believe in the Light is to dispel
the darkness. A knowledge of good overcomes evil. The consciousness of
abundance dispels want and pours the contents of the Horn of Plenty into
our uplifted bowl of acceptance. John tells us that there is no lie in the truth.
The truth never contradicts itself; it never denies us our good; it evermore
proclaims the Divine Presence in everything, through everything, and
around everything. If God is Allness, then there is no otherness. Kwang-
Tze tells us that anxiety will not save us, because anxiety is unbelief. Jesus
also tells us to take no anxious thought for tomorrow. The Chinese sage said
that perfected people find that they already have everything within themselves, after which they discover the same in others. This corresponds to the
teaching of Jesus that the blind cannot lead the blind. We must know the
truth about ourselves before we can know it about others.

I know that the truth is in me, perfect and complete. I know that I manifest the truth, the whole truth, and nothing but the truth. I know that the
truth makes me free. Today it frees me from the burden of care and anxiety.
Every form of fear, every sense of burden is dropped from my consciousness and I walk the way of truth lightly, joyously.

Today I Am Resolved to See Only the Good

He brought them out of darkness and the shadow of death,
and brake their bands in sunder. —PSALM 107:14

Sin is an obstruction in the heart; an inability to feel and comprehend all
that is noble, true and great, and to take part in the good. —THE TALMUD

We all wish to be brought out of darkness into the light. To be free from the
bondage of fear, superstition, and want, the mind must be riveted on freedom. The thought must rise transcendent over bondage. If we do this, then
we are brought from the shadow of darkness into the light of the glorious
freedom of God. The Talmud tells us that if we would be free from sin (mistake) the mind and heart must be open to enlightenment. Ignorance of the
Truth is the great sin or mistake from which spiritual enlightenment alone
can give freedom. But what is spiritual enlightenment other than an increasing capacity consciously to become aware of the Divine Presence as
peace, joy, and harmony? If we are to know the Truth that makes us free, we
must first recognize the essential nonreality of evil as being a thing within itself; we must equally know the essential absolute reality of good, not only as
the Supreme Beneficence, but as the Absolute Power.

Therefore, today I am resolved to see only the good, and whenever evil,
in the form of lack, fear, pain, or uncertainty, presents itself, I shall endeavor
instantly to recognize its native nothingness, to know that it is entirely relative. I shall make every effort to see through this limitation to that which
is boundless and free. I shall proclaim the glad tidings of the freedom of
the Kingdom of God in my experience and in the experience of everyone
I contact.

Today I Recognize That I Am a Perfect Being, Living Under Perfect Conditions

All things were made by him; and without him was not
any thing made that was made. —JOHN 1:3

There is naught whatsoever higher than I. . . . All this is threaded
on Me, as rows of pearls on a string. —THE BHAGAVAD-GITA

All things are threaded on the Divine, "like rows of pearls on a string." Spiritual intuition tells us that beauty is at the root of everything. Ugliness is its suppositional opposite. We must sense not the opposite but the Reality. It is this Divine Presence that we are to recognize. For every apparent opposite we are to supply a realization of the truth about that opposite. In this way we supply a spiritual sense that is transcendent of the form that the material sense has created. In this way we can look at, in, and through a difficulty or a difficult situation, until we perceive the truth at the very center of its being. Thus the devil, that is, evil or false appearance, is transmuted into an angel of light, for there is naught beside God. If everything enduring and true comes from God, the Creator, then we may be certain that no matter what the appearance is, the reality is always perfect. This is why Jesus tells us to judge not according to appearances, but to judge righteously. We shall always judge righteously when our knowledge is based upon the certainty of the Divine Presence, perfect at the center of everything.

Today I recognize that I am a perfect being, living under perfect conditions, knowing that the good alone is real. I will also know that good alone is the only thing that has any power either to act or to react. Everything that I do, say, or think today will be done, said, or thought from the spiritual viewpoint of God in everything.

There Is a Subtle Power Within Me— The Essence of Spirit

For, lo, he that formeth the mountains, and createth the wind, and
declareth unto man what is his thought, that maketh the morning
darkness, and treadeth upon the high places of the earth,
the Lord, The God of hosts, is his name. —AMOS 4:13

The Atman [the real self] is permanent, eternal and
therefore existence itself. —RAJA YOGA

The great prophet Amos tells us that "The God of hosts" is the name of the
Power that forms the mountains, creates the winds, and declares Its presence in the sanctuary of our own thought. This poetical description of Spirit
brings a sense of lightness, of peace, and of transcendent joy. Amos seems to
have lifted the load of life in his declaration that the Spirit treads upon the
high places of the earth. This transcendent thought of God should ever be
with us, and, like Jesus, we should walk over the waves of human distur-
bance rather than being submerged by them. Our lesson tells us that the
Atman, which means the real self, is eternal and permanent, and here the
text swings into the profound observation that Spirit exists within Itself.
Life does not depend upon something outside itself, but immediately pre-
cipitates itself in our experience when we recognize it. It is this divine recognition that gives us transcendent power, and we may rely upon this law for
it is absolute. "Look unto me, and be ye saved, all the ends of the earth."

There is a subtle power within me, the essence of Spirit. I am sustained.
I am guided. I am guarded. I am kept in the way of peace, prosperity, and
joy. Every atom of my being is vibrant with life, alive with deathless self-
existence. There is something within me today that sings a celestial song,
which exalts. This song finds its echo in everything I do, causing the deaf to
hear, the blind to see, and awakens the paralysis of fear into life and action.

The Peace and Power of a Conscious Recognition
of the Divine Presence Is with Me Today

Now the Lord is that Spirit: and where the Spirit of the Lord is,
there is liberty. —II CORINTHIANS 3:17

My fifth name is All good things created by Mazda,
the offsprings of the holy principle. —THE ZEND-AVESTA

We all desire to experience liberty and to know that the all-comprehensive Mind and Principle is in the very words we speak. The Zend-Avesta tells us that all good things are created by Mazda (the principle of light). Here we have a concept of liberty, of light, and of freedom accompanying our words, a Divine Authority imparting a creativeness to our thought. The creative power of Spirit is in our word in such degree as we become conscious of Spirit. We know that words of love overcome thoughts of hate. We know that peace will heal confusion and that a sense of power will overcome the belief in weakness. All our work should be built upon the supposition that good overcomes evil, not by combating, but by transcending it. The non-combativeness of Spirit is the principle back of the law of nonresistance that Jesus so plainly taught. The Spirit has no opposites; It is always joyous, perfect, and free. There is no difference in the essence between our spirit and the Spirit. Our spirit is the Spirit of God in each of us—the two are one.

The peace and the power of the Divine Presence is with me today. Therefore, I walk calmly, knowing that I am enveloped in the Divine Presence. I am fully conscious that my word liberates every bondage, whether it be in myself or in others. I know that my word is the law of good automatically executing itself, irresistibly proclaiming itself, inevitably fulfilling itself.

I Know That I Live in the Changeless Reality

And the world passeth away, and the lust thereof: but he
that doeth the will of God abideth forever. —I JOHN 2:17

All that is with you passeth away, but that which
is with God abideth. —THE KORAN

Neither the Will of God nor the Nature of God can change. Reality is the
same "yesterday, today, and forever." That which was is, and that which is
will remain. As human beings, our nature is spiritual. The only thing about
us that can change is that which ought not to be permanent. We are changeless beings living in a changing world. Thus all of our experiences are bound
together on a thread of continuity that James Russell Lowell called "the
thread of the All-Sustaining Beauty which runs through all and doth all
unite." It is wonderful to know that something permanent, substantial, and
eternal stands in the midst of our being, and, I believe, watches with joy the
eternal change taking place. To the Spirit these changes are merely variations of experience. The Spirit is never caught, tied, or bound. Ugliness may
seem to exist for a brief moment but Beauty, like Truth, endures forever. All
that is evil passes; as our Hymn of Faith says, it cannot exist even for a moment when faced by the Divine Reality. Everything that we now experience
objectively will change, as it ought to, "but that which is with God (of good)
abideth."

I know that I live in a changeless Reality. I am not disturbed by the passage of time, the movement around me, nor the variations of experience
through which I go. Something within me remains immovable and says,
"Be still and know that I am God." This I Am, which is God within me, is
substantial, changeless, and perfect.

Today I Have Implicit Confidence in the Good, the Enduring, and the True

Though an host should encamp against me, my heart shall not fear: though war should rise against me, in this will I be confident. —PSALM 27:3

When one cherishes no fear of anything, when one is not feared by anything, when one cherishes no desire, when one bears no hate, then is one said to have attained to the state of Brahma. —THE MAHABHARATA

Holiness is the best of all good. Happy, happy the person who is holy with perfect holiness! . . . The will of the Lord is the law of holiness. —THE ZEND-AVESTA

Fear is the only thing we shall be afraid of. It is not the host encamped against us, nor the confusion of war around us, that we need to fear; it is a lack of confidence in the good that alone should cause concern. Through inner spiritual vision we know that evil is transitory, but good is permanent. We know that right finally dissolves everything opposed to it. In confidence, then, and with a calm sense of peace, we know that the truth never fails to win every issue. The power of good is with us. The Power of the Spirit is supreme over every antagonist. Then we should cherish no fear, and when we neither fear nor hate we come to understand the unity of life, and then, our lesson tells us, we have attained to the state of Brahma (conscious union with God). Thus the Zend-Avesta tells us that "holiness is the best of all good," and it adds that there is no difference between the Law of Holiness (Wholeness) and the Divine Will. Since the Nature of God is peace, then the Will of God is toward peace; since the Nature of God is love, then the Will of God is toward love. "Who knows not love, knows not God, for God is love."

Today my heart is without fear. I have implicit confidence in the good, the enduring, and the true. I enter into conscious union with the Spirit. I am happy, whole, and complete in my Divine Self. Therefore, with joy I enter into the activities of the day, and with confidence I look forward to tomorrow, and without regret I remember the events of yesterday.

I See God in Everything, Personified in All People, Manifest in Every Event

Theirs was the fullness of heaven and earth; the more
that they gave to others, the more they had. —KWANG-TZE

'Tis Love Itself that worketh the one harmony of all.
Therefore, let us sing the praise of God. —HERMES

We are the children of God; and if children, then heirs;
heirs of God, and joint-heirs with Christ. —ROMANS 8:16–17

Jesus said, "Give and to you shall be given." All the great scriptures have announced this central and transcendent truth, realizing that every act carries with it a sequence, bringing the result of this action back to the self. This is what is meant by Karma, for Karma means the fruit of action. Emerson called it the Law of Compensation, and Jesus proclaimed the same law in his teaching that as we sow, so shall we reap. This is why Kwang-Tze tells us that the more we give to others the more we have. Walt Whitman also refers to this when he says, "The gift is most to the giver and comes back most to him." This all means the return of the self to itself. The great apostle did not tell us to forget the self; he merely told us to also remember everyone else. We are to view ourselves each in the other and behold God in all. Hermes tells us that when we realize Love as the great harmony, we shall all sing the praise of God. Before we can do this we must perceive this harmony in one another and in everything. Thus, everything that seems separated is united at the root. "Over all, in all, and through all," the "sustaining Beauty" of the inevitable "seed of perfection" to which Robert Browning referred as nestling at the center of our own being.

I see God in everything, personified in all people, manifest in every event. The Spirit is not separated from the person or the event; It united each to Itself, vitalizing each with the energy of Its own being; creating each through Its own divine imagination. I, too, am an instrument of Its perfection, and today I recognize my union, which is perfect and complete.

Today I Uncover the Perfection Within Me in All Its Fullness

Again, the kingdom of heaven is like unto treasure hid in a field; the which
when a man hath found, he hideth, and for joy thereof goeth and selleth
all that he hath, and buyeth that field. —MATTHEW 13:44

Success [in the attainment of objects] forsaketh the person whose heart
is unsteady, or who hath no control over his mind, or who is
a slave of his senses. —THE MAHABHARATA

In the place of heaven there is no fear of any kind: . . . none fears decay.
Without either hunger or thirst, beyond all grief [all] rejoice in
the place of heaven. —KATHA UPANISHAD

Who would not be successful in the true sense of the term? For there is no
success without happiness and a sense of certainty. There is something eternal about success. There is no grief in success, because one who is truly successful is no longer sad. That person knows the things of this world are but
temporary, that treasure is in heaven. Jesus likened it unto a treasure hid in
the field, and he said we would sell everything we have that we might purchase this field and uncover the hidden treasure. This treasure, the Mahabharata tells us, cannot be found while one is a slave to objective appearances
or lacks control over one's thoughts. All of this means that success, even in
our objective undertakings, depends, first of all, upon stability of mind,
consistency of purpose, and concentration of effort. The kingdom of heaven
is already hidden within us. The field that contains this hidden treasure is
our own soul. The priceless pearl is covered by the hardened shell of experience. We must learn to see God at the center of our being.

Today I uncover the perfection within me. In its fullness I reveal the indwelling kingdom. I look out upon the world of my affairs, knowing that the
Spirit within me makes my way both immediate and easy, for I know that "it
is not I, but the Father that dwelleth in me, he doeth the works."

I Know That I Understand How to Speak the Word of Truth

It is the spirit that quickeneth: the flesh profiteth nothing: the words that
I speak unto you, they are spirit, and they are life. —JOHN 6:63

And where do name and form both cease, and turn to utter nothingness?
And the answer is, "In consciousness invisible and infinite,
of radiance bright." —BUDDHIST TEXT

This lesson tells us that the objective world is quickened by the indwelling
Spirit. The words of Truth are life unto every form they animate. All words
that are spoken in a realization of the Divine Nature are words of Truth and
all such words give life. "It is the spirit that quickeneth." Our lesson also
tells us that all objects, that is, the entire objective universe, comes from
One Substance. This Substance is differentiated, that is, manifest in many
forms. It looks as though the cause were dual because the forms are all different, but our lesson clearly states that we must not fall under this delusion
of a dualistic character, but, rather, penetrate the Unity back of all form. In
our text from Buddhism, we get the idea that there is a place where both the
objective name and form cease to exist as things in themselves. There is an
invisible consciousness that radiates all forms. This does not mean a denial
of the objective world, but, rather, an affirmation that it is an effect projected from, by, and within a transcendent cause that has complete control
over it.

I know that I understand how to speak the word of Truth. I know that
the invisible Power of the Spirit is with me. I know that my world is peopled
with forms of light, with the Divine Radiance. I know that I am a perfect being, living under perfect conditions with other perfect beings in a perfect
God.

I Enter into the Limitless Variations That the Divine Spirit Has Projected into My Experience

For all flesh is as grass, and all the glory of man as the flower of grass.
The grass withereth, and the flower thereof falleth away: But the
word of the Lord endureth for ever. —I PETER 1:24–25

The unreal hath no being;
the real never ceaseth to be. —THE BHAGAVAD-GITA

The Bhagavad-Gita tells us that unreality has no existence, while Reality cannot cease to be. Our lesson also states that all of the effects of the Spirit are themselves real and that there is nothing different from the Divine Spirit. Jesus tells us to judge not according to appearances. However, he did not tell us that appearances are unreal. The unreality of appearance lies not in the thing of itself, but rather in our interpretation of it. If we spiritually interpret the universe, we shall understand it, enter into it, become one with it. We shall see that the bird, the rock, the mountain, and the river are spiritual manifestations of the joy of the Divine Mind. The illusion is in seeking to interpret them as being separate from the Infinite. The blade of grass may wither and petals fall from the flower, but the idea, "the word of the Lord endureth forever." This lesson teaches us that there is not only the fundamental unity; there is also an eternal variety. Without this variety life would become stagnant.

Today I enter into the limitless variations that the Divine Spirit has projected into my experience. I know that all things are good when rightly used. I perceive that all experience is a play of life upon itself. I enter into the game of living, then, with joyful anticipation, with spontaneous enthusiasm, and with the determination to play the game well and to enjoy it.

I Am Alive, Awake, and Aware. My Spiritual Eyes Are Open

For now we see through a glass, darkly; but then face to face:
now I know in part; but then shall I know
even as also I am known. —I CORINTHIANS 13:12

O ye people, earth-born folk, ye who have given yourselves to
drunkenness and sleep and ignorance of God, be sober now, cease from
your surfeit, cease to be glamoured by irrational sleep! —HERMES

If ye knew God as God ought to be known, ye would walk on the seas,
and the mountains would move at your call. —THE KASHF AL-MAHJUB

"For now we see through a glass, darkly." How familiar this passage is to all
of us, but what does it mean other than that our vision is clouded by a material sense of things? Hermes tells us that we are both drunk and asleep,
that we are ignorant of God. Emerson tells us that once in a while we awake
from our slumber and look about us to perceive the world of reality, but too
soon sink back again into sleep. And from another ancient text, quoted
above, we are told that if we knew God as we ought to, we would be able to
walk on the seas, that the mountains would come at our call. All progress is
an awakening. Every new scientific fact is a discovery. This also is an awakening. It is really true that we are largely asleep, dreaming away the hours.
"Awake thou that sleepest, and arise from the dead, and Christ shall give
you life." It is indeed high time that we awake from this sleep. No one can
awaken us but the self. Let us, then, make every endeavor to arouse the
mind to reality and to penetrate the gloom of fear and superstition, to cast
aside doubt and uncertainty, to behold the Light, which is eternal.

I awake! I awake! I awake! I am alive, awake, and aware. My spiritual
eyes are open. As from a long night's sleep, I awake!

Today I Bestow the Essence of Love Upon Everything

The Law of the Lord is perfect, converting the soul: . . . The statutes of the Lord are right, rejoicing the heart: the commandment of the Lord is pure, enlightening the eyes. —PSALM 19:7, 8

For the Self-begotten One, the Father-Mind, perceiving His own Works, sowed into all Love's Bond . . . so that all might continue loving on for endless time, and that these Weavings of the Father's Light might never fail. —THE CHALDAEAN ORACLES

But love will the God of Mercy vouchsafe to those who believe and do the things that be right. —THE KORAN

"The Law of the Lord is perfect" and the Law of the Lord is Love. We are made perfect in the Law when we enter into the communion of love with one another and with the invisible essence of Life. Love is the fulfillment of the Law, that is, we never can make the most perfect use of the Law unless that use is motivated by love, by a sincere desire to express unity, harmony, and peace. We should not hesitate to express our appreciation for people, things, and events. There is too little enthusiasm about life. We sacrifice hope on the altar of unbelief and fail to extract the essence of Reality from the invisible, because we refuse to rejoice in our human relationships. Love will not remain abstract. Its power of transmutation in human events comes only as we catch its vision and mold it into human experience.

Today I bestow the essence of love upon everything. Everyone shall be lovely to me. My soul meets the soul of the universe in everyone. Nothing is dead; everything is alive. Nothing is ugly; everything is beautiful; everything is meaningful. This love is a healing power touching everything into wholeness, healing the wounds of experience with its divine balm.

Today I Walk in the Light of God's Love

God is a Spirit: and they that worship him must
worship him in spirit and in truth. —JOHN 4:24

I the Father of this universe, the Mother, the Supporter, the Grandsire,
the Holy One to be known, the Word of Power. —THE BHAGAVAD-GITA

The Tao produced One; One produced Two; Two produced Three;
Three produced All things. —TAO TE CHING

Our lesson tells us that God is the Father, the Mother, the Supporter, and Grandsire. It tells us that from the Oneness of God proceeds the Law, the Essence and the Word. Then it tells us that God is Spirit. Wonderful indeed is this conception of the union of all life, which Jesus proclaimed in the ecstasy of his illumination, "I and the Father are one." All cause and all effect proceed from the invisible Spirit. We are one with this Spirit and cannot be separated from It. Our word has power because our word is the action of God through our thought. Power is. We use it; we do not have to create it. Let us seek to use the power of our word more generously, with a greater idea of its beneficence, its abundance, and its availability. When we learn to believe, then our belief is increased. Receiving much, we shall receive more; giving everything, we shall, in return, receive all. Let us be willing to die to the lesser in order to become resurrected into the greater. This is the true meaning of that thought that we must lose our lives in order to find them. Naturally we must let go of ignorance if we would gain knowledge; we must stop walking in darkness if we would walk in the light.

Today I walk in the light of God's Love. Today I am guided and my guidance is multiplied. I know exactly what to do, exactly how to do it. There is an inspiration within me that governs every act, every thought, in certainty, with conviction and peace.

I Believe in Divine Guidance and I Know That Underneath Are the Everlasting Arms

The eternal God is thy refuge, and underneath
are the everlasting arms. —DEUTERONOMY 33:27

All this universe has the [Supreme] Deity for its life. That Deity is Truth.
He is the Universal Soul. —CHHANDOGYA UPANISHAD

But God will increase the guidance of the already guided. —THE KORAN

If God is our refuge, why is it that we refuse to avail ourselves of this divine security? The Psalmist tells us that "the Lord is nigh unto all them that call upon him . . . in truth." This can have but one meaning. We cannot call upon God in truth unless we enter into the Divine Nature in truth, that is, we cannot expect love to become hate, nor peace to enter into confusion. If we would call upon God in truth, we must become like the truth. This is the seemingly unfathomable mystery of the infinite, invisible Essence that surrounds us. Jesus tells us that if we abide in Him, then His words will abide in us, and we shall ask for anything that we will and it shall be done unto us. The everlasting arms are beneath, but they bear us up only when we enter into the truth. The Koran tells us that God increases our guidance once we have guidance. This is a mystical way of saying that if we believe in Divine Guidance, then we will be divinely guided. "Act as though I am, and I will be." "Believe and it shall be done unto you."

Today I believe in Divine Guidance. Today I believe that underneath are the everlasting arms. Today I rest in this divine assurance and this divine security. I know that not only all is well with my soul, my spirit, and my mind, all is well with my affairs.

I Bless Everything and Know That All Good
Will Multiply in My Experience

But whoso looketh into the perfect law of liberty, and continueth
therein, he being not a forgetful hearer, but a doer of the work,
this man shall be blessed in his deed. —JAMES 1:25

It [God] was not created in the past, nor is it to be annihilated in the
future; it is eternal, permanent, absolute; and from all eternity it
sufficiently embraces in its essence all possible merits. —THE MAHAYANA

James tells us that we should look to the perfect law of liberty, follow its precepts, and then we shall be blessed in our deeds. This means to keep the eye
single, or centered, on the Presence, the Power, and the Responsiveness of
Spirit. The Law of God would have to be a law of liberty, since bondage
could not come from freedom any more than death could be born of the
Principle of Life. We often wonder why we are so limited, and too frequently project the blame for our limitations upon the universe itself. This
is a psychological trick that we play in ignorance of the true facts. Limitation is not imposed upon us by the universe, but through our own ignorance. Every discovery in science tends to prove this. The Invisible takes
temporary form in our experience. Fortunately, none of these forms is permanent. We should look upon them as the play of Life upon Itself. In our
own experience we are privileged by the Creative Wisdom to become cocre-
ators in our personal affairs. The Divine Creative Spirit embraces every
possible action. No greater freedom could be found or given, and we should
daily open our consciousness to the Divine Influx, expecting greater wisdom, more definite guidance, and more complete self-expression.

Today, I lift up my consciousness and receive a more abundant expression. I bless everything and know that all good will multiply in my experience. I expect the good. I live in a state of joyous anticipation, as well as
quiet realization. I expect the All-Good to manifest in my experience today.

Today I Speak My Word, Knowing That It Will Not Return unto Me Void

He is in one mind and who can turn him? —JOB 23:13

Mind is Brahma; for from mind even are verily born these beings—
by mind, when born, they live. —THE UPANISHADS

The Mind, then, is not separated off from God's essentiality,
but is united unto it, as light to sun. —HERMES

Job tells us that God is of one mind, and Jesus clearly taught that this one Mind includes our own thinking. Emerson also tells us that "there is one mind common to all individual people." It is this eternal and perfect Mind that we use. "Let this mind be in you which was also in Christ Jesus." The Mind of God must be peace, joy, and perfection. We enter into this divine state of Being in such degree as our own thoughts are peaceful, joyous, and perfect. To practice the Presence of God is to practice the presence of Perfection, of Wholeness. This Perfection and this Wholeness include joy, peace, and the fulfillment of every legitimate desire. Hermes said that our mind is united to God's Essence as light is united to the sun, that is, we are individualized rays of the universal Light. And the Upanishads say that everything is born from Mind, lives in It, and by It. "In Him we live, and move and have our being." We live in Mind and our thoughts go out into Mind to be fulfilled. This is the principle of spiritual mind healing and demonstration. Each one individualizes this Universal Mind in a particular, unique, and personal way. This is our divine inheritance. But we have drawn too lightly upon it, not fully realizing, as Jesus did, the limitless significance of our relationship with the Infinite. We should learn more fully to enter into our divine companionship.

Today I make a greater claim upon good. Today I speak my word, knowing that it will not return unto me void. It must accomplish and prosper, not because of the power of my will, but because I am willing to let, to permit, to accept guidance, power, and peace.

I Shall See God Reflected in Every Form, Back of Every Countenance, Moving in Every Act

The spirit of God hath made me, and the breath of the
Almighty hath given me life. —JOB 33:4

We created man: and we know what his soul whispereth to him,
and we are closer to him than his neck-vein. —THE KORAN

After long meditation and much deep reflection, having passed through the confusion of human experience, Job finally arrived at the conclusion that the Spirit of God was within him, and that the breath of God was his life. We all have traveled this same pathway of experience—the journey of the soul to "the heights above"—and always there has been a deep inquiry in our minds: What is it all about? Does life make sense? What is the meaning of birth, human experience, and the final transition from this plane, which we call death? Somewhere along the line we too must exclaim with Job, "The spirit of God hath made me and the breath of the Almighty hath given me life!" With the Koran we must realize that the Divine is closer to us even than our physical being. Nothing can be nearer to us than that which is the very essence of our own being. Our external search after Reality culminates in the greatest of all possible discoveries—Reality is at the center of our own being. Life is from within out. We must no longer judge according to appearances, but, rather, base our judgments on the assumption that the God-Mind dwells within us, proclaims or reflects Itself through us into every act. Thus the search after Reality culminates in the realization of the ever-present good. The search, at this point, should cease, and we should at once enter into our Divine inheritance, no longer as searchers after, but now as users of the highest gift of heaven.

I feel that my search is over. I feel that I have discovered the Great Reality, and today I shall speak this Reality into every experience I have. I shall see God reflected in every form, back of every countenance, moving in every act.

I Know That Every Apparent Death Is Resurrection; Therefore, I Gladly Die to Everything That Is Unlike Good

Yea, though I walk through the valley of the shadow of death,
I will fear no evil; for thou art with me; thy rod
and thy staff they comfort me. —PSALM 23:4

Unhappy is he who mistakes the branch for the tree,
the shadow for the substance. —THE TALMUD

We are taught that we must gain a knowledge of that which cannot pass away. The Talmud says that unhappy conditions arise when we mistake shadow for substance. Even the valley of the shadow of death causes no fear when we arrive at the consciousness of the Psalmist who, from the exaltation of his Divine deliverance, proclaimed, "thy rod and thy staff they comfort me." The rod and the staff of Truth is the realization of the substantiality and the permanence of that which cannot change. We are ever renewed by the passage of the Divine Light through our consciousness. "Behold, I make all things new." The revitalizing, regenerative power of Spirit flows from the consciousness of wholeness into our physical organism and into every objective act, when we give the realization of the Divine Presence free passage through our thought. Emerson tells us that in these moments we are conscious that we as isolated beings are nothing, but that the Light is all. Thus he admonishes us to get our "bloated nothingness" our of the way of the Divine Circuit. How wonderful to realize this possibility to which he refers—nonresistance and nonburden. Let us, then, learn to let the burden slip from the shoulders of personal responsibility and enter into our divine union with enthusiasm.

I know that every apparent death is a resurrection. Therefore, gladly, today, I die to everything that is unlike the good. Joyfully I am resurrected into that which is beautiful, enduring and true. Silently I pass from less to more, from isolation into inclusion, from separation into oneness.

A Prayer for World Peace

The earth is the Lord's and the fullness thereof.

I know there is but One Mind, which is the mind of God, in which all people live and move and have their being.

I know there is a divine pattern for humanity and within this pattern there is infinite harmony and peace, cooperation, unity, and mutual helpfulness.

I know that the mind of humankind, being one with the mind of God, shall discover the method, the way, and the means best fitted to permit the flow of Divine Love between individuals and nations.

Thus harmony, peace, cooperation, unity, and mutual helpfulness are experienced by all.

I know there will be a free interchange of ideas, of cultures, of spiritual concepts, of ethics, of educational systems and scientific discoveries—for all good belongs to all alike.

I know that, because Divine Mind has created us all, we are bound together in one infinite and perfect unity.

I know that all people and all nations will remain individual but unified for the common purpose of promoting peace, happiness, harmony, and prosperity.

I know that deep within each person the Divine Pattern of perfect peace is already implanted.

I now declare that in each person and in leaders of thought everywhere this Divine Pattern moves into action and form, to the end that all nations and all people will live together in peace, harmony, and prosperity forever.

And so it is.

ABOUT THE AUTHOR

Ernest Holmes (1887–1960) was an internationally recognized authority on religious psychology and the founder of the Religious Science movement. In addition to the classic work *The Science of Mind,* he was the author of several other inspirational books, including *This Thing Called You, Creative Mind and Success,* and *This Thing Called Life.*